THE LIVE ALBOM

■ The best of Detroit Free Press sports columnist

MITCH ALBOM

Published by the Detroit Free Press
321 W. Lafayette Blvd.
Detroit, Michigan 48231

Cover design and illustrations: Dick Mayer
Front and back cover photography: Mary Schroeder
Editor: Tracee Hamilton
Copy editing: Brad Betker
Project co-ordinators: Dave Robinson, Bill Diem

Manufactured in the United States of America

Library of Congress Cataloging in Publication
Number: 88-070362

ISBN 0-937247-06-5

INTRODUCTION

For more than two years, Mitch Albom has been commenting on a variety of people. Here, and on the back cover, the tables are turned.

"Albom has aplomb. Albom is a balm. Albom is not a bomb. Albom is not a bum. I have been reading Mitch Albom ever since he was the writer to be named later in the deal that sent me to Los Angeles. Most people, me included, think Detroit got the best of it."

Los Angeles Times columnist Mike Downey

"Mitch Albom has style, a nice attitude in his point of view, never pretentious, the mark of a pro in that he makes it look easy."

Birmingham novelist Elmore Leonard

"Mitch is a good guy, a guy you can cut up with maybe a little more than the other writers. . . . Mitch is one you can have a little more fun with."

Lions punter Jim Arnold

"He's fairly young, and I can relate to him pretty good. We talk about everything from hockey to music to people to football. He's pretty good to talk to. The questions that he asks and the things he writes about are realistic. He writes things that people want to read about. . . . He's got a great job."

Red Wings captain Steve Yzerman

"Mitch is one of two writers in Detroit who might kill the Lions, but he does it with class."

Lions defensive tackle Eric Williams

This book belongs to the Free Press as much as it does to me. Without Dave Lawrence, Kent Bernhard and Joe Distelheim, I would not have this job. Without Dave Robinson, I would have no boss to complain to. Without our sports desk, I would be on the English Teachers' 10 Most Wanted List. And without Tracee Hamilton, this "collection" would be a bunch of scribbled pages in search of a stapler.

May I therefore dedicate what follows to all of them — and most of all, to my parents, who never taught me a thing about writing, but taught me everything else.

TABLE OF CONTENTS

1985

1986

1987

ABOUT THE AUTHOR

Mitch Albom came to the Detroit Free Press in August 1985 from the Ft. Lauderdale News and Sun-Sentinel. His work has appeared in numerous national magazines, including Sport and Sports Illustrated.

Mitch, who was born in May 1958, was named the top sports columnist in the country in 1986 by the Associated Press Sports Editors.

1985

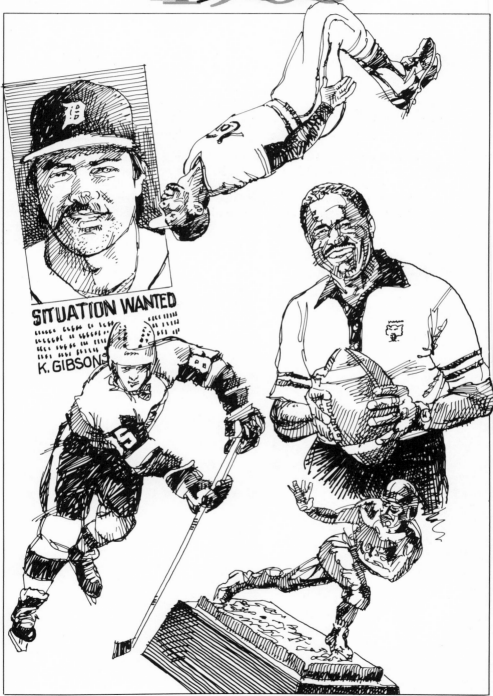

SITUATION WANTED

K. GIBSON

GIVE ME SPORTING CHANCE, AND I'LL GIVE IT BACK

August 4

Let's start with an old joke.

On a plane trip home after a football game, Buck Buchanan, a massive lineman for the Kansas City Chiefs, was sitting next to a sports writer. Buck had the aisle seat. The sports writer was by the window.

Dinner came, and they ate.

Soon Buck fell asleep.

The flight got very bumpy. The sports writer, who had a weak stomach, began to feel queasy. He wanted to get out to the aisle, but he didn't dare disturb Buck's sleep. So he stayed put.

Finally, it was too much. The sports writer leaned over to grab the air-sickness bag. Instead — to his shock — he got sick all over Buck's lap.

The big football player stirred, opened his eyes, saw the mess and mumbled, "Grmphuh?"

The sports writer looked up innocently.

"Feeling better, Buck?" he asked.

You need reflexes like that in this business. Challenging moments always arise.

Like starting your column in a new newspaper, which is what I'm doing today.

Writing for a new audience can strum your nerves a bit. But not for long. I don't know you yet, but I do know sports. And so do you.

The way I figure it, with sports being as monstrously big as they are, we already have a lot more in common than not.

Besides, sports have a way of bridging gaps between people. Like when Casey Stengel caught a pitcher sneaking back at 4 a.m. from the tavern.

"Drunk again," Stengel scolded.

"Me, too," the pitcher said.

See? Togetherness.

We'll get along just fine.

As for my background, I figure too many details here would bore you. Let's just say I've worked for a number of newspapers and magazines, some very big, some very obscure.

I've lived in American League cities, National League cities, been on assignment in Boise, Boston and Berlin, and I still find that just when you figure you've seen everything in sports, along comes pro wrestling.

I once worked in a city where the baseball team came back from 14 games out to win the pennant and the World Series. Take heart, Tigers fans.

But most sports writers don't get too caught up in time or place. It's the nature of the beast.

I knew of a New York writer who was fired from his job. Then, 11 years later, he was rehired by the same newspaper. In his first column back, he wrote:

"As I was saying when I was so rudely interrupted 11 years ago. . . ."

Reflexes.

So what can you expect from this space four times a week?

Some opinion, some heart, some frankness. Some laughs.

Some out of the ordinary. There's a side of the sports leaf that rarely gets turned over, a human side that I like to peek at now and then.

Otherwise, it's hard to predict. Except that, whether my tone be scolding or sympathetic, I try to be honest. That doesn't change.

This is not always a pretty job. Sometimes you have to write that the good guys lost, or that somebody's favorite baseball hero in the whole world just checked into the rehab clinic.

Still, sports are the only show in town where no matter how many times you go back, you never know the ending. That's special.

And, for the most part, sports are fun. Even the silly things can be worth reading about.

So in the end, that's all I ask.

Read.

You may not always agree with what I write, and I may not care for the shredded copies of my column you send back in an unmarked envelope.

That's OK. A column is just one person's view. Read it before your coffee, or after your coffee. You can dunk it in your coffee if you like, though I suggest you read it first.

The only thing I'd resent is if you didn't bother to read it at all.

I'll always try to make it worthwhile.

One other thing. Some people apparently look at a new job in Detroit as something to be endured or tolerated.

Well, maybe that's right for them. I, for one, am thrilled to be here. For sports, they don't make towns any better than this one.

Enough said. Starting tomorrow, I ask your attention, your reaction, your letters, your laughter and, once in a while, the benefit of the doubt.

After all, even Buck Buchanan let that sports writer live. I think.

EDDIE ROBINSON WINS EVERYTHING BUT FAME

September 13

Midnight. Forty young black men get on a bus in Mississippi. Their coaches follow. Then the assistants. The trainer. They are all black. Eddie Robinson, the head coach, gets on last, still in the suit he wore on the football field hours earlier.

The air is cold and still. You can hear crickets. Robinson nods, and the bus rolls. Seven hours and 400 miles will pass before the players get home to Grambling, La. This is how they travel.

Robinson leans against the window, his forehead creased with age lines, and holds out a roll of mints. "Want one?" he asks. Then he begins to reminisce, his voice a whisper over the engine.

The stories. Fascinating. Horrible. Of the 1940s, and the lunch-meat sandwiches he used to prepare for his players because blacks were not allowed in the restaurants.

Of the 1950s, and how they broke down somewhere in the Deep South, and the nearest mechanic picked up a wrench and yelled, "Don't bring that nigger bus in here."

Of the 1960s, and how some players came from such poor backgrounds, "they did not know how to use a knife and fork."

Eddie Robinson took them all. Taught them all.

Where you expect anger in his voice, there is none. Where you expect resentment, there is none.

I took this bus ride with him a year after he won his 300th game. Now, in his 44th season, his foot is in the door of history again.

He is about to pass Bear Bryant as the college football coach with the most victories of all time.

And where you expect recognition, there is none. Not the kind Eddie Robinson deserves.

Remember that when Bear Bryant was starting out at Maryland, Eddie Robinson was already at Grambling, coaching football. A one-man staff.

And when Bear Bryant was making a name for himself at Kentucky, Robinson was at Grambling, coaching football. And hosing off the field, and directing the girls' drill team.

And when Bear Bryant was turning into a legend at Alabama, Robinson was still at Grambling, coaching football. And writing the game stories for newspapers that generally didn't print them. And when Bear Bryant passed Amos Alonzo Stagg in all-time victories among college coaches,

Robinson was still at Grambling, coaching football. And sending his 200th player to the pros — though his quarterbacks were almost always given new positions. "Not smart enough," the pros said.

For decades, black athletes in the South came to Robinson, for they had little choice. If they wanted to play college football, it had to be at a "black" college: a Grambling, an Alcorn State, a Southern.

Eddie Robinson took them, molded them, won with them, made sure they graduated.

And when, in the 1960s, the previously all-white schools were integrated, the black schools were suddenly shunted aside. Their programs sank as their would-be players were wooed away by promises of network TV and fancy stadiums.

Robinson would not complain. "I watched black kids risk their lives to integrate society," he said. So he settled for the also-rans. The leftovers.

And he taught them. And he won with them.

Time magazine once asked him about the irony of it, and he shrugged. "Some build the roads, some drive over them," he said. "We're getting there."

Well, maybe and maybe not. Saturday marks the start of Grambling's 1985 season, with Robinson only four wins from breaking Bryant's career mark of 323 victories. And I don't hear much fuss, much Pete Rose-type hoopla.

Oh, there's an article here and there. But you can bet if he were white and at a major school you'd know Robinson's name backward by now.

And meanwhile, he goes on, still on a tiny budget, still making the midnight bus rides, still driving the Louisiana back roads to recruit players.

He is 66 now, and how many men owe him their football careers? Tank Younger, Willie Davis, Ernie Ladd, Buck Buchanan, Doug Williams. And how many less famous owe him their diplomas, their manners, their pride?

Remember Ralph Ellison, the brilliant black writer, who called himself an Invisible Man because people refused to see him?

Eddie Robinson has been invisible. Too long.

No doubt there are some who don't want Bryant's legend eclipsed — and particularly by a black man. Tough. It's going to happen.

And when it does, it might be worth noting that Bryant did not have a black athlete in his program until 1970. The same year Grambling finally got a sprinkler for its football field.

Some build the roads, some drive over them.

This college year belongs to Eddie Robinson. And sadly, too few of us know it.

THANKS FOR SHOPPING AMERICA, PETR

October 7

Petr is getting a new car. He does not know what kind. But he hopes it will be very fast.

We are in a Chevrolet dealership. Petr is sitting in a chair, looking at the ceiling. Petr's translator, Ivan, is doing the talking, because Petr speaks no English.

"K-l-i-m-a," says Ivan, spelling Petr's last name. "He is new hockey player for Red Wings. . . . Yes. . . . He make lots of money, don't worry."

Ivan laughs. Petr laughs, too, even though he has no idea what's going on.

Petr is 20 years old, with a broad frame, thick blondish hair, and the beginnings of a first mustache. He has been in America less than three weeks, since defecting from Czechoslovakia. He was sneaked away in the night, leaving his family and friends behind.

Now he has a big NHL contract, and many newspaper stories about him, which he cannot read. And, in a few moments, a new automobile. His own.

It was part of the contract. A fast American sports car. Welcome to the USA.

"I want you to give him the key, very special, OK?" Ivan whispers to the dealer. "So we can take picture."

The car is brought out. A black Camaro Z28. Very sleek. Petr stares. He never owned a car before. He runs his hand along the hood. Along the side. Along the window with the sticker that reads $15,800.

"Wait, Petr! We take a picture," Ivan says.

The dealer comes out with the keys. He puts his arm around the hockey player. Petr smiles widely. There are spaces between his teeth.

Click. Click.

We are driving in Petr's car. Rrrummm! Petr is at the wheel. Rrrummm! His foot slams on the gas, then quickly to the brake, then back to the gas.

"It's a good thing . . . there is traffic . . . ahead of us," says Ivan, as he jerks forward, then backward, then forward, "or else . . . we be dead."

Petr pushes the electronic mirror adjuster button. Bzzzt. It is one of a dozen extras that came with the car. Ivan tried to explain them all to Petr, but isn't sure how much he absorbed. Bzzzt. The mirror moves up, down. Bzzzt. Left, right. Bzzzt. Petr smiles.

"Good?" he is asked.

15

"Good," he says.

Back in Czechoslovakia, it is nighttime. Petr's father is no doubt sleeping, tired from his job at the ice rink. His mother? Who knows? Perhaps she is dreaming of her son, imagining his new life in America.

Bzzzt. Up goes the mirror. Bzzzt. Back down.

How long would it take someone in Czechoslovakia to earn $15,800? Petr is asked

Ivan laughs. Petr laughs, too.

"I think 10 years," Ivan says.

P ull in here," says Ivan, pointing left. Petr looks at the finger, then turns.

K mart.

We march to the men's section. Petr — who defected with only one bag of clothes and personal mementos — needs underwear. He is about to take a road trip with the Red Wings.

"Here," says Ivan. Petr opens the box of bikini briefs by Brut Faberge. He feels the material and makes a face. Nylon. No good.

He settles on a box of blue and white cotton ones, size large. "That is L," says Ivan, pointing at the letter on the box. Petr mouths the L sound.

"He must work on his English," Ivan says.

We go to the counter. A young male cashier, about Petr's age, looks up. "Will this be cash or charge?"

Petr just smiles. Petr always smiles. "Cash," says Ivan. He says something in Czech. Petr reaches into his pocket and pulls out a wad of bills, fives mixed with twenties mixed with hundreds, mixed with ones. The cashier's mouth drops open.

"Here," says Ivan, picking out the bills. Petr glances around at the counter merchandise. Film. TV Guide. Halloween masks. Peppermint patties.

On the ice he will do what comes naturally. He will do well. But how strange the rest must all seem. One month, your native country. The next month, across the world, across the culture.

And no going back.

"OK, Petr," says Ivan.

Petr puts his money back. Car down. Underwear down. Rest of America to go.

"Thank you for shopping at K mart," says the cashier, but Petr only looks at him blankly and walks away.

TARP TELLS ALL: 'WHY I ROLLED OVER COLEMAN'

October 15

ST. LOUIS — At first, the tarp wasn't talking.

"Get away from me," it mumbled. "I don't need no cheese-head reporters around me now."

Hours earlier, the tarp had committed the most heinous crime of this National League playoff. During batting practice, it had rolled up the leg of an unsuspecting Vince Coleman, the Cardinals' prize rookie, trapping him under the weight of its 1,200 pounds until teammates could pull him free.

Coleman escaped with minor bruises and cuts, but was forced to miss Sunday's and Monday's games. Now the police were bringing the tarp down to the station. The charge: attempted man-smother.

Suddenly, the tarp made a break for it. It hopped into the stands and tried to hide as a foul pole. The police spotted it when it began to flap in the wind. They slapped on the cuffs, which wasn't easy, because the tarp was 180 feet long.

"Why'd you do it?" a reporter screamed.

"Did you mean to roll over all of Coleman, or just his legs?" another hollered.

The tarp was silent, as tarps will be.

"Were you trying to make a political statement?"

"What did you plan to do with him once you had him rolled up?"

"Mr. Tarp, I'm from People magazine. Is it true you only did this to impress Jodie Foster's pillowcase?"

The tarp shifted uncomfortably. There was an awkward silence. Finally, it spoke.

"Look," it said, "if you want to ask me questions, at least ask them to my face. You're all standing at the wrong end."

The reporters scurried to a more appropriate position.

"It's a frame-up," the tarp began. "I was just doing my job. It rains, I unroll. I'm automatic. It ain't my responsibility to look out for dumb rookies."

"But isn't it a strange coincidence that it was Coleman — the Cardinals' best base-stealer — that you trapped?" someone asked.

The tarp said nothing.

"Someone said you were seen talking with Tommy Lasorda the other night."

Silence.

"And how come you're blue? Shouldn't you be red like everything else here?"

More silence.

"Hey! Lookit this!" a reporter hollered. He'd found a tag in the tarp's far corner. It read Made In Los Angeles.

"Let go! Let go!" the tarp yelled, its voice unsteady. "OK. I give. A guy came by Saturday night wearing a Dodgers jacket. I was just hanging around my cylinder. He pulled out $500 and said it was mine if I could take out Coleman, who was burning the Dodgers with his speed.

"Do you know what $500 means to a poor tarp like me? I live in a hole, for cripes' sake. I never seen that kind of money in my pockets. Come to think of it, I never seen my pockets."

The tarp grew somber. It wrinkled up.

"This ain't an easy life, you know. Rainy days always get me down, so to speak. How would you feel if every time you came out, people booed? Then you just lie there, face in the dirt, soaking wet.

"I coulda been somebody. I coulda been a parachute, maybe. But no. I came from the wrong side of the mats.

"My dad was a shower curtain. My mom was a rubber sheet. What chance did I have? Now I'm going to the Big House. I've heard stories about that place. They cut you into place mats, rags, Hefty trash bags."

The policemen took their positions around the tarp, getting ready to carry it off.

"Coleman!" a reporter yelled. "Quick, tell us about Coleman!"

"I didn't mean to hurt him," the tarp said. "But when I came out of my hole on Sunday, there he was, so near, so easy, so unsuspecting.

"I couldn't help myself. I rolled onto his shoe and I lost control. Next thing I knew it was the ankle, the shin, the knee. I heard voices inside my head saying, 'Go for the nose!' I was mad! Mad! Ahhhahahhaha. . . ."

The thing was coming unraveled. Everywhere. It rolled left, then right, then left again. A temper tarptrum.

It took 37 policemen to finally lift it and slide it into a converted moving van. "Watch your hands and feet," the sergeant said, "it could still be dangerous."

"What a life," mumbled the tarp.

The squad cars were started. The sirens whirred. Justice would be served. Baseball would go on.

"Any last words?" a reporter hollered.

"Yeah," grumbled the tarp, as the van pulled out. "No offense, but I hope it rains all day."

FANS CAN'T GET ENOUGH OF LIGHT-HITTING OZZIE

October 16

ST. LOUIS — They would not leave.

"OZ-ZIE! OZ-ZIE! OZ-ZIE!"

Not one. Not a soul dared move. The game was over, but all 53,708 were on their feet, screaming for him to come back out, and if they had to stand there until the start of next season, damn it, they would.

"OZ-ZIE! OZ-ZIE! OZ-ZIE!"

What in sports is more dramatic than a home run in the bottom of the ninth? What raises an explosion in your larynx more than a home team's sweep of three straight playoff games? What goose-bumps you more than a little man getting a big hit when he's not supposed to, watching the ball arc high, high, high . . . gone!

Ozzie Smith, little Ozzie Smith, singles hitter Ozzie Smith, did all that for St. Louis Monday with one left-handed swing of lumber.

It was quick death. A screaming bullet across a Midwestern sky. This game had been tied, 2-2, for six innings — it felt like a week — and Smith had two strikes on him and there was nobody on base. To be perfectly honest, people were squirming in their seats, figuring this game was going into extra innings for sure.

And then — bang! It was over. It was victory. The ball caromed high off a right-field pillar — home run! — the crowd sprang to its feet, singing the name as he circled the bases and was swarmed by his Cardinals teammates.

The players disappeared quickly. But the people would not leave. Not a one.

"OZ-ZIE! OZ-ZIE! OZ-ZIE!"

The man they were waiting for had begun the game by running out to his shortstop position and doing a back flip, flipping his body in midair, like happy people do in the movies. Happy Ozzie Smith. Bouncy Ozzie Smith. Fielding Wiz Ozzie Smith.

But Slugging Ozzie Smith? Wait a minute. This is a man with a whopping total of 13 home runs in eight major league years, a switch-hitter who had never hit a home run left-handed before in his life.

"I wasn't trying to do that," he would later admit. "I was just trying to get a hit and I got under it and the next thing I know, I'm seeing the umpire giving the signal."

And fireworks were being sent airborne, and the scoreboard was flashing: "California Here We Come!" and the Cardinals were suddenly one game away from the pennant.

And the chant began.

"OZ-ZIE! OZ-ZIE! OZ-ZIE!"

Oh, for a moment like that. Smith would later call it the highlight of his career, and there was even a glaze of vindication on that home run ball. Smith signed a contract before this season worth $2 million, and people had questioned how a lifetime .238 hitter warranted such money, no matter how great a wizard he was in the field. He bristled inside every time he heard the criticism.

But glory comes in all sizes. Even to a player with Smith's build — roughly that of your average high school junior. What little guy hasn't dreamed of winning a big game with a home run? This was the dream personified.

Someone would ask him the difference between that left-handed at-bat and all the previous ones.

"The end result," he would say, and everyone would laugh.

But there was more. For no at-bat mattered as much since he'd put on a Cardinals uniform three years ago. The Cardinals had dropped the first two games to Los Angeles in this series. They had lost their star rookie, Vince Coleman, to a freakish accident. This was possibly Smith's last appearance in St. Louis this year.

And the crowd wanted one last look, just in case.

"OZ-ZIE! OZ-ZIE! OZ-ZIE!"

Finally, he came back out, sprang out, like a novelty snake from a can, raised his hands above his head and shook to the thunder of his own name.

What a roar! The St. Louis arch itself was shaking.

Thanks to Smith's home run, the Cardinals had won three straight games in unusual fashion, and had risen from the ashes of a 2-0 deficit to pull ahead in this series, 3-2.

Anything seemed possible now. A home run in the bottom of the ninth has that effect.

Thirty minutes later, in the din of honking horns and distant screams of celebration, a handful of people still lingered atop the Cardinals' dugout. One was a white-haired man in a dirty jacket. His eyes were half-closed and he had a twisted look on his face that said he'd been drunk for hours.

No matter. He slapped his hands together in a feeble attempt at rhythm. "Oz-zie! Oz-zie! Oz-zie!" he gurgled.

The song will last a long time.

REINHOLD NEVER BENT, BUT STEEL IN HIS LEG DID

November 13

ANN ARBOR — Football is full of symbols. The penalty flag. The goalposts. For Mike Reinhold, it's a stainless steel rod, 21 inches long. That's what doctors inserted into his right leg two years ago, after a hit from a Minnesota lineman shattered his femur into three pieces, and left him twisted like a rag doll on the field.

For nearly a year, Reinhold and the rod shared the same flesh. He could press on his thigh and feel the object inside him. How strange. But then, all sorts of strange changes were taking place. He had remained in a Minneapolis hospital weeks after his Michigan teammates had flown home. Thanksgiving came and went, and he passed it in a hospital bed, flat on his back, eating lukewarm turkey that some alumni had brought him.

The leg had suffered a terrible break. But the break from the team was harder to take. As Reinhold said, "College football is like a big machine. When a cog is damaged, it's replaced."

And even as he lay in bed, he knew it was happening to him. His place had been taken.

He had never been hurt before. Never been too injured to play. Just as some young men are musicians, and some are scholars, he had always been a football player. And now he wasn't.

It was as if someone had stolen his last name.

No one expected to see Reinhold in a Michigan uniform again. Most would have been happy to see him off his crutches, which he had to use for eight months. "He was one player," Bo Schembechler said, "that I figured would never come back. No way. The injury was just too severe."

The rod remained inside him. Iron Leg, they called him. It even brought a few laughs — like when Reinhold passed through the metal detector at an airport and the alarm went haywire. But more often, he could feel the piece rubbing against his hip bone, a reminder that he was still part hardware, still not quite normal.

His weight had dropped from 225 to 185 in four weeks. He felt weak. One day, around Christmas of '83, he hobbled into an empty weight room and tried a bench press. He had been lifting 330 pounds before the operation. He set the bar at "a joke" weight of 135. Eight repetitions and he was exhausted. "I was back to nothing," he said.

All during this time, he was still living with other players, other healthy players, and when they would leave for practice, there was the loneliness

21

you feel as a child when the door slams and you are suddenly alone in the house. Your inclination is to run out after your loved ones, to catch them before they leave you behind.

In a way, that's what makes an injured player such as Reinhold want to come back so desperately. "As a football player you feel special," he said. "But when you're out, not playing, you just feel like, I don't know. . . . Normal. And alone."

One night the following summer, Reinhold attended a wedding in his hometown of Muskegon — where he'd been a high school star — and the questions were all about when he'd return for U-M. They echoed inside. That night, at 3 a.m., he put on sweats and pushed himself through a grueling neighborhood run, "touching every mailbox and telephone pole along the way."

From then on, if the trainers told him one mile, he ran three. If they told him a half-dozen weight lifts, it was a dozen. He did hours of work that he wasn't supposed to, swimming, running, jumping rope, too eager to let common sense be heard. He did it alone, except for the 21 inches of cold steel inside him. And when he returned to the hospital, it took the doctors more than two hours to remove the implement. Reinhold had put himself through a private hell that would astound even Schembechler in an effort to get back.

When the doctors removed the rod, it was bent.

R einhold is back now — as a middle guard instead of a linebacker — on a Michigan defense that is the finest in the nation. This weekend, he returns to the haunted house in Minneapolis (the Metrodome) where the injury took place.

"It'd be lying to say I'm not a little nervous," he admitted. "I went through hell up there."

What brings college players such as Reinhold back? Mostly, it's the sense of belonging. Of feeling special. And in that way, they are no different from most of us at college age. They cling to the team as others cling to their friends, their fraternity brothers, their bands, their student government. Being injured is like being a child forced to watch a family picnic through a window.

"The whole time I was hurt, I just kept visualizing coming through the tunnel with the other guys," Reinhold said. "When I finally got to do it again, it was like coming home."

He still has the rod from his leg. He says he may make something out of it. No need. The curve in the object is testament enough to his will.

The steel bent. He didn't.

HORROR OF PELLE'S DEATH: IT HAPPENS EVERY DAY

November 15

As a kid in Philadelphia, I played a lot of ice hockey. It came with the territory. The Flyers were the only winning team in town. So if you wanted to feel good, you put on skates, grabbed a stick and picked a Flyer to call your own.

In those days, it was Bernie Parent, the star goalie, whose name was invoked most often. You would stand in the net and a puck would come zipping in, and in your mind's eye you saw yourself as Parent, the last seconds of the game ticking away, and a surge of adrenaline coursed through your veins and for the briefest of moments you were he — and you slapped away the puck and screamed, "What a save! Bernie Parent!" just like a radio announcer.

Play-acting. The ground floor of hero worship. Certain players just inspired it. Parent was one. Pelle Lindbergh was another.

He was just 26, but he had inherited the job that once belonged to Parent, and he was great, leading the Flyers to the Stanley Cup final last season. Many ranked him as the NHL's best goalie.

And as late as last week, on the same ice where we once played, kids were slapping away pucks while shouting his name. They are quiet now.

Early Sunday morning, on his way home from drinking at an after-hours club, Lindbergh slammed his red Porsche 930 turbo into a schoolyard wall in Somerdale, N.J.

He is dead. His two passengers are hospitalized.

When they peeled away the wreck, red paint was embedded in the concrete. It's still there. On a school wall. Call it the goodby lesson.

There is no question Lindbergh was driving drunk — his blood-alcohol content measured at twice the legal limit. Because of that, some people are saying "he got what he deserved."

But there's no satisfaction in this. Just as there is none in turning Lindbergh into a tragic hero. His death was not heroic. On the contrary. The horror is how very ordinary it really was.

Listen to how a coach who knew him described Lindbergh: "He was a fun-loving fella who loved to be around people. Everybody liked him. . . . He always had a fast car. He liked to drive fast."

Sound like anyone you know? I can rattle off a dozen guys who fit the description. They work hard. They play hard. None is a criminal. None is a bad guy. They merely possess the right birth certificate and a set of car keys.

So before we walk away from Lindbergh's corpse with the comfort of "that's him, not me," remember he was not known as a chronic drinker. Nor was he guzzling Wild Turkey or grain alcohol the night he died. Just celebrating a victory with drinks served at your average bar. And that includes beer. The innocence we associate with that beverage — "When it's time to relax. . . ." "Here's to good friends. . . ." — masks the rope we are getting to hang ourselves.

Drunk is drunk. No matter what the pedigree.

Or the age. Today, even as Lindbergh's family mourns his death, we hear about a Michigan State basketball player named Scott Skiles, who was arrested last week and charged with drunken driving, his second such offense. The last time he was reportedly too intoxicated to get past the letter D in the alphabet. Yet he's back on the team after a one-game suspension — an exhibition game, at that.

The cry is that Skiles got off easy because of his status. The real crime is that with such a slap on the wrist, he may never realize how closely he was dancing with death. And he may try it again.

If there was somehow a bridge to where Pelle Lindbergh is now, what message would he send back to Skiles? Would he listen?

Maybe your kids are hockey fans. Do them a favor. Tell them Pelle Lindbergh's story. Tell them of his glories on the ice, and what he left behind off of it — a family, a pretty fiancee, an hourglass full of untapped happy moments.

Tell them how, like most of us, he was no doubt convinced that tragedy would never darken his doorstep, even as he staggered into the car for the final ride of his life. Include the gruesome ending, for it would be a grave injustice not to.

Children grow up. Some play sports. When they win, they celebrate, and if they're old enough, like Lindbergh, they may celebrate with alcohol. That will not change. Not tomorrow, and not in years to come — when even those apple-cheeked kids playing hockey in Philly reach the age of cars and beer.

But maybe, when they sit down behind the wheel, eyes droopy and equilibrium fuzzy, that old spirit of youth will flush through them, and they'll hear that make-believe radio announcer — "What a save! Pelle Lindbergh!"

And they'll hand over the keys.

If there's any good in his death, it will be in this moment. May we all be that smart when it comes.

DIVISION III BACK MAKES HIS MARK ON THE HEISMAN

December 5

Quincy, Mass. — Rita Dudek works in a convenience store. Sells everything from toothpaste to Hawaiian Punch. Once a week she puts out the magazines — "It only takes me an hour," she says — cutting open the bundles and placing them on the shelves. Last week, after she put them out, she found herself checking the customers who walked past. She couldn't help it. Were they looking at the new Sports Illustrated? At the cover? Were they looking?

For there, beneath a headline that read "The Thinking Fan's Vote for the 1985 Heisman Trophy," were three faces with a box next to each: Bo Jackson of Auburn, Chuck Long of Iowa and someone named Joe Dudek of Plymouth State, an obscure Division III college in New Hampshire.

And Dudek's box had a red check in it. On the cover. Of Sports Illustrated. The magazine's choice for the Heisman Trophy winner.

Joe Dudek. Rita's son.

Joe Dudek?

This has really changed everything," said Joe Dudek, dressed in a corduroy sports jacket and red tie. He was sitting in a restaurant in Medford, Mass., awaiting a local sports banquet. Friends and teammates were mingling. Dudek himself looked unspectacular — crewcut hair, a slightly crooked smile, average football build. A little small, actually.

But in this small-town restaurant, he almost glowed. Violinists dream of Carnegie Hall, oilmen of the Forbes 400. But if you carry a football, like Joe Dudek, you fantasize about the cover of Sports Illustrated.

With a check mark. The room was buzzing.

"Did you see that article?"

"Hey, he's great. I'm not surprised."

"Is he going down to New York for Heisman ceremonies?"

"Did you say he was going to New York?"

"Hey. You think he's got a chance?"

Dudek found out about the cover only the night before it came out. He and his girlfriend drove to the first open newsstand and bought a copy. They read it in the car. Five times.

The article is mostly a tongue-in-cheek comment on the overblown big-name Heisman candidates. And its writer never met Dudek. Just spoke to him over the phone.

But a cover is a cover, and in these parts, it was like Rocky Balboa being

25

given a shot at the heavyweight title. People Dudek had known for years began asking for his autograph. The phone rang. Reporters arrived. TV camera lights glared. The phone rang. Channel 7, Channel 56, the Boston Globe, the Boston Herald. Could they have a minute? The phone rang. At the family Thanksgiving, Joe Dudek was a celebrity. His nieces and nephews drew crayon signs: "Hurrah for Joey!" Agents are circling. The pros are interested.

An article that criticized the hurricane of Heisman hoopla created a little storm of its own.

Not that the article is without merit. In his four years at Plymouth State, Dudek, 21, scored more touchdowns (79) than any other collegian ever to wear a helmet. He gained 5,570 yards (a Division III record). In his final game two weeks ago, he ran 34 times for 265 yards and two touchdowns before he was taken from the field by ambulance, exhausted and injured, with four minutes left.

He has received no silver-spoon treatment. No scholarships. Dudek, the youngest of eight kids, pays to go to school, and owes more than $10,000 in student loans. He lives in a regular dorm. He never played in a bowl. Division III? The farthest he has traveled to play is Schenectady, N.Y.

But now. The cover. The Heisman check mark.

"I know what people think," Dudek said. "It's a Division III school. Who do they play? But guys here play football because they love it. To me, the hits are just as hard, the holes are just as tough to get through."

Sadly, the Heisman voters are less understanding. It will be awarded this weekend. Jackson or Long will get it. Joe Dudek will not win. No. Will he?

"I know I won't," he said. "I'd be thrilled to even finish in the top ten. But I have the magazine. Nobody can take that away. Playing out here in Division III, there's usually nobody to tell you if you're any good or not. This tells me that maybe I at least belong with those other guys, you know? That means a lot."

A new Sports Illustrated arrives at the convenience store today. Rita Dudek will cut the bundles and put them out. A new cover. A new face. The week is up.

"That's OK," Joe Dudek said. "I'm kinda looking forward to the next week's issue, the letters to the editor they get for picking me."

He laughed. "That should be pretty interesting itself."

GIBBY, YOU NEED A JOB?
PUT IT IN THE WANT ADS

December 11

Poor Kirk Gibson.

A baseball star without a contract.

Nobody wants him. Except the Tigers. And he doesn't want them. Not at their latest offer.

"Hard Times For Free Agents," read the cover of Sports Illustrated last week, above a photo of Gibson. He was looking angry.

Who'd have thought being talented, rich and handsome could bring so many problems?

Well. I have an idea. It is time for action. It is time for Kirk to do as any businessman would. When supply exceeds demand, there is only one answer.

Take out an ad.

SITUATION WANTED: Young, strong baseball player seeks long-term, mutually beneficial arrangement with major league club. Let me make you great! Location no object. Climate no object. Uniform no object. Money an object. Contact agent.

This could run in the New York Times, the Atlanta Constitution, the Kansas City Star, and any other newspaper in a major league city.

But newspapers are just the beginning. Let's talk magazines. Lots of ads in magazines. Like Rolling Stone:

THIS GUN FOR HIRE! He's free. He's loose. And he's ready to rock your town. Kirk Gibson. For a limited time only. Feel the power. Grrrrrr.

Or Business Week:

INVESTMENT OPPORTUNITY: High-yield professional athlete available at depressed rate due to sudden drop in market conditions. Low risk of injury. Proven ticket seller. Make your money back in no time. Serious investors only, please.

Or even Soldier Of Fortune magazine:

ATTN. MAJOR LEAGUE OWNER: If you are a mouse, you can stop reading right now. But if you are a man, this message is for you. Show your courage. Show your guts. Sign on the dotted line and get yourself five years' worth of baseball power. My name is Kirk Gibson. I can say that proudly. Can you?

You see how powerful words can be? But let's not forget pictures. It's hard to sell these days without pictures. How about this:

DO YOU KNOW ME? I'm a talented, exciting baseball star in the prime of my career. I was the MVP of the American League championships in 1984. I can grow a beard in six seconds. I drive the woman fans crazy. And — are you ready? — I'm available. Yes. You can stop rubbing your eyes now. Get out your American Express card. Let's talk turkey, turkey.

And then there's the personals. Oh, yes. The personals are very big these days. Kirk Gibson could advertise in the personals. It might work.

SINGLE WHITE MALE, 28, tall, athletic build, seeks meaningful relationship with other sports lovers who enjoy standing in the sun, signing autographs and spitting tobacco at anything that moves. Sincere, honest, sensitive. I want to share. Turn-ons? A fastball down the middle, a sizable bank account. Turnoffs? Shaving cream, sports writers. Interested? Let's get together. Write BOX 23, Detroit, MI. All inquiries confidential.

Too wordy? OK. Let's go with something simple.

FOR SALE: HR httr. Mint Cond. Looks gd., runs gd. Must see!

Maybe Gibson could get into one of those Dewar's Profile whiskey ads. That would be good:

NAME: Kirk Gibson. EDUCATION: Michigan State, Tigers dugout. OCCUPATION: Baseball star. PHILOSOPHY: "If I'm not worth five years and $8 million, I'll vomit." SCOTCH: Dewar's White Label.

Of course, some baseball owners do not read newspapers or magazines. Some do not read at all. Otherwise, they would read their balance sheets and die of heart attacks.

But owners smoke cigars. This means they need matches. And what is on the cover of every good matchbook? Why, an ad. How about that?

CAN YOU DRAW THIS FACE? If you can, and you own a baseball team, you might have a new career — as boss of the greatest free agent in baseball today. Write for more info.

Anyhow, there it is. The power of the ad. With the right campaign, Gibson's problems will soon be over. Someone will bite. Someone always bites. How do you think those hair-weave people stay in business?

Of course, if the someone who bites is someone other than the Tigers, Detroit readers can look for another ad soon in their favorite publications.

WANTED: Right fielder for major league franchise. Must be powerful, fast and not hung up on material possessions. Great opportunity for right individual. Contact the Detroit Tigers.
Hurry. Please.

ALVIN HAYES HAS A FIGHTING CHANCE

December 18

Alvin Hayes looks out the window. Then he looks at the clock on the wall. It's 9 in the morning and he's waiting for the car to pull up so he can get the hell out of here and back to the real world for a few hours. Rehab centers are better than prison, he figures. But not much. "Like the Army," he mumbles. They check your every move, give you penalty points if your bed isn't made right, and, ho, God forbid you get caught hiding anything when they strip-search you. Forget it. You're dead.

So he waits for the car, his long arms dangling by his side, his gym bag packed and zipped, and as each minute passes he figures this is the morning his uncle gives up on him. But eventually the car pulls up, and Alvin Hayes gets in, and the two men drive away.

This is a story about a boxer and a cop and it begins deep in the city, the east side of Detroit, in a section where hope dies with the alarm clock and you don't get dressed without a pistol. Not if you plan on running the streets. Here there are no carports and no croissant shops and the words "getting high" don't mean sneaking some marijuana in the upstairs bathroom; they mean crashing in somebody's one-room apartment, free-basing cocaine until the money runs out.

This is where Alvin Hayes — once the fifth-ranked lightweight boxer in the world — could be found last spring. Mixing cocaine with baking soda, melting it until it hardened into a ball, chopping the ball into little pieces, and then smoking it until it jolted his nervous system like a drill through a tooth. He felt on fire. For about three minutes. And then he had to do it again.

"Thirty times a day," he says. "At least. I would go through $3,000 a day sometimes. I had to keep going."

He had the money. For a while, anyhow.

Boxing had given it to him.

Too Sweet Hayes, they called him, mostly because of that angelic face, the high cheekbones, the babykins smile, and that long, tall, nail of a body that looks too frail to take a hit, much less give one. But, ah, it could do both. Hayes was slick. Quick. A strong puncher. Great moves. Did a dance routine to Michael Jackson music at the start of his bouts that ignited the crowds.

People were talking about Alvin Hayes, never louder than on the June evening last year when he fought Jimmy Paul in Las Vegas for the United States Boxing Association lightweight title. The last night of his old life.

29

T hose were the good days. Had to be. His childhood wasn't much fun. No money, father takes off, kids run the streets. Have you heard this song before? Yeah. Well. It's as common as air in Hayes' neighborhood. Juvenile court became his second home. And as soon as he was old enough to be tried as an adult, he was. They sent him away at 17 for carrying a pistol and violating probation. Four years.

But boxing. That he could do. He started late — he was 21 when he laced up his first glove. But it came naturally. For a while he was knocking out everyone they put in front of him. Nineteen of his first 22 fights were KOs. All were victories. "I thought the guy would become a world champion," says Stuart Kirschenbaum, the Michigan boxing commissioner. Hayes was making as much as $10,000 a bout, and he seemed to have found a way out. TV was after him. Promoters. Fans.

Sometimes a little success is the right medicine.

And sometimes it's the worst. Hayes had been taking prescription pain pills following an operation on his hand. Tylenol with codeine. "I started taking one a day, then two, then three and four," Hayes says. He became addicted. He began guzzling cough syrup. Codeine again. When he stopped using them, a few weeks before the Jimmy Paul bout, he went through a withdrawal, he says, that left him as weak and powerless as a balloon on a tether.

He got in the ring with Paul that night and got his butt kicked. Knockout. Sixth round. His first loss.

Soon after, his manager bailed out. Hayes went into a shell. A girl he knew came around and said, "Do you wanna get high?" and we've already told you what that meant. Hayes said OK. It was stupid. He knows it.

"I figured I could just do it once," he said, reciting the junkie's epitaph.

He gave her money for cocaine.

Within weeks he was free-basing all the time.

A rich man is a target in Hayes' neighborhood, and a rich man with a weakness for drugs might as well have a bull's-eye painted across his face. People came over. The money went fast. He fought again and lost. He used the purse money for more cocaine, until it was all gone.

One morning an acquaintance called him and said he had a way they could make some money. It was snowing. They drove to a stereo store. "Wait here," the friend said. He came out with a stereo. Hayes wasn't too coherent at the time, but he saw a cop car across the street and instinct was enough to tell him to run. The police chased him, tackled him, arrested him.

A few months later, he was arrested again, on a breaking-and-entering charge. He says he was so high that night, he doesn't even remember what happened. This time he went to prison.

He called his mother. "I said, 'You gotta get me out of here,' and she said she wasn't gonna get me out because I'd only get in trouble again."

Other relatives ignored his calls. He was alone. He couldn't stand it. He took the cord from his windbreaker and made a noose. He tied it to the bars, then slipped it around his neck. He was only pretending to kill himself, he says, figuring "that way they'd have to come get me out."

Next thing Hayes knew, he was in a hospital. Northville Psychiatric Hospital. With a band on his wrist.

At 25, Alvin (Too Sweet) Hayes — who had electrified the Detroit boxing scene more than anyone since Thomas Hearns — had hit bottom. Rock stinking bottom. For two weeks he sat there screaming at doctors, "I ain't crazy! I ain't crazy!" while patients in the ward pawed at him for cigarets.

The windshield wipers squeak as they clap back and forth, flicking away the snow. We are inside the car that picks up Alvin Hayes every morning from the rehab center. Sam Williams' car.

Sam Williams is a cop, and a cop really shouldn't be getting too involved with criminals, especially drug addicts. But Sam Williams is also Alvin Hayes' uncle. And that counts for something, he figures.

Williams is 40 years old, thickly muscled, and street-wise enough to be soft-spoken. Five years ago, while on patrol, he was attacked by a drunk with a knife. He pulled out his gun. The guy kept coming. Williams could have fired. Self-defense. Instead he let the drunk get closer, closer, until the blade was within inches of his gut. Then he swiped at the drunk's arm and punched him helpless.

When Sam Williams spoke to the nurses at the hospital and they told him about Hayes, something clicked. Without knowing it, it was happening again. He was letting the danger come closer, in order to save a life.

"Let's go," Williams says. He and Hayes get out of the car and trudge through the snow and into the Coleman Young Recreation Center. Into the boxing ring.

It is time to train for the fight.

Oh, yes. There is a fight. Thursday night. Cobo Arena. The return of Alvin (Too Sweet) Hayes, after eight months of hell.

Roll the credits. Begin with Sam Williams.

When Hayes stood in a courtroom a few months ago, ready to be sentenced, Williams asked to speak to the judge privately. He asked that his nephew be placed under his jurisdiction. A policeman's jurisdiction. The judge agreed.

And when Hayes was put in a rehab program for his drug problem, Williams agreed to pick him up each morning before work, drive him to the gym, come back at lunchtime, take him to another gym, pick him up in the

31

afternoon and get him back to the rehab center by the 5 p.m. deadline.

"I don't know why I'm doing it," Williams says. "I know he could slip back to his old ways. Maybe I'm crazy. But everything Alvin's done wrong has been on account of drugs. He was high both times he was arrested. These guys he hung around with, he couldn't resist them."

Williams figured if he could shake the cocaine dust off Hayes, he'd find his nephew. And bring him back.

So he laid down the rules. Said he couldn't keep Hayes from jail, if that's what the courts wanted. Said the first sign of drugs, Hayes was out. Said things had to be his way or no way.

Alvin Hayes said OK. Quickly.

Sometimes, all people are looking for is a little caring.

At the end of the day, when the sparring and the weight work and the jumping rope are finished, Hayes and Williams, the boxer and the cop, drive back to the rehab center. The snow is still falling, and Hayes, sitting in the backseat, talks softly about the things he has done. The people he has hurt.

He says he is sorry. You can believe that or not. But when his voice goes raspy and his eyes tear up, you give him the benefit of the doubt.

"If I got high again," he says, "I think . . . I'd just take myself to the police and tell them to lock me up. Instead of me gettin' high again, I'd rather kill myself. I'd . . . rather die.

"When I lost to Jimmy Paul, it hurt me. I felt real bad. But it don't hurt nothing like when I think what I did on account of drugs."

Back at the rehab center, Hayes gets in line for dinner: macaroni, string beans, salad, green Jell-O. He spills some water and quickly wipes it up. There are penalty points if he doesn't, and Hayes says he's playing by the rules. No matter what. He has three months left on his time here, then he must face a judge again. The judge could sentence him to three to five years in prison anyhow.

But he has been clean from drugs since July. And that's what this is all about. At one point he is asked what he would tell a 17-year-old in the east side who was carrying a pistol and feeling cocky. He launches into a speech as if the youth were sitting across the table.

"Look here," he says, "tell me if I'm right. You think nobody can tell you nothing. You think it's all about money, right? School can't teach you nothin', right? What you gotta learn is how to make some money, right?

"You think you're too slick to get in trouble? You'll get caught eventually. It might not be that bad at first but it'll get worser and worser. You'll wake up one morning and be an addict."

He is breathing fast. "People gonna tell you stuff you don't want to hear, but believe me, you'll wish you'd listened to it later. You don't want to go through what I gone through. Because I . . . don't . . . think . . . you'll make it."

His eyes are wide, as if listening to his own speech. He exhales, picks up his fork, and starts poking at the Jell-O. He doesn't say anything for a few minutes.

There's no payoff to this story. No moral. No Cinderella slipper. Fact is, Alvin Hayes spent the last couple of days in jail over a traffic violation. It never ends.

Or maybe it does. The drugs were the problem. The drugs seem to be under control. Caring was a problem. Sam Williams has cared. Boxing was the way out, and boxing is on the verge of coming back into the life of Alvin (Too Sweet) Hayes.

If hope is the ground floor of salvation, then the guy has at least a fighting chance.

On Thursday morning, the car will roll up to the rehab center and Hayes will hop in. And on Thursday night, when the fight is over, win or lose, that car will go back to the center and Hayes will be strip-searched before being readmitted.

He won't make big headlines. After all, he's fighting a nobody. A relative beginner. But that's OK.

Sometimes the longest road is the one that takes you back to square one.

1986

FEAR AND LOATHING IN A $23 MILLION PARTY STORE

January 26

NEW ORLEANS — Listen, boss. The kid was a professional hustler, I don't care how high his voice was. He had a shoe-shine brush and a jar of polish and he was about nine years old, but he didn't fool me; he was on the make just like everybody else in this city during Super Bowl Week, the biggest, liquor-crazed, money-soaked pep rally of the American calendar year. And the little newt had his eye on my shoes, which made me nervous.

"I betcha I can tell you where you got those shoes," he said.

"How much?" I said.

"Five bucks," he said.

I thought about it. And I figured, what the hell? Maybe the kid'll be psychic and I'll get the Super Bowl score two days early. Then I can clean up on every bookie in New Orleans and take a nice long vacation.

"OK. Five bucks. Tell me where I got my shoes."

He pointed to the street sign. "Right now, you got your shoes on St. Peter's Street. Now gimme my money."

Get it? OK, OK. There are worse ways to go down. I paid him. Besides, compared to the general swill that was flying around here by then, the kid actually made sense.

Anyhow, boss, I just wanted to tell you this before we go any further, so you don't balk when you see the entry on my expense account, under the heading "social research." It won't be the only one. And they won't all be five bucks, either. But OK. I'm jumping the gun a little.

This was the week that was, the Super Bowl XX countdown, and here, holed up in my peach-colored hotel room, with old newspapers and dirty socks and several half-filled glasses blocking the door, I am trying desperately to get it all down before deadline comes or I pass out, both of which must happen sooner or later.

You wanted me to document the past six days, do a diary sort of thing, right? And I thought it was a pretty good idea at the time. I'm not so sure anymore. Super Bowl week can get pretty weird, and how many lunatics can you squeeze into one piece without illustrations? Personally, I think this whole adventure started going downhill the minute Jim McMahon's butt turned into the week's hottest story. But a deal's a deal. Here goes nothing:

Monday: This was the day the players arrived, and the day every strip joint on Bourbon Street nailed up a "Welcome Super Bowl XX!" sign to let the tourists know it was OK to get smashed there, right alongside the locals.

I came in around 10 a.m. My cab driver wore a cowboy hat. Called himself Dirty Harry. Right, I figured. He told me to bet on the Patriots with three points. He had a sticker on his window that said "This Cab Protected By Smith And Wesson." So I said, "Patriots, huh? Good advice. Thanks, friend." It's starting, I thought. The weirdness.

Because the players were due to arrive soon, there were already TV film crews scouring the hotel lobby. They knew the big stars such as McMahon, Walter Payton and Refrigerator Perry by sight, but with everyone else it was, "Psst. Is that guy a Bear or a Patriot?" And it would turn out to be a bellhop.

You don't find a lot of intelligent behavior during Super Bowl week. Face it. It's six days of waiting for a football game to start. Nothing is happening, and you have about a trillion reporters who have to file something by six o'clock. Which is why you get great stories such as how the mayor's wife is betting a gallon of gumbo on the Bears, because blue is her favorite color.

I might as well talk here a little about Bourbon Street, because it will come up again. Bourbon Street is the jugular vein of this city, coursing through the French Quarter with every sort of sin known to man, many available by credit card. "Girls! Men! Topless! Bottomless!" Name it, they got it, all set to the rhythm of a Dixieland beat, and washed down with a big red drink they call a Hurricane, which I suppose comes from the way you look after you finish one. As in, "Hey. What hit you? A hurricane?"

Bourbon Street has no memory. At dawn they come by and sweep up the bottles and the bodies and they juice the bugger back up and start over again that night. Which is why a lot of people want the Super Bowl to be here full time. What better place for a disposable celebration?

So at 3 p.m. Monday, Bourbon Street was sedate with the soft sound of a distant saxophone, like something out of the Old South. And by 10 p.m. there were a thousand bug-heads staggering in the middle of it, wearing sunglasses and headbands, and screaming, "GO BEARS! KICK A—!"

I tell you, boss, the place comes alive like instant soup. Just add liquor and, boom, it's lit.

Tuesday: Between 9 and 11 a.m., the Bears and Patriots players were scattered around the field of the Louisiana Superdome, a cavernous indoor stadium big enough to house five or six cruise ships. It was the first of several full-scale encounters with the world's media. We're talking thousands of reporters here. You have Japan and Australia rubbing elbows with Fargo, N.D. Print journalists fighting for space with radio and TV. All of them trying to circle the same half-dozen "name" players — Payton, McMahon, Perry, Tony Eason, Craig James, Andre Tippett. It's not a good mix. Newspaper guys have little tolerance for TV types, especially when they stick a boom mike up their noses. It can get ugly.

What was said? Oh, let's see. Irving Fryar refused comment on reports that his wife cut him with a knife. Julius Adams, 37, the oldest lineman in football, said the wait had been worth it. So did Steve Grogan, John Hannah, Billy Sullivan and about 50 other people. McMahon sat in the middle of a mob and chewed tobacco. He said he had a sore butt and he was flying an acupuncturist in to treat it. You'd have thought he just predicted the day the stock market would crash.

By the way, boss. I found out the Chicago Tribune has 27 people here covering this. We have two — Curt Sylvester and I. Don't worry, though. Nothing those extra 25 reporters are gonna get that we won't.

Tuesday night we saw some players walking Bourbon Street for the first time. Steve Nelson, who has been a Patriots linebacker for about a zillion years, bumped into Gary Fencik, the free safety and token Yuppie of the Chicago Bears, in front of a female impersonators' club. Now, because Fencik graduated from Yale and Nelson went to North Dakota State, I'm not sure what they had to talk about. But I got close enough to hear Fencik say, "I'm just thrilled to be here," and then they split apart and this little geek with a cigar stepped up to Fencik and shoved a hand at him and said, "Gary, pleased to meet you. We just hired someone from Yale to join our firm." Fencik sort of nodded, then turned and high-tailed it down the street like a jackrabbit. I think he suddenly realized this wasn't a football field. And it sure as hell wasn't Yale.

Wednesday: By now McMahon's rear end was front-page news, which goes to show you how little really goes on here during this week. Over eggs and grits — cooked industrial style and served to two thousand hung-over sports writers — Bears coach Mike Ditka insisted McMahon's butt was for real. "He's hurting," Ditka said. So were the sports writers. In several minutes they would be turned loose inside a giant ballroom with every player seated at his own table, identified by a magic-marker sign with his number and his name. And there would be only 10 seats per table. First shoved, first served. It takes more than eggs to prepare a man for a nightmare like that.

Meanwhile, the whole city of New Orleans was starting to look the same. Everywhere you went people were wearing headbands that said "Rozelle" — McMahon had worn one in the NFC championship game in defiance of the commissioner, which I'm sure teed off old Pete, because he wasn't getting a cut. Face-painting was big. There is nothing quite like asking a middle-aged woman for the time and seeing P-A-T-S! across her forehead.

By Wednesday night, I saw a man belly-flop onto concrete along

Bourbon Street, while his friends stood by and applauded. There was an old piano player who played "C.C. Rider" and made horn sounds and called himself "The Human Trumpet." There was someone in a Bears suit and someone dressed like Paul Revere, and some bimbo hanging from a telephone pole, screaming, "ALL CHICAGO IS GOOD FOR IS LANDING THE AIRPLANE" — he swooped one way — "AND TAKING BACK OFF!" — he swooped the other way. Several listeners thought he made perfect sense. Things were sinking.

Thursday: A buddy of mine, whom we'll call J.S., rolled into town and asked to crash on the spare bed in my hotel room, and I said OK. We woke up Thursday morning to hysterical voices. "My God, they've come for us!" J.S. screamed. But it was the clock radio. A report that McMahon had called the women of New Orleans "sluts," had prompted every half-brained morning deejay to incite a riot. Women were calling in with insults of their own to McMahon, screaming them across morning drive time.

It would turn out to be only a drop in the barrel of weirdness that day. There was a photo of McMahon mooning a helicopter. Payton was complaining about lack of recognition for his career. Eason was rumored to have the flu. Tony Franklin said his Super Bowl dream was "to win the game with a 60-yard kick, run into the locker room and jump into a hot tub with Heather Locklear and a bottle of Dom Perignon." Hell, he could have done most of that on Bourbon Street that night.

By the end of the day, the McMahon thing turned out to be a complete lie, giving new meaning to the phrase "what journalistic standards?" Meanwhile, there wasn't a TV screen in town that wasn't running the Bears' "Super Bowl Shuffle" — a mindless rap song video that only proves Steve Fuller can't dance to save his life.

I saw a baby with a Rozelle headband. A baby? Two female impersonators singing a Bears fight song. Acupuncture needles selling at an all-time high. Odds were put out on who would score the first touchdown Sunday, and Refrigerator Perry was listed at 12-1.

Speaking of odds, did you realize, boss, that in 1803 we picked up the whole state of Louisiana for $23 million from the French — and Sunday we'll bet about $30 million alone on the Bears' ability to eat up a quarterback by halftime?

It was clearly time for a Hurricane.

Friday: How can I describe Friday to you? Maybe this way. Friday is the long-awaited day that every slimeball, lounge lizard, air-brained, doughnut-eating, semi-plastered chewing-gum mutant head shows up at the hotel and immediately stakes out a spot in the elevator. That way no matter when you need to get to your room, it's absolutely impossible unless you want to walk 23 flights of stairs marked FIRE EXIT: KEEP OUT.

The press conferences were dwindling. With the game just two days away, players were off-limits. Only Ditka and Raymond Berry, the Patriots coach whom the media had nicknamed Mr. Snooze, were available. There was plenty going on without interviews. The SWAT team had already been in the Hilton once that morning, sweeping the place because of a bomb threat.

Bourbon Street was sheer insanity by this point. You needed a nut card just to get out there. J.S. and I made it over. Someone ran by in a rabbit costume, followed by a girl dressed like Alice. "Did you see the rabbit?" she asked. We just shrugged. It's best not to encourage these people.

Friday night is traditionally the commissioner's party — the NFL's All-Out Blowout for 3,000 executives and media. About two zillion pounds of oysters and lobster and shrimp, washed down with two zillion mixed drinks, all sprinkled with the appropriate number of stars — Diana Ross, Doug Flutie, Ahmad Rashad, Michael J. Fox — mixing in like common folks. Someone spotted Sonny Jurgensen, the old Redskins quarterback, and asked about the difference between football today and when he played.

"You mean besides fun?" he said.

Saturday: Madness. You couldn't make a phone call from the hotel because the switchboard was so jammed. People were sleeping in the lobby chairs, while rocks bands pounded away. Someone spotted Bill Murray. Bill Murray? A torrential rain fell on the city — some divine sign, no doubt — which only kept people running and drinking indoors. There was Frank Sinatra. Frank Sinatra? A Patriots rally was held in Jackson Square — a few thousand crazed and soaked New Englanders whooping it up before the serious nighttime drinking began. J.S. told me there was a full moon predicted for this evening. "Great," I said. "That's all we need." I had visions of werewolves, Minnie Mouse and Rambo trashing my hotel room.

This was getting to be too much, boss. Every nonsensical word a football player had uttered was reported 200 times. The desk people were wearing furry ears. Every cheese-head had a drink in his hand, if not a bottle.

I needed air. I wandered back to St. Peter's Street. I wanted another crack at that kid.

"Betcha I know where you got those shoes," he said. The little thief.

"Tell me where I bought them," I said.

"I'll tell you where you got 'em," he said.

"Uh-uh. Tell me where I bought them."

He just shrugged. Another kid came over. About the same size. He was wearing a cap, and one of his eyes was closed. There were stitches around it.

"I'll tell you what you paid for those shoes," he said. "For five dollars."

A new challenge. All right, kid. At this point I was sure I had him.

"You're on. Tell me what I paid for 'em."

"You paid money for 'em," he said.

I owed him five. I reached into my pocket. All I had was a ten. His eyes lit up.

It was getting late. Just hours before the big game. Somewhere in the city, McMahon and his sore butt were resting on cotton sheets. Payton was down the hall, probably meditating. Eason was sneezing, and Berry was praying for a miracle, or maybe just throwing up. On Bourbon Street people were hanging out of windows and spilling champagne and hollering gibberish that they would never remember the next day. The moon was out. The music was thumping. This was the Super Bowl, I thought. And the game hasn't even started.

Next thing I knew, the kid was gone. So was my 10 bucks.

IF YOU HAVE THE MONEY, BEARS HAVE THE RHYME

January 28

NEW ORLEANS — "OK. OK. Quiet in the studio. Bears, are you ready? This is the moment we've been waiting for. The follow-up to the 'Super Bowl Shuffle.' Do it right and it could be a gold record — not to mention huge video sales. Big bucks, fellas. It'll be great. OK. Mr. Perry, try not to drool quite so much this time. And Mr. Fuller, don't dance. Just, uh, sort of stand there, OK? Remember, guys, let's sing on the beat, not in between it. All right. Is everybody ready?"

"YEAH! ... Of course! ... DO IT! ... I'm hungry. ... WOOO! ... Where's the broads?"

"OK. Cue the drums, Mort. Places, everybody. Ah-one, ah-two, ah-three, ah-four. ..."

WE ARE THE BEARS, SHUFFLIN' CREW,
DID YOU MISS US? WE'RE BACK FOR TWO.
WE'RE SO BAD WE KNOW WE'RE GOOD,
GONNA BE RICH, LIKE WE KNEW WE WOULD.
WE'RE NOT HERE TO DO SOMETHING FUNNY
WE'RE JUST HERE FOR SUPER BOWL MONEY

"They call me Sweetness, I like to dance,
I wanted to score but I never got a chance,
They gave it to the fat man, instead of me,
I got the bruises, he got the TD,
Won't get mad, or knock over a fountain,
I'll just go home and run up a mountain."

"I'm the rockin' QB, my name's McMahon,
Super Bowl's over now here's my plan,
I'm gonna have pizza with Pete Rozelle,
He and me got some headbands to sell,
Then maybe I'll go, and shave my head
Drink some beers, wind up under the bed,
Chew some tobacco, shoot off a gun,
Do 'Rolling Stone' then become a nun."

WE ARE THE BEARS, WE WON, WE OUGHTA
THAT WAS NO GAME, THAT WAS SLAUGHTA,
WE'RE NOT HERE, TO DO NOTHING RASH,
WE'RE JUST HERE FOR SUPER BOWL CASH,
PAY UP (drums) ba-ba-ba-ba-ba-ba-ba-ba-ba-ba

"Ditka's the name, Coach for short,

You don't like it I'll take off your nose,
Everything I do, I credit George Halas,
He taught me coaching, and poetry, too,
Some say I'm mean, some say stupid,
but I bet I can make this rhyme. . . . uh –."

WE ARE THE BEARS, SHUFFLIN' CREW,
COME TO COLLECT OUR SUPER BOWL DUE
WE ATE 'EM UP, THAT'S WHAT IT'S ABOUT,
TASTED LIKE CHOWDER, WE SPIT 'EM OUT
WE'RE NOT HERE, TO PUT ON A SHOW
WE'RE JUST HERE FOR SUPER BOWL DOUGH.

"Sackman's comin', his name is Dent,
Now it's the Bears who're gonna get bent,
They coulda signed me, for 300 grand
Now they can come and kiss my hand,
Maybe a million? Maybe two?
I'm the MVP, what's it worth to you?
I'm not here, to dig some ditch
I'm just here to get Super Bowl rich."

"Willie Gault, number 83
Lippett and Tippett now bow to me
That's why I'm quitting, as Bears receiver,
To realize my dream as host of 'Dance Fever.' "

WE ARE THE BEARS, 46-10,
YOU DON'T BELIEVE IT WE'LL DO IT AGAIN,
WOULDN'T BE PRETTY, WOULDN'T BE NICE,
YOU'D HAVE TO SIT THRU HALFTIME TWICE
WE'RE NOT HERE, HUNTIN' FOR DUCKS,
WE'RE JUST HERE FOR SUPER BOWL BUCKS

"Fencik here, I went to Yale,
Biff and Dougie flew in from Vail,
Muffy and Missy gave me two big kisses,
Beating Harvard was never like this is,
We crushed the Pats by more than thirty,
I didn't even get my uniform dirty,
I'm not here, looking for a block,
I'm just here for my Super Bowl stock."

"My name's Eason, you don't know me,
Folks in New England used to call me Tony,
But after Sunday they sold my home,
Took my dog, disconnected my phone,
Can I join you, in any form?

Carry your helmets? Clean your dorm?"

**WE ARE THE BEARS, THE ONLY ONES,
THROW THIS GUY OUT ON HIS BUNS!**

"They call me Fridge, I'm the rookie,
I may be fat but I'm no dumb cookie,
I scored a touchdown, that was the plan,
Then I knocked out my own man,
I'm tired of jokes about my weight,
Next year I'm gonna weigh 408,
I'm not here looking for the green stuff,
I just came for those vanilla cream puffs —."

"Buddy here, last name's Ryan,
Folks think a head coach's job I'm eyein',
Is it true? I really wouldn't know,
(dial 999-8760)."

**WE ARE THE BEARS, CALL MTV,
GOODBY SPRINGSTEEN AND SHEILA E.
VIDEO STARDOM HAS OUR VOTE,
SHOVE THIS RECORD DOWN THEIR THROAT
WE'RE THE BEST, HEAD OF THE CLASS,
ALL YOU PATS CAN KISS OUR ... RINGS!**

"OK. Cut. Cut. That's a wrap, fellas. Thanks."

"GREAT! ... Nice job. ... Hey, man, you sounded awful. ... LET'S EAT! ... Who sounded awful? ... Get off my foot, pea-brain. ... WOOO! ... Where's the broads?"

"Hey, yo! Mister producer!"

"Yes, Mr. Perry?"

"What're we calling this thing, anyway?"

"We're going to re-create an old dance craze, Mr. Perry. We're calling it The Hustle."

A MOMENT OF MADNESS, A WEEK OF SORROW

February 9

The coach speaks in a whisper, and the young wrestlers gather around him in a semicircle on the purple mats. They listen. They say nothing. A few of them are big and muscular. Others are smaller, their skin soft. They are teenage, but they are still children, really. And children should never have to witness a murder, especially not to one of their own. But it happened inside Romulus High School, and now everybody here must learn to live with the nightmares, and it is not easy.

This is a story about a moment of madness, about a young life snuffed out for no reason except the rush of anger that kids enjoy because it makes them feel grown-up, makes them feel tough, makes them carry a weapon. And then something tragic happens, a knife goes into someone's chest, and they want to be kids again, but they never can be.

How could it happen that an 18-year-old senior, captain of the football team, goes to school in the morning and never comes home? And now there are broken pieces of dreams all over the place, and teachers hugging students, and flowers wilting on classroom desks — flowers left over from last Tuesday, the first time anyone can remember a funeral service taking place in a high school auditorium.

How could it happen? That was the question that buzzed through the parking lot that day, through the hallways jammed with reporters, and through the auditorium itself, where some 800 friends and family — most of them barely old enough to drive a car — listened quietly to prayers and eulogies for Robert O'Day, whose body lay in a coffin just in front of the stage.

And a few miles away, in a Wayne County youth home, a 16-year-old boy from Inkster — who had never met Bobby O'Day before putting a knife into him — was being held in custody, facing a charge of murder.

Romulus High lies hard off Interstate 94, just a few miles west of Metro Airport, so that at any given moment there's probably a plane flying overhead, landing or taking off. But inside, Romulus could be any high school, a spidery maze of hallways and classrooms and glass trophy cases and white porcelain water fountains. Bells ring every hour, and the kids scream and their sneakers squeak on the linoleum tile floor, and then the bells ring again and the doors close and it is quiet.

On the last day of his life, Bobby O'Day came here expecting, as usual, to go to class and then to wrestling practice. And to have a few laughs with

46

his friends in the hallway, and maybe to put his arm around his girlfriend. He was, by everyone's account, simply a great kid, a strong kid, a football player and wrestler who had taken high school popularity to the mat and won easily. His handsome face fairly leaps off the yearbook page. He was 18, tall and well-built, on the lip of becoming a college heartthrob. He had hoped to attend Western New Mexico University, because his parents, who own a family printing business, planned to move to New Mexico to open a new shop once he graduated.

"Everybody we asked about the kid had nothing but praise for him," said Mike Martinez, an assistant coach at Western New Mexico who recruited O'Day. "His work habits, his attitude — you couldn't find anything wrong with him."

O'Day's coaches had sent reels of film out to Martinez, along with a letter from the student himself stating how much he would like to "contribute to the program" should it offer him a scholarship. Martinez was looking over the film about the time the bell rang at Romulus on the afternoon of Friday, Jan. 31. The last school bell Bobby O'Day would ever hear.

W hat actually happened that afternoon is sketchy. It will be for some time, because these are children involved here, and in this society we still protect children, even when they take a life.

What is known is enough. It is too much. There was a scuffle the day before between a wrestler and a freshman student in the hallway. Scuffle? Maybe just a bump. One of those mindless, "Who are you bumping?" kind of things that led the non-wrestler to say, "I'm gonna get you." And the next day, around 2:30 in the afternoon, he came back with friends, all bloated with that violent sensation that makes teenagers think they're important when they act tough. And one of the friends had a knife.

They were looking for the wrestler. An assistant coach, Norman Butler, tried to get rid of them. Just then the wrestler they were looking for came out of the locker room. A fight broke out. A fight? Maybe just poking and jabbing. Butler tried to break it up. It was then that O'Day arrived, saw what was going on, and jumped in to help his teammate.

It wasn't his fight. He didn't have to get involved. That should matter, shouldn't it? But it didn't. O'Day picked the wrong guy, and while the two kids who had started the whole stupid affair were exchanging harmless blows, the wrong guy, according to witnesses, pulled out a six-inch pocketknife and stabbed O'Day, stabbed him once, but once in the chest is enough. The outsiders fled. And O'Day, bleeding and stunned, staggered back into the locker room where his teammates were dressing. And he collapsed. There was screaming. Shock. Within seconds O'Day was stretched out on the concrete floor and someone had a shirt stuffed over

47

the wound and it was soaking up blood fast.

Wrestling coach Wayne Schimming was in the school office when someone screamed, "Bob's been stabbed!" and he sprinted down the corridor and pushed through the doors and saw a crowd around the handsome athlete whom he had often thought of as his own son. Every coach has one kid who gets a passkey to his heart, and Bobby O'Day was it for Schimming. The two had spent countless hours together. "I hope my own kids turn out like him," the coach had said. He was sure Bobby would place in the state tournament this year, that he would get a scholarship, and now here he was covered with a bloody shirt and his eyes were closed.

"My first thought was just to get to him," Schimming said, "to comfort him." He pauses on the memory and his voice drys up. "I don't know about, you know, medically, stages of consciousness but . . . he . . . when I got to him, he wasn't responding to me."

No goodbys or final words. That is the way it happens in real life.

A caravan of cars followed the ambulance to Westland Medical Center. Schimming stayed with Bobby's parents and told them over and over "how much I loved him. How much we all loved him." A doctor called the parents into a room. They asked Schimming in, also. He came out after a few minutes and approached a group of his wrestlers in the hospital waiting area. He told them the only way he knew how, which was the simplest way. "He died," Schimming said.

There is no justice that follows. No satisfaction in a suspect being apprehended. There is only irony, layer after layer, peeled back like the skin of an onion. It began when O'Day was stabbed in a fight that he knew nothing about. And it continued when the family returned home from the hospital that night, still stunned by the news, and not 10 minutes later the phone rang and it was Mike Martinez, the recruiter from Western New Mexico.

"Hello, is Bob there?" Martinez asked.

"This is Bob," said Mr. O'Day, who shared his son's name.

"The one who plays football?"

"No," the father answered softly. "My son is dead. He was killed today."

Martinez apologized and hung up quickly. He never mentioned that he was calling to offer Bobby a scholarship.

I t is one week after it all happened, and Wayne Schimming still wears the look of a shell-shocked man, as if someone had just clubbed him from behind and he is about to buckle at the knees and crumble. His thick neck and torso are stiff, his tie seems to choke him, and his blond hair frames a face that is taut with the fight against tears.

"Right now," he said Friday morning, when asked how he was feeling,

"I'm wondering how I'm going to get through the day."

School was canceled for two days following the incident. The first was for the teachers to decide how best to handle the grief. The second was for the funeral.

Like most funerals, the service held for Bobby O'Day was a curious blend of sweetness and horror. The question of "Why did this have to happen?" could not be answered. And yet high school athletes from around the state, wrestlers whom O'Day had pinned to the mat, football players he had tackled, fellow teenagers who had envied his abilities, people who knew him and people who had never heard of him until he was a victim, came together to pray and weep for him. Many of the teenagers — children, really, despite the eye shadow and the leather jackets and the grown-up armor they wear — had never faced a life loss before.

Their pain came in every direction and every form. One student carried carnations from the casket with him for several days until a guidance counselor finally told him to "let go." One wrestler asked to quit the team, despite his excellent record. He had been in the locker room when it happened and has not returned since. The student who provoked the incident is transferring. The wrestler whom he bumped is off the team for now. Butler, the assistant coach who was in the middle when it all happened — and who now must forever fight the demons of "Why didn't I? . . . Why couldn't I? . . ." — is still too upset to say anything.

There is no sharing the grief of the parents.

O'Day was a slice of all of them, all they had given him and all they wanted to be — one part athlete, one part student, one part leader, one part charmer, one part loving son.

He lived for everything. He died for nothing.

"It was terribly senseless," said Romulus superintendent of schools Dr. William Bedell. "It was just two young men being macho; unfortunately, Robert O'Day is dead."

The wrestlers begin to stretch on the purple mats. Though there are 35 to 40 kids on the team, there are only eight here today. It is snowing outside and Schimming says he hopes that's the reason, but he knows better. These kids are hurting. They are confused. Schimming brought a radio into practice because he felt the music might keep the room from being ghostly silent. But except for the music, it's pretty quiet anyhow.

Schimming goes downstairs to make a phone call, and walks back through the locker room where it all happened, and it all happens again inside his head. "It's in my mind all the time," he says. He mentions how difficult it was to get the kids to even dress for a practice in that room. How empty the first practice was without Bobby leading the exercises.

"He's just ... not there," said the coach.

In wrestling there are moves called "escapes," designed to free the wrestler from the grasp of his opponent. Roll your hips out, spin your shoulders, get free. But you can roll Bobby O'Day's death around into a hundred positions and you can't escape its senselessness and horror. And you can't escape the sad fact that in days to come, when these Romulus High School students find themselves face to face with another person's danger, a voice inside is going to say, "Don't get involved. Remember what happened to Bobby."

The locker room is quiet and clean now. A water fountain is locked on and there is a small splashing sound that won't stop. Taped on the window to the coach's office are several notices about college scholarships, and a plainly typed copy of a poem called "Don't Quit," a verse common to locker rooms around the country. Part of it reads:

"Life is queer with its twists and turns
As every one of us sometimes learns ...
So stick to the fight when you're hardest hit
It's when things seem worst that you mustn't quit"

Schimming shakes his head. He's worried about the other wrestlers who aren't here. It has never happened before, and there's a big tournament coming up and he's not sure what to do about it.

"I feel like crying right now, I really do," he says, and then he turns before the tears can start and heads back to the muscled children who are waiting for him upstairs, no longer as young as they used to be.

SKILES CAN ONLY WAIT FOR THE REST OF HIS LIFE

March 23

KANSAS CITY, Mo. — It was too early for heartbreak. The sun was just creeping through the huge glass windows. The plane wasn't ready yet, and the airport was filled with the lonely echo that comes in those ungodly hours before the coffee shop opens.

It was the first morning of the rest of Scott Skiles' life, the first morning he was no longer a college athlete but a young man with memories behind him and a prison sentence in front of him. It was a hell of a morning, really, and Skiles was coming in on no sleep. "Not one minute," he said, shaking his head slowly. You don't sleep when your insides are on fire.

He was dead now, but seven hours earlier he was still alive, because he was still playing basketball, and anyone who has seen this clenched fist of a man knows if ever a human being needed a ball in his hands for survival, it was Scott Skiles. And, damn, the ball was there, right where he wanted it, in his hands, as the final seconds of the big game against Kansas ticked away, and the score was tied and the crowd was screaming and he was racing up the court with defenders chasing him and his eyes were locked on that basket, as if the last lights of his life were up there waiting inside the red steel rim.

"I had eight seconds," he said softly, narrating it all over again. "I should've dribbled that baby up, 25 feet from the hole. Then I should've pulled up and shot a normal jumper and hit it for the game-winner. . . . I had it in my hands. And I failed."

The shot he fired instead was an off-balance jumper from around 17 feet. It careened off the rim. The clock ran out and the game went into overtime and his team, Michigan State, had nothing left. The Spartans lost a few minutes later, 96-86. They were out of the NCAA tournament.

It wasn't his fault. No way. There was a malfunctioning clock and bad officiating and two missed free throws by teammates and a dozen other good reasons why the blame should fall anywhere but on the pale white shoulders of Skiles, whose gritted-teeth style of play had literally carried the Spartans this far, the regional semifinal, way past anyone's wildest expectations.

Besides, Friday night's game was such a thriller, people left saying, "There was no loser tonight." But Skiles didn't buy it. He blamed himself. And in the showers afterward, as the water ran over his head but the loss would not wash away, he turned to his teammate Larry Polec and quietly said, "It's over, isn't it?" and Polec could only nod yes, it was over.

What do you do when the buzzer sounds and there's no going back? You are a senior. You are history. What do you do? You don't sleep, that's for sure. "I talked with my folks for a half-hour, I talked with my grandparents. I went upstairs and got into bed. I tried to sleep, but I just rolled around."

He sighed deeply. His eyes were bloodshot and he wore a green cap over his stringy blond hair. His face was marked by a few pimples, the kind that surface on college skin when things get sweaty.

Here in the morning light, with cinnamon gum in his mouth and his hands tucked in his coat pockets, Scott Skiles looked very young. Too young, it seemed, for all that has happened. Too young, certainly, for the jail cell that awaits him.

But heroes are cast in all kinds of colors, and to understand Scott Skiles you must be able to mix the golds of glory with the deep blues of tragedy, for here was a young man splashing through both. It is doubtful we will soon see his likes again, a 22-year-old twister playing an entire college basketball season with the threat of prison hanging over his head.

He was forever on the front pages of newspapers this year for his 27.7 scoring average, his dazzling passing game, his fiery leadership. And because he was going to jail. A 30-day sentence for violating the terms of his probation with a drunken-driving arrest last November. Skiles had been arrested before: in August 1984, charged with marijuana and cocaine possession, and in September 1984, charged with driving while intoxicated.

After the most recent episode, people had called for Skiles' expulsion, for Skiles' head, for Skiles' coach's head. And at the same time, other people were calling for him to light it up night after night in the gym for the glory of old MSU.

"It's been more difficult than anyone will imagine," he said, leaning forward in the airport chair as he waited with his teammates for the flight back home. "There are a lot of things about the arrests that I'm sure will die with me. I just know I'm damn lucky to have gone to Michigan State. When I got into trouble people didn't say, 'Let's find a way we can phase this kid out.' They stuck by me.

"And this year . . . well, I don't know if I could have played basketball anywhere else with all that happened."

All season, Skiles was greeted in foreign gyms with chants of "GO TO JAIL!" or "D.U.I!" Some fans waved plastic bags of sugar at him to suggest cocaine.

He had bigger problems. Like the jail sentence that comes this summer. "Sure I'm scared of jail," he said, when asked. "It'd be inhuman not to be scared of it. But isn't that what jail is supposed to be about?

"The thing is," he added, his voice lowered now, almost pleading, "I don't want to drive drunk. I mean, I don't want to go out and kill someone on the road. God, that's the last thing I'd want to do. I just made a . . . mistake."

He leaned back, quiet. In that last word was the unmistakable plea of conscience, and anyone who had ever messed up in life would have had a hard time not feeling something for the guy.

But Skiles is not usually that fortunate. His manner doesn't evoke sympathy. He lacks the sweetie-pie countenance of a Magic Johnson or an Isiah Thomas. What can you do? Some guys buy with their looks and some guys pay for them. Skiles just happens to have the flaring eyes of a marine sergeant in a barroom brawl. And that's during lay-up drills. Even when he grins he has the look of someone who has just gotten away with murder.

How did Jim Valvano, the N.C. State coach, describe him? "Whenever I watch Michigan State on TV I'm afraid to turn the channel because I keep thinking Skiles is gonna jump out of the set and say, 'What the hell do you think you're doing?' "

But it's this same ferocity that is responsible for all the victory in the MSU program this year. And there's the dilemma. You can't have one without the other. Skiles is a fist-wielding, bad-mouthing, rile-'em-up kind of player on the court. The words "sit down" might as well be written in Swedish for him. Skiles bled from the knee all game in MSU's tournament win over Washington. Yet he scored 31 points. He led the upset charge against Georgetown even though he had a piercing sciatic nerve injury. He scored 24. "You can count on Scott to spill his guts on the floor," said Polec. And that's what the Spartans needed.

If Skiles had played like a choirboy, MSU fans would have been watching "Dallas" Friday night.

Friday night. The Goodby Game. It has already replayed itself "too many times" inside Skiles' head, and this was only in the airport on the morning after. A man walked by with an overstuffed garment bag. Another man passed reading a newspaper. Skiles didn't notice. He slumped in his chair and his eyes went far away when he described those last two minutes.

"It all happened so quick. I thought when (MSU freshman) Mark Brown was at the line, and we were up, 80-78, if he could have made one foul shot we'd have won it. He didn't. But I missed a foul shot before him and Larry (Polec) missed one before him, and if we'd have made them, Mark wouldn't have had to be there.

"Then there was the thing with the clock malfunctioning. It's a shame that had to happen in such a big game. Even worse than that was the officiating. I hope those officials aren't working the Final Four because they're not very good. They made a lot of bad calls on both sides."

Several of those came on Skiles early. He was tagged with three fouls and forced to sit for the last seven minutes of the first half.

"That was the worst feeling in the world," he said of walking to the bench. "The worst."

Well, probably the second worst. There was, and always will be for Skiles, that final shot. You have to fully understand this young man to realize that he had every expectation of winning that game with that shot, every expectation of doing the same thing three more times, until the NCAA crown was painted green and white. If there is such a thing as winning by sheer will, Skiles already has a half-dozen games in his back pocket. And Friday was almost there.

"I don't think it's any secret that I thought that I could win the whole thing for Michigan State," he said. "That's the way I feel. That's the kind of confidence I had.

"When I came down the floor, I knew I had Polec on my left and Vernon Carr on my right. After I missed the shot, right before the overtime, Vernon told me he was open. In retrospect, I probably should have passed it to him. But I don't know, I just felt like I had to put a shot up there."

Someone suggested that the place was insanity, thousands of screaming Kansas fans thumping their feet and waving banners. Who could think straight in such a blast furnace?

Skiles waved off the suggestion. "I've won with that stuff before," he said. The message was clear. If he was passing out of the college ranks on a disappointing note, well, so be it. There would be no easy excuses.

Then came an odd question, a question that could only be asked of Skiles, and in whose answer you catch a glimpse of something: If he could do one thing over and make it come out right — the trouble that is sending him to jail or that final, off-balance jumper — which would he choose?

He thought about it for a few seconds. He decided on an answer. "I guess I'd choose both," he said finally.

But he couldn't help it. It showed. His heart was on the side with the net.

They were calling his flight.

"You know, I don't know how I'm going to get home," he said suddenly. "My car's not even there. I'll have to get a ride from somebody. Maybe I'll stick around. Maybe I'll go home to Plymouth (Indiana). I had 100 percent confidence we'd be advancing to the Final Four. It's my responsibility. I'm taking the blame. It's something I have to deal with the rest of my life."

He reached for his bag. He was dressed like a civilian. His college basketball career was abruptly over. He said he hoped to be drafted by an NBA team, but college is not the pros and he thinks "the scouts don't like me that much." He also knows he could be serving his jail term when the NBA draft takes place.

"I really hope I can avoid that," he said softly.

There were a lot of us who screamed for justice when Skiles was arrested. There were a lot of us who screamed for a miracle when Skiles brought the ball up in those last regulation seconds. None of us ever knew what was going on inside of him. And most likely we never will.

The final colors of a man's life belong with the gods. But in the early morning light of an airport gate, with all the crowds and the cameras and the celebrations gone, with him sitting there chewing gum, a cap on his head, no jump shots, no waving fists, no siren call of glory, the sweetest moments of his basketball life probably behind him and nothing immediately ahead but a summer and a jail sentence, it was hard not to cast Scott Skiles as some sort of hero, even a tragic one. It seemed only fair.

"I'm very, very sad my career is over," he said finally. "I don't know if I'll ever play like this again. I may make it in the NBA, I may not.

"But you know, it doesn't matter. As far as I'm concerned, my quality years were played at Michigan State. No matter what happens. And I'll tell you this. In my mind, my hometown is East Lansing, Michigan. And it always will be."

He got up, pulled out his ticket, and walked slowly through the carpeted corridor of the rest of his life, his head neither high nor low, but staring straight out at what was in front of him.

WEBBER COLLEGE: BEST TEAM YOU NEVER SAW

March 28

BABSON PARK, Fla. — The gym is empty now. Just two baskets staring at each other across a hardwood floor. Flies circle overhead. The air is sticky. It's hot. It's still. It's dead. It's over.

Dies the season, dies the program. Almost nobody knows what went on here at Webber College and almost nobody ever will now. Most American eyes this weekend are on the NCAA Final Four in downtown Dallas. Millions will watch it. Millions will bet on it. It's a big story.

But this is a better story.

This is a story about a chance of a lifetime, a deal you'd be crazy to take and crazier to pass up. This is a story of a tiny college and its gunslinging president, named Buck, who gave a basketball coach, named Nick, a chance to bring a handful of kids from the streets of New York and Baltimore and Buffalo down to the middle of nothing in Florida, to an auditorium with two backboards nailed to the walls and red ants crawling on the floor, and to work a miracle.

And they almost won it all.

This is a story about the Webber College Warriors, who disappeared forever last week, and who might have been the best college basketball team you've never seen. They just ran out of time.

Imagine the conversation. You're a young basketball player who couldn't make Division I — maybe grades, maybe lack of recruiting — so you've been playing junior college ball, or maybe not playing at all, and you're just hanging around in August 1983 trying to decide what you should do next and the phone rings.

"This is Nick Creola," the voice began. "I'm the new coach at Webber College. I'm looking for a man of your caliber. I'll give you a full scholarship, you'll play right away, you'll get a chance to see sunny Florida. If you're interested, there'll be a plane ticket waiting for you next Thursday. Come down. Look around. If you like the place we'll sign you right there."

This was the sales pitch Creola used on his prospects — all of whom he'd collected in two weeks' time — and as he drove to the Orlando airport that Thursday he still had no idea how many of them would buy it. "I had no recruiting budget," he said. "What else could I do?"

He had taken the job himself only a few weeks before. Who takes a coaching job in August? At Webber College no less, a tiny business school on the curb of the Bible Belt, with 450 students and no gym. Heck, the whole basketball idea was just a publicity stunt by the school president.

It was a gimmick. An investment in advertising. It was crazy. Which means it was just the kind of thing G.W. (Buck) Cleven, a former bomber pilot turned college president, would do. Cleven, 67, is a big man, with white hair and ice-blue eyes. He rules Webber. He calls himself "a benevolent despot," keeps a .357 Magnum in the desk drawer, and once fired a shotgun at joyriders who were disturbing his campus. Get the picture?

Only now he wanted a basketball team. A nationally renowned basketball team. Get some ink for his college. So he hired Creola, who is short, tanned, muscular and a winner.

Creola was a successful junior college coach at Jamestown, N.Y. — his team was ranked No. 1 in the nation — and back then, in 1983, he was 40 and single and figured this Webber thing might help him move up in the coaching ranks. Of course, he had no idea whom he'd be coaching.

And then he got to the airport.

"I looked around the baggage area and there were five or six big black kids, and they were talking, some of them knew of one another, and I said to myself, 'Holy jeez. This town is in for the shock of their lives.' "

Why? Because this is not New York or Baltimore. This is the South, and changes come slowly, and Webber College is mostly white. It's hardly the setting for a supersonic, inner-city-type basketball team. Drive out to Webber. If you can find it. Take Route 27 to Fat Boy's Barbeque, turn right, and keep going. Don't look for any other landmarks, because there aren't any. Just some orange groves and baked grass as hard as bristle. And after a few miles, it's just sort of there. A handful of small yellow buildings. Webber College.

It was here that Creola brought players such as Rockin' Rodney Jones from Buffalo, and Big Joe Farmer from the Bronx, and Dennis Pope from Baltimore and Carl (Jete) Jeter and his brother Gary, and Joe Patterson, who can dribble the ball behind his back and between his legs and over his head while on one knee. Brought them into an auditorium with no air conditioning — it had to be at least 100 degrees — pointed to the makeshift baskets and said, "Let's go, let's get started."

The floor was carpeted — carpeted? — and the ball kept skipping away. Gnats stuck to the wet skin of the players. One player took off his socks and wrung the sweat out like a sponge. Creola, wearing shorts, leaned down on one knee to watch a drill and jumped up yelling, "What the hell?" and there were red ants all over his legs chewing on him.

A fight broke out that first practice, a fight between two players, and the others instinctively rushed in and broke it up. And then they looked at each other, sweat washing their faces, and there was a sudden realization that they either died through this separately or lived through it together.

"I owe you guys the chance to be national champions," Creola said that first day. "How can you get beat? How can you get beat with what you're going through here?"

They had nothing. But nothing plus desire is no longer nothing. It's a beginning.

There are only about 120 people on this earth who can tell you about that first game. It was played in a local high school gym and the few students who came brought their books, figuring on early boredom. Creola's new team marched in: eight blacks, two whites, two Cubans and the coach. The first tap went up and Rodney Jones, a 6-foot-5 forward who can jump high enough from a standing position to bang his head on the rim, took the ball in for a reverse dunk. Heads turned. What was this? The Warriors laughed through that game, won it by something like 50 points, with alley-oops and slams and jams.

And they kept winning. They would later say their practices — in the hellhole of a gym — were harder than their games. It was movie material. These kids, mostly from northern cities, whirling and juking and sending a buzz through the state. Winning? Is that the word for 141-62? And 137-50? And 95-36? All real scores from Webber victories.

"The word spread on us like wildfire," Creola said. Once during a game against an NCAA Division II opponent — which is like Cyclops playing Harpo Marx — the big-school coach came over to Creola and promised to "take it easy" on his kids.

"Thanks," Creola said. The Warriors won by 22 points.

By the time that season ended, Webber was 34-5 and won the national championship of the National Little College Athletic Association. It wasn't magic. It was more like chemistry. The players were all similar; all good, flashy players who had somehow missed the boat for bigger schools. They had three common denominators: Creola, the dunk and poverty.

"The first time I had Joe Farmer at school," says Creola, "he opened up his suitcase and there was only a toothbrush inside. I said, 'Joe, where's your clothes?' And he said, 'Coach, I'm wearin' them.'" Creola raised money to buy Farmer and several others a decent wardrobe. He and assistant Steve Prevesk ran bingo games every Sunday night to help pay for the players' books.

Creola was tireless, selling ads for programs, coaching, phoning recruits, coaching, playing psychologist, coaching.

"We were like his family," says Jones. And they were all alone.

Let's face it. This was a team full of sleek, street-smart black players in a white Southern school in a white Southern community in a region where Ku Klux Klan activities were more than an occasional rumor.

There were incidents. A black player and a white student scuffled in a bar. Ugly feelings arose over the players' dating some of the white female students. This is a place where such emotions still bubble close to the surface. So when the school threw a party that first year to wish the team well in post-season play, most students boycotted.

But in the second year, things seemed to cool down. People got more used to the idea. A new gym was built. A real gym.

Things should have gotten easier. They didn't. Prevesk remembers returning from summer vacation and hearing this from Cleven:

"Cleven said, 'Now listen to me, you son of a bleep. See this hand? This is my wedding ring. See this hand? This is my national championship ring. I don't need any more rings. Now we do things my way.' "

Those were the first notes of the death song. Cleven had bragged about how the team he dreamed up would win a title in its first year, and now that the Warriors had done it, he wasn't sure he wanted them around anymore. "We were stealing his thunder," Creola said.

Meanwhile, the Warriors had moved up a class, to the National Association of Intercollegiate Athletics, and were finding a different problem. No one would play them. Ten Division II schools were within a 90-mile radius, and not a single one wanted Webber on its schedule. The reason was obvious: They were afraid of losing.

Instead, Webber had to take games as far north as Georgia and as far south as Miami. The players traveled in a Dodge van, drove eight or nine hours, ate at McDonald's, listened to Walkmans, talked. Once they broke down in a town called Yeehaw Junction, and a few players got out to roam around. Then someone spotted a bull behind a fence and the players ran back into the van. "Half these guys had never seen a bull in their lives," Prevesk said, laughing. "They didn't know what it was going to do."

They kept winning. It was a simple formula: Run fast. Lots of offense. A pressing defense that stole the ball often. And dunk, dunk, dunk.

"Every player on the team dunked," Creola said. "People used to come out just to see our warm-up drills. We had an alley-oop play from halfcourt that was our trademark. It was beautiful."

That season the Warriors went to Hawaii with money Creola had raised, and they beat everyone they played — including Chaminade, which had knocked off national powers Louisville and Southern Methodist. The team wound up 32-5 and made it to the district semifinals of the NAIA. There was talk of moving up yet again, to Division II. Things looked good.

And then the roof fell in.

T he experiment was called off.

Buck Cleven — who had once been quoted as saying, "We're using basketball to let people know we're here. After that, the heck with it" — announced that Webber was dropping basketball after the 1985-86 season. A "one-year moratorium," he called it. "It will never come back," interpreted Creola.

The coach was crushed. So were his players. But at Webber, Buck Cleven makes all the rules. All the players could do was go out in a blaze. Go for the NAIA national title. And they went for it. Won 24 regular-season games and lost only one. Averaged more than 100 points a game. Led the nation in scoring.

And a funny thing happened.

Support.

People began to come out to the games. Signs started popping up. The racial tensions that had once existed had eased, if not to where we dream, at least to where we can coexist.

"A lot of times this school isn't fun," Prevesk said. "It's too small. But the team was something fun. Something to rally around."

Webber won its district championship and was headed to the nationals in Kansas City. In the last home game, the crowd actually stood up when the players were announced, and when the first basket was scored, a roll of toilet paper was thrown out on the court.

The Warriors' last home game. Their first roll of toilet paper.

It certain ways, it was as big as a victory can be.

There is no happy ending. Webber lost in the first round of the NAIA national tournament by four points. The program is over. The players are without a team. The coach is looking for a job. The gym is empty.

"It's taken a few years off my life, I'll tell you that," Creola said. "But what a few years! I wouldn't trade them."

It's tough to say how good the Webber Warriors were. Creola rated them a "low Division I team." Maybe. Who'll know now? No one good would play them. Their creator gave up on them.

Things are quiet around Webber now. Most players plan on transferring. So do other students. "I don't know 10 people coming back here," says Prevesk.

For a brief moment something special happened here. Something was taken from nothing, some colors of life were mixed together, black and white, and though there were problems at the beginning, toward the end they were learning how to get along. Basketball was teaching them. And one gets the feeling this is the way the game was before the NCAAs and TV cameras and recruiting violations.

Dies the season, dies the program. And it rests there, inside the quiet gym near the orange groves. The arc of what might have been, going stale with the heat.

MARATHON'S GHOSTS HAD LAST SCREECH IN '86

April 22

BOSTON — He was running alone before it was halfway over. No one breathing down his neck. No footsteps to worry about. The other 4,738 runners in the Boston Marathon were all behind Rob de Castella, way behind him. So for the last hour of the race, right to the finish line, his only companions were the police motorcycles and the press truck. It was a sterile victory. But then, the whole thing was sterile, wasn't it?

This used to be an event where winning was glory enough, it had to be enough, because there was no money. You crossed the finish line after 26.2 miles and entered a parking garage under the Prudential Building. They gave you a laurel wreath and a cup of yogurt. Only if you won. Otherwise, no laurel wreath.

But, you know, change, change. So when de Castella came across Monday in 2:07:51, first place, a Boston Marathon record, he was marched around the corner where a new blue Mercedes-Benz was waiting. Prize No. 1. He sat in it while photographers snapped away. Then he got out, and headed for Prize No. 2. A $60,000 check. He walked across the street, past a massive outdoor TV screen, and a massive sound system, and giant inflatable yellow Nike shoes hanging from the side of the Westin Hotel, none of which had ever been at a Boston Marathon before.

Coming the other way was a man named Bill Rodgers, who has won this race a few times — back before the $30,000 winner's check, and the $25,000 bonus for breaking the course record, and the $5,000 additional bonus for finishing under 2:10:00. Rodgers is probably too old to win here anymore. But he ran. And now he gazed at de Castella, the toast of the Australian sports scene, and said, "Fantastic, fantastic."

"Where did you finish?" de Castella asked.

"Fourth," Rodgers said.

"Great race," said de Castella.

And he kept walking.

So much for memories of the past. This event tastes corporate now, sweetly coated, marshmallow-filled. De Castella, 29, is maybe the biggest name in marathoning — he has won in the world championships, in Rotterdam, in Fukuoka — but he never ran here before because there wasn't any money. He felt a marathoner gets only two or three races a year, and why blow yourself on one that doesn't pay when there are so many that do?

Tradition wasn't enough. Not for him, and ultimately not for the race organizers. So the Boston Marathon finally went modern this spring, adopting prize money and a corporate daddy — John Hancock Mutual Life Insurance Co. — after 89 years of pure amateurism. And hel-lo. Along came Rob de Castella. World-class champion. His time Monday was more than six minutes faster than last year's victory by Geoff Smith (2:14:05).

You get what you pay for.

De Castella, a trained biophysicist who looks like a cross between Clark Gable and Sean Connery, ran an intelligent, steady race. And after he'd run through Hopkinton and Framingham, past the Wellesley co-eds and the Boston College crazies, after he'd streaked past the leafless trees and curled into downtown Boston and broken the tape and the course record, he was ushered not into the garage but into a grand ballroom in the Copley Plaza hotel, where the ceilings were trimmed with something gold and eight chandeliers gazed down from above.

There weren't any chandeliers in the garage, if I remember correctly.

D e Castella talked about his race. It was an impressive time. "My legs were sore during the last few miles." That was about it.

His wife, Gaye, sat in the front row, watching. She is a triathlete, as well as a commentator for Australian television.

"Do you need the Mercedes?" she was asked.

"Well, yes," she said. "We have a Subaru here in America. And he has an Alfa Romeo back in Australia. But we could use it."

OK. It's not that de Castella did anything wrong. Of course not. He won. It's not that Ingrid Kristiansen, who won the women's title, $30,000 and a Mercedes, did anything wrong.

It's simply that this event has changed. Anyone who has ever been here before could feel it. It has jumped up in class, maybe ensured its survival. But it has traded in the idea that someone could endure 26.2 agonizing miles of running just to say he'd won it. And it got chandeliers in exchange.

Toward the end of de Castella's press conference, someone pulled a fire alarm and a horn-like screeching made the ballroom sound like a submarine on red alert.

De Castella looked around, confused. The horn kept screeching. Finally, de Castella laughed for what seemed like the first time all day. "I hope we don't have to make a run for it," he said.

It was the only moment of spirit in this suddenly plastic environment. The only moment anybody really let go. You know what I think? I think the ghosts of Boston Marathons past pulled that fire alarm. That's what I think.

AT 18,000 FEET, EVEN CAST CAN'T KEEP GIBSON DOWN

April 24

This was where Kirk Gibson belonged. Up in the clouds, 18,000 feet high, looking out through an airplane window at the land masses below.

"That's Niagara Falls, I bet," he said, leaning over for a better view. "Yeah. And out there. See that shoreline? That's Lake Ontario. I'll betcha it is."

His eyes were alive, his voice had that high pitch to it — he gets that way when something interests him — and all told, it was a pretty happy moment, except that his left leg was propped up against the bulkhead wall, straight out, and his left foot was swallowed by a cast and a flesh-colored bandage. It was the size of a Thanksgiving turkey. "Oooh," he would say occasionally, when the ankle started throbbing. And then he'd close his eyes for a second, he'd swallow, and then he'd look out the window again and identify Buffalo.

He was flying home, back to Detroit. He was out of it. The night before he had gone down trying to scurry back to first base in a game between the Tigers and the Red Sox, and his foot seemed to catch on the bag, and the rest of him twisted horribly, and a second later he was writhing in pain and cameras were snapping. The star of the team. Hobbling off the field. Ugly.

"You could hear the thing pop," he said, staring at his toes sticking out of the cast in front of him. "The Red Sox's doctor came running out. Did you see him? He said he could hear the ligaments pop from the dugout."

Gibson sighed. A middle-aged woman across the aisle had been staring at him, as had most of the people in the first-class cabin. The woman leaned over.

"It was terrible," she said, as if Gibson didn't know. "We were there last night. We saw it."

"Yep," said Gibson.

"We saw it," the woman repeated.

Everybody saw it. Fans in the stadium watched from their seats. Fans at home watched on TV. The radio broadcast it. The late news reran it. Maybe it shouldn't be such big stuff, but in a baseball-crazy town in April, it is. Everybody saw it.

But nobody saw this.

Nobody saw Kirk Gibson, alone, slouched in an airport chair, his injured foot propped up on crutches, his hand over his eyes. This was early Wednesday morning at Logan Airport in Boston, and Gibson's plane was late by two hours.

He tried to lose himself in a newspaper. But the ankle was throbbing. The doctors said he'd be out three to six weeks with a "severe sprain." An examination today will prove if that's all it really is.

Gibson shifted in his seat. He'd been up most of the night. He didn't take the painkillers. "I don't like codeine," he said. His blue sweatshirt dangled loosely. He needed a shave. To his right was his briefcase. To his left was a wheelchair.

A wheelchair?

It was an unsettling picture. Kirk Gibson in a wheelchair is like Superman hailing a cab. Better Gibson should be out in right field, chasing a line drive, or at the plate, whacking the hell out of the ball. Leading the Tigers. Slapping high-fives. Hitting home runs. He is 28. A wheelchair? No.

But this is the flip side of sports. And nobody saw it, except the people at the airport, who mostly gaped and made comments as he wheeled past.

"You with a baseball team?" one old man asked.

"Yes," Gibson said.

"Which one?" said the old man.

A young woman brought up her 10-year-old son.

"Mr. Gibson broke his foot," the woman said.

"He did?" the kid said.

"No, I sprained it," Gibson said.

"Oh," the woman said. "That's worse."

It went on like this for the than two hours. Autographs. Handshakes. Quips. Autographs. Anyone who thinks celebrity is some big thrill should sit in an airport coffee shop with Kirk Gibson sometime. How many little girls did he have to pinch? How many businessmen made small talk? This isn't his job. His job is baseball, battling pitchers and racing across the outfield.

How much would he rather have been out at a ballpark, taking batting practice? Instead of sitting there, listening to the same tired questions. "How'd you do it?" "Is it bad?"

Is it bad? The guy was in a wheelchair, with crutches across his lap.

W ell. Could it be any other way for Kirk Gibson? Everything he does is magnified. There is no peace. When he hits two home runs on Opening Day, he is virtually canonized. And when he tells some nagging fan to get lost, it's liable to end up in the gossip columns. The baseball field is Gibson's sanctuary from all that. Only now, as he made his way onto the plane, left crutch, right crutch, he knew the sanctuary had been taken away. Three to six weeks.

"The next few days are really critical," he said, settling into his seat. "I have to stay inactive. I'll go home. Try not to walk around too much.

Tomorrow's an off-day. Before this happened, I was planning to ride my horse."

He wiggled his bare toes. "I don't know. Maybe I can ride it anyhow. Maybe I will."

Ride a horse? With a sprained ankle? Well. Such is the spirit of Gibson, the same stuff that lets him smack a home run when it's most needed, or tell a stranger to bleep off without hesitation.

"Will you go to the games while you're on the disabled list?" someone asked.

"Oh, yeah, I'll go to the park for treatment," he said. "If I can get a seat where I can stretch out my leg I'll stay for the game. I'll be out there."

"The Tigers will miss you," someone said.

"Well, yeah, but this happens," he said. "Now we'll see the character of the team."

"What will you do until you're well?" someone asked.

He shrugged and opened a bag of salted peanuts. "I've got a lot of things to read, you know? I'm about a month behind in my business stuff. And I'm studying for my pilot's license. I hope to buy a plane after the season. So I'll study. I'll read the manual."

It seemed odd to think of Kirk Gibson reading in April and May. Odd to think the baseball season will unfold without him — even for three to six weeks. But the whole injury was odd. Very odd. Everybody saw it.

"I still can't figure out what happened," Gibson said. "I spoke to my wife, and she said, 'It was really bad. It was worse than when you got hit in the mouth by that pitch. I wish I was there with you.'"

He laughed off her concern. And you can be sure if he could have laughed this injury off, he would have. This is a guy who once played a college football game with a separated shoulder and refused to be helped off the field when it happened because the other team was taunting him.

But Tuesday night in Fenway Park, he had to be helped off. By two people. That's how you know it was bad. He let them help him off. Three to six weeks. The words stung.

As the plane soared over Massachusetts and New York, Gibson shifted the angle of his leg. He was in pain.

"Will there be a wheelchair waiting for me in Detroit?" he asked a flight attendant.

"Do you have one of your own?" she said.

"No," he said, laughing. "I don't have my own wheelchair. I'm young. I'm healthy."

He paused for a second.

"Most of the time."

Maybe it was the hour. Or the quiet hum of the plane engine. But for that entire flight it was a different Kirk Gibson than what most people expect. A reflective person. An easygoing person. Bad luck often brings out a sour side of a man. But up there, tucked safely in the clouds, away from the phones and the minicams, Kirk Gibson seemed, well, at peace. Bum ankle and all. He told stories: about surprising his wife's daughter with a horse for her birthday; about listening to flight instruction tapes in his Sony Walkman; about the baby he and his wife are expecting in September. He watched the window. He identified four types of clouds. And Lake Huron. And Lake Erie. The skies agree with him.

Toward the end of the flight he was laughing, even at himself. When a stewardess came over with a Detroit newspaper and asked for his autograph, he looked at the front page and found a photo of him writhing in pain. He thought for a second, and then he wrote beside the picture: "OUCH! Kirk Gibson."

Nice.

"Can't do anything about it," he said, when someone remarked on his pleasant disposition. "The injury happened when I was playing hard. I can't be sorry about that. I'll be back soon enough. I'm a fast healer."

At one point, as the plane descended, he was squirming from side to side, the future pilot, talking loud enough for the whole cabin to hear. "That's St. Clair Shores," he said, pointing out one window. "And that's Belle Isle. Right there. And over there, that's. . . ."

He was in control again. A brief moment. Way up high. The passengers smiled at their geography lesson.

For a man who can barely walk, Kirk Gibson was taking things remarkably in stride.

The plane landed. A wheelchair was waiting in the corridor that connects to the terminal. Someone handed him his briefcase.

"Thanks," he said.

"No problem," came the answer.

"No, really," he said. "Thanks a lot."

Two flight attendants began to wheel him down the corridor. From 20 feet away you could see the first poking of a TV camera lens through the terminal door. Then another. And another.

"Here we go," one flight attendant said.

"Oh, my," said the other.

Through the door they came, and it was insanity. A crowd three-deep of photographers, reporters, TV people, onlookers. All of them pushing around this man in a wheelchair, fighting for a better angle. At first Gibson said nothing. Then he said quietly, "Come on, let me get by." Then he said it a little louder. The swarm followed him, sticking like wet cotton. A TV man asked how he felt.

"Fine, until you guys showed up," he said.

And, you know, that may be the one comment the crowd will remember. An ornery answer. And they'll return to their offices and tell a few people who'll tell a few people. And the "annoyed athlete" side of Kirk Gibson will be rehashed. And they'll never know the other side.

More's the pity. Because there is a lot there.

Eventually the crowd grew so that Gibson stopped his wheelchair, got on his crutches and did some TV interviews, as the camera lights and the midday sunshine combined to leave him half-blind as well as half-crippled.

It is the price he pays for who he is. And he is paid well. But it was hard, watching Gibson, not to think that he is better suited to 18,000 feet, his thoughts on the clouds, his sight line nothing but blue-and-white carefree sky.

Not today. Not for a while. For now it's rehab. It's waiting. It's X-rays. It's a cast and a cast of thousands. And it's pretty clear the time will pass slowly for Kirk Gibson, back here on earth.

DERBY HORSES WEREN'T NEARLY THIS BEASTLY

May 4

LOUISVILLE, Ky. — The beasts were pawing at the gates.

"START THEM UP!" someone screamed.

"WOOOH!" screamed someone else.

Only the gates stood between them and mad glory. The beasts were restless. The beasts wanted to run.

"IT'S TIIIIME!" someone screamed.

"DO IT!" screamed someone else.

A cop checked his watch. There were about 75 cops there, billy clubs by their sides, safe on the other side of the gates, away from these wild animals. The cop with the watch looked up. He nodded.

The locks were lifted. The gates swung open. And the beasts charged toward the track. They were carrying sleeping bags and blankets. Some had been out there for hours, some all night long, sleeping on the sidewalk just a few feet from the white-spired grandeur of Churchill Downs racetrack — where the Kentucky Derby would be run that afternoon for the 112th straight time.

These were human beasts. And the worst kind. The kind without tickets.

They had begun camping out at 6 p.m. the night before. They had come to claim the last spot available: the infield. The Churchill Downs infield. Twenty dollars gets you a section of grass there as big as your rear end, where you can sit all day and bake in the sun and shower with beer. It's the only way in here for the regular guy who can't pony up $127.50 for a lousy reserved seat.

So they came — thousands of them. They shivered through the night. And now their faces were twisted, their eyes droopy, their hair matted, their breath stale with sleep and booze. But there was no time for that. It was 8 a.m., Derby Day, the gates had been opened, and so they were sprinting like crazed beasts toward the tunnel that went under the track and spilled onto the infield grass, sprinting for the best spots before someone else got them. And I started to sprint with them.

I don't know why. It was just a sudden mass frenzy, like running with the bulls through the streets of Pamplona. Only here I was racing against two long-haired bikers with shades and folding chairs and a cooler.

"Get the quarter-pole spot!" yelled one.

"Go left outta the tunnel!" yelled the other.

We were breathing hard, locked in a desperate 400-yard dash. Suddenly it was all that mattered. That spot. It was me or them. Survival of the fastest. Our legs pumped. It was early morning. The horses were somewhere in their stables. The debutantes were home, picking out their Derby Day outfits. The Kentucky colonels were enjoying their breakfasts before coming out to the track.

And there we were, two bikers, one journalist, charging down the concrete, panting and sweating like the beasts we had come to bet on. . . .

How exactly I ended up in the middle of this deranged race is fuzzy. A blur. There was something about a strip joint and a waitress and a street party at 4 a.m., and mint juleps and motor homes and a woman who told me the best way to sneak whiskey into the Derby was to hide a flask inside a loaf of bread, because "they never look there."

I'm not sure how this all fits together, even now. But I figure that's one of the side effects of the depraved illness they call Derby Fever; a euphemism for 48 hours of decadent, liquor-soaked behavior that gets ugly every few hours, like clockwork.

You might as well know right off that there are two sides to this most famous of horse races. What you see on TV — the lime green knickers, the hoop skirts, Millionaires Row, the Derby breakfasts, the box seats, the cultured talk about the fine breeding of horse No. 3 — all that is one side.

Then there's the other side. Where the real beasts perform.

I was on that side Saturday morning. And the bikers were a step ahead of me. . . .

But wait. Let's back up two days. The idea here was to witness the Derby from the street up. Leave the horse details to our racing writer and just go for the color. So, naturally, when we blew into Louisville in the wee hours of Thursday morning ("we" being myself and Jimmy S., a friend who likes to accompany me on these sick little jaunts), we asked the cab driver to immediately recommend an action spot. He suggested a club called the Green Light Lounge.

Never ask a cab driver. The Green Light Lounge — whose sign read "DERBY FANS: CHECK OUT OUR FILLIES!" — proved to be a seedy little strip joint that charges you a dollar to walk in the door. You get 30 seconds for your eyes to adjust to the dark, and then the female dancers saddle up alongside you.

"Buy me a ticket?" said a brunette in a red dress cut down to the imagination.

"Ticket to what?" I said.

"That's how we work it here," she said. "You buy me a ticket, I can sit with you."

"How much is a ticket?" I asked.

"They start at 12 dollars," she said.

Jimmy and I exchanged glances. We figured neither of our bosses would mind that little item on our expense accounts, considering the information we could get. Right, boss? We bought the ticket. She sat down.

In five minutes we learned more about Derby week than was contained in all those colorful books they stuff in your media packet. Nancy (that was the name she gave us) said she worked in a nursing home in eastern Kentucky most of the year, but always came to Louisville during Derby Week. Said she could clear $800 for five nights' worth of smiling and dancing and wearing skimpy dresses.

"I get all kinds," she said, lighting up a cigaret, "high rollers, motorcycle guys. Friday night before the Derby is the busiest. It's nonstop. The bar stays open until 6 a.m. This is an unbelievable week."

Nancy said tickets to sit with her — and only sit with her — ran up to $50 a pop, depending on how much the Derby tourists felt like spending. I asked her how many minutes you got for 12 bucks.

She looked at her watch. "You're on overtime now, sweetheart," she said.

Suffice it to say it was a late night. But in the interest of a fair picture, we hit the track early on Friday morning. And I mean early. Like 6:30. I don't know why horsemen insist on getting up before the sun. Maybe because it keeps reporters from asking too many questions, as most of them are asleep standing up.

Anyhow, it was worth seeing, because the difference between Churchill Downs at sunrise and Churchill Downs in the middle of the fifth race is like the difference between Wisconsin and Beirut. In the morning hours, the horses graze quietly while the trainers talk softly about their chances. You hear the occasional thundering of hooves around the track. And then it's quiet again.

It's here, along the backstretch, where writers fall in love with horse racing. It's in the bleachers where they come to loathe it.

When the gates open, the whole scene changes. Especially on Derby weekend. The entire range of human condition comes through these doors, from the down-and-out war vet in a wheelchair to Don Johnson of "Miami Vice." That's part of what the Derby is about, they brag. Everybody gets a peek. Everybody gets to hunker down a wager on Snow Chief or Badger Land, and to spend five or six hours in Derby glory.

They just don't all spend it the same way.

Friday went by quickly. The afternoon was the running of the Kentucky Oaks, the filly version of the Derby. It was a prelude of things to come. Churchill Downs was packed. People set up beach chairs in front of the building-sized tote board that flashes the odds. They sat there all day, watching numbers change. They never saw a horse. And they were still happy.

That's because Churchill Downs is less a racetrack than a stage on Derby weekend. A place for the busted to stare at the loaded. Hats. Hats are big at Derby time. Bowlers and Stetsons and big round things with flowers and ribbons and pink veils hanging down.

That's what I remember most. And girls hawking mint juleps as they hawk programs at Tiger Stadium. And people waiting in line for the bathrooms, for water fountains, for wagers. Every hotel room in Louisville was gone. Every decent restaurant was running double shifts. Rates were triple on everything. The locals were charging up to $30 for desperate visitors to sleep on their porches. If you behaved yourself, you might get to use the bathroom.

Jimmy S. and I ate that night at some rib joint that boasted five video screens. There were horseshoes on the walls. And a two-hour wait. When a table cleared, people who'd been standing began to fight over the empty chairs. A guy who said his name was Mister Wonderful got in a tug-of-war with a young woman. "This chair stays here," he growled. I had a lousy feeling about the night after that.

Still, nothing, at least nothing short of a full-scale nuclear alert, could have prepared me for the streets outside Churchill Downs late Friday night. How do you describe it? It was as if MTV, Hell's Angels and "The Rocky Horror Picture Show" had let out onto Central Avenue and multiplied by a thousand. Teenage kids staggering on top of one another. Beer cans rolling across the street. Old men rocking on their porches with shotguns under blankets. An auto body shop with a craps game being run inside. And screams. Screams that rose like sudden smoke, rose out of nowhere, people just screaming to a crescendo, then stopping. In the daylight it would have been weird. In the darkness of 2 a.m. it was a signal to head for cover.

We were moving quickly back to the car when we passed a stocky cop from the sheriff's office.

"Any trouble yet, officer?" I asked him.

"Nah," he said, slapping his nightstick. "Just some fighters, and some boys trying to sell that Mary Jane You-Wanna stuff. Nuthin' too bad."

Just then a buddy of his came up and slapped the cop on the back. "HEY YOU REDNECK!" the buddy yelled. "WHICH WAY TO FAIRYTOWN?"

"Let's get out of here," I said to Jimmy. He didn't argue.

On our way to the car we passed the locked entrance to the general admission infield section. It was still six hours away from opening but already dozens of people were tucked into sleeping bags against the bars, trying to keep warm.

"I been here six straight years," said a guy from Florida. "I ain't

71

missing this one." Next to him were four college roommates with three cases of Budweiser. Before the night would end, there would be several arrests and more than one ambulance visit. Nothing unusual, as the cop put it.

Across the street from the gate was an all-night drugstore. It had a grill going, and the sizzle of sausage mixed with cigar-choked conversation. Under normal conditions, you wouldn't set foot in the place. Tonight it was paradise. People nursed their coffee and pie, staying warm and safe for a few extra minutes until the waitress booted them. It was, after all, a long way until 8 a.m.

Which sort of brings us back to where we began this weird tale, the footrace against the bikers. Let's just call it a draw. The three of us burst out of the tunnel and into the infield and realized, panting, that there was no big rush. The place was massive.

As the hours went by it filled up. Kids in football shirts. Old men in caps and jackets. There were Port-O-Lets and betting windows and refreshment stands out there. The drinking began almost immediately.

"Get started now," hollered some geek in a rose hat. "Gonna be a long day."

That was the truth. Three hours passed before the first race. By that point, the infield was half-filled and mostly crazed. Girls had stripped down to bathing suits. Guys had binoculars. Cassette players were blasting. Beer and whiskey were going down throats at a record pace. Bodies were crouched over racing forms, and wherever you stepped, you just missed somebody's stomach.

But that wasn't the weird part. The weird part was when the races started, and for the rest of the afternoon, the horses raced around all this mutant madness. It was like being in a demilitarized zone on the 50-yard line of a Cowboys-Redskins game.

To keep from going completely insane, I kept switching locations. I stopped by the paddock, where they bring the horses before the races. By midafternoon, people were 10 deep all around, which can get the horses pretty spooked, especially when some drunken fool screams, "AWW RIIIGHT!" directly into their ears. Last year, something like that happened, and a horse bridled and broke into a sweat. "Ruined him for the race," said an observer.

Then there was the Paddock Lounge, which is a few hundred dollars and several light years away from the infield. Here — as in the other Churchill Downs restaurants — were white shoes beneath white slacks beneath a white sports jacket and a white hat. Here were women with shoulder pads beneath their silk dresses and tall men who looked as if they should be on a fried chicken bucket, flagging down waitresses and saying,

"How 'bout a few of those mint juleps, little darlin'?"

This was the glitter and romance they write about. The exclusive corporate booths were not far away. A hunch bet over here was a year's income for some of the infield types.

"I've got 10 grand on Badger Land. . . ." said some bug-head with a polka-dot ascot.

"It's in the breeding. . . ." said his silver-haired partner.

The air smelled of fine food, Derby pie and money.

By 3 p.m. the infield was a sea of drunken humanity. The whole place seemed to sway. People were singing, rolling on top of each other. The lines for the beer were exceeded only by the lines for the Port-O-Lets, both of which were beyond sanity. It was Woodstock without music. Half-clad bodies waving at clouds. Tents pitched 20 feet from the betting windows. And no rhyme or reason to the cast. An old black man studying the racing form sat next to three teenage girls, whose blanket bordered a motorcycle king with a boom box. A bare-chested guy watched his wife reach into his wallet.

"Get out of there, woman!" he yelled. "You been in there enough." She took the money anyhow.

Across the way in the exclusive boxes sat Walter Cronkite and Cornelius and Marylou Vanderbilt Whitney. I sat there in the infield, with my back to a fence. Jimmy S. had fallen asleep next to me, and his face was getting sunburned. I thought about Cronkite. And about the redneck cop. And Mister Wonderful. And the woman with the loaded bread loaf. I thought about the money being tossed out on this Derby race, some $13 million. I thought about Nancy the dancer, and how she was probably on a bus back across the state by now, with $800 in her pocketbook that she didn't have last week.

The contrasts were too much. The whole thing was too much. There were only minutes before the big race. The only sensible thing to do, it seemed, was to head for shelter.

Which is why they invented the press box.

From high above it all, safely inside the working media room, a cup of coffee to the left, a TV monitor on the right, it was possible to actually get a grip on this weird and greed-soaked affair. Here were hundreds of thousands of people, dressed up and drunk out and swollen like peacocks, all there ostensibly for a two-minute horse race. But come on. That was garbage. Maybe one in five knew anything about horses. The others either knew high heels or seersucker suits or how to puncture a beer can with a fountain pen. For them, this was a party, and the horses were a convenient excuse.

When the trumpets sounded for the Derby race, everybody rose. They joined in a version of "My Old Kentucky Home," but not too many got the words right. The horses entered the gate. Then the bell, and they were off. For two minutes everybody was together, eyes on the track instead of each other. But two minutes is still only two minutes. And soon the two minutes were over. The horse named Ferdinand won. A major upset. A 17-1 shot. The lucky winners waved their tickets and toasted their foresight. The rest ripped up their stubs, dropped them on the ground and stomped on them as they made a gigantic cattle run for the exits.

"Well, there you have it. . . ." the TV announcers said. That's it for this year. The Derby was over. The beasts had run again. But I knew better. I knew most of them were out there in the parking lots. I took a long sip from my coffee cup. For the moment, I was staying put.

WORDS FAIL ENGLISH AS HE SAYS GOODBY

May 6

He sat in an office behind smoked-glass windows. He wore a sports jacket and a button-down shirt. No pads. No helmet. These were the final 60 minutes of Doug English's football life. He was going out as a civilian.

"You OK, big fella?" a front-office guy asked.

"I'm OK," English said.

"You mind waiting here until the press conference?"

"Well, I don't have any other plans," English said.

Nice guys finish last. Someone said that once. But that wasn't what was burning inside Doug English now. He was used to being last. Last out of the pile. Last to stagger off the field. Last to drop. Last would be fine. It was going out first that was killing him.

But going out he was, retiring at age 32. A neck injury had decided it. A ruptured disk. It had caused him to miss the last six games of 1985. It had put him under the knife. And finally, it had brought him to the team doctor on Sunday, seven months after it happened.

Here was the verdict: As it is, you'll suffer from arthritis and maybe degenerative bone problems. Play, and you could end up crippled.

"The bottom line," English said, lowering his eyes, "was that he could not pass me to play football."

He choked on the words. Here he was, a 6-foot-5, 258-pound lineman, who'd been slamming into giants since high school. And one sentence cut him down. You want to kill a football player? Tell him you can't pass him to play.

"When I heard the news," he said, "I said to myself, 'Well, let's push it. Let's beg. Let's try and talk these guys into something to let me keep playing.'"

He paused. "But the doctors can't do that. They have to live with themselves. They don't want to go to some alumni function 10 years from now and see what I've become."

He crossed his legs. He rubbed his hands over his face. He looked at his watch. Forty-five minutes left on the career. Through the office windows you could see the first TV trucks arriving, and the camera crews getting out.

Do you realize," he asked suddenly, "that outside of my parents, I've been more involved with this team than anything in my whole life?"

He sighed. These are the discoveries you suddenly make. All the time he was out there, 10 years with the Lions, earning four trips to the Pro Bowl, rolling in the melted butter of glory, he never stopped to consider the time. Now he was counting it up. And counting it down. Thirty-five minutes. Thirty minutes.

"How much does football mean?" he was asked.

"It's me," he said. "It's my identity."

Maybe it would be easier if someone had speared him. If some player had done the dirty deed. Then he could focus the anger, blame somebody. But no, he said. It happened sometime during a game against Chicago last year, in a frozen wet Soldier Field, and all of a sudden he felt a tingling in his hands and fingers. Parts of him went numb. Then he fell a few times for no apparent reason. He stayed in the game until the fourth quarter, and no one will ever know how much damage that did.

"Why didn't you come out?" someone asked.

"I didn't want to abandon ship," he said. "I hate coming out of a game when we're losing. It's too easy. You see a lot of guys doing it. The only fights I've ever had with my coaches were over coming out of a game too soon."

Twenty-five minutes left. A PR man poked his head in and recited the plan: A photographer wanted a quick shot on the field. And then, the press conference.

"All set?" the PR man asked.

Doug English stood up. He took a breath.

"Let's go," he said.

He walked to the tunnel, passing stadium workers and an occasional teammate.

"How's it going?" they'd say.

"Everything's OK," he'd say.

And he'd keep walking.

It's easy for media types to call Doug English a nice guy. He has always cooperated with reporters, laughed with them, spoken candidly. But you don't need newspapers for good reviews. Try anywhere.

Try the kid with a brain tumor whom he befriended in the hospital last year. English called him Monday morning to tell him he was retiring. Try the secretaries in the Lions' offices; they light up whenever he comes into the office. Try the guys sweeping up the Silverdome. Try the Muscular Dystrophy Association. Try anyone on the streets of Detroit.

"Whadya think about Doug English?" you say.

"Great guy," they say. And they've never met him.

The coaches like him. His teammates like him. Oh, maybe a few resented the attention he got. But more were likely to chow down with him in the unofficial Thursday Night Club, in which players gathered at an area restaurant to blow off some steam before zeroing in on Sunday's game.

Thursday nights. He would miss those.

"It's the players," he'd said, when asked what hurt the most about leaving. "Guys like Keith Dorney (his roommate) and Bill Gay and all of them. You live with these guys, fight with them, cry with them.

"I mean, what's a sport anyway? It's a billion-dollar business of watching people play a game that doesn't mean nothing. So it's the people that count. I can't say how much it hurts to be leaving them."

Back in 1980 he had left voluntarily. Took a year off. He was disillusioned, depressed. Tired of 2-14 seasons and taping his legs from thigh to ankle every day. But a year away renewed him. He came back with a daydreamer's desire never to wake up outside of football again.

Now, for the last time, he was walking down the tunnel as a Detroit Lion. Twenty minutes to go.

He passed a cleanup crew and stopped to shake hands with one of the custodians.

"Doug English! How you doin'?" the custodian said.

"OK," English said. "I'm, uh, fixing to hang it up in a few minutes. Gonna call it quits."

The custodian just stared, forgetting to remove the smile from his face. "Nawww. Uh-uh," he said.

"Afraid so," English said quietly.

He kept walking. The photographer posed him in the middle of the field. Across the way were a dozen rookies, tossing a football. Some knew who he was, this guy in the sports jacket and button-down shirt. Some didn't. They just stared, then went back to their catch.

F ifteen minutes left in the career. English walked through the carpeted corridors of the Lions' offices, picking up followers like the Pied Piper. A few secretaries fell into line behind him. A few front-office people. Coach Darryl Rogers. General manager Russ Thomas. The PR staff. They all squeezed into the elevator. English towered above everyone.

"Kind of tight in here," he said.

Everybody laughed.

The door opened. The ensemble walked down the otherwise deserted hallway. Several Lions players — who had just finished lunch — were coming the other way. Demetrious Johnson saw English and held open his arms, as if he were a relative just arriving from a long flight.

"Heyyyy," Johnson said, hugging him.

"Heyyyyy," said English, hugging back.

That was better than words. English broke away finally and walked on, on through the press lounge where the other ball players were eating. At the front table sat William Gay, one of his closest buddies. They exchanged glances.

"Just tell 'em you got tired of it," Gay yelled after him.

"Yeah," said English, forcing a laugh.

On they marched. Got within five feet of the press conference door. Inside were the microphones, the notepads. The finish line. And suddenly Doug English, who never wanted to come out of the game, disappeared behind the nearest door and closed it behind him.

No one followed him. No one wanted to watch. Through the narrow glass you could see Doug English wiping the tears from his eyes and trying to catch his breath.

N o one will be around when Doug English is 50 and aching with the simplest of movements. No one will know how he feels today, waking up without a Detroit Lions locker to call his own.

All you have is what you see. And here is what you saw.

Darryl Rogers introduced him with kind words. English stepped up to the microphone, and threw out one last joke.

"I know the only way to get you media guys out here is to offer a free lunch," he said.

Everybody laughed.

Ten seconds. Doug English swallowed hard.

"With the exception of my family. . . .

Five seconds.

"And the Good Lord. . . . "

Somewhere a distant gun was fired. Time had expired. No more football. No more Thursdays. Nevermore.

". . . this has been the best thing in my life. . . ."

The cameras clicked. The microphone meters jumped. Doug English, dressed in a sports jacket and button-down shirt, was out of it. He was over.

He was saying goodby, ending a career. In his years in the game he'd taken down countless opponents. Now with his farewell, with the saddest kind of tears, he was cutting down an old expression, right across the knees.

Sometimes, nice guys finish first. And it hurts like hell.

'JAIL AIN'T NO HOTEL' FOR SCOTT SKILES

May 21

PLYMOUTH, Ind. — It was a church wedding on a spring afternoon, and the couple was posing for snapshots. Scott Skiles watched silently through a window in the building next door. He knew the groom from high school. He wanted to yell out something — congratulations, maybe. But he kept his mouth shut, because if he yelled the guard would come and close off the window and there would be no outside at all, not even this little glimpse from behind the iron bars. And if there's one thing you learn in jail, it's to hang onto every little thing you get.

Where did Scott Skiles go after his brilliant basketball career at Michigan State? Here is where he went. To the Marshall County jail. Fifteen days for violating probation with a drunken-driving charge. He walked in on a Friday morning, handed over his watch and his wallet, undressed, put on the undershirt and the pants and shoes, and followed the guards. He was supposed to stay alone. A private cell. It would be easier, he figured, than taking any crap from inmates who knew who he was. This jail was in the middle of his hometown, and he'd been a high school hero. Once.

The guards opened the door. The room was dark and tiny with no windows. He stepped inside and the concrete began to creep closer to him. The hell with privacy. "I'd rather go in with other people," he said.

So in he went, with five other inmates, one toilet, one shower, one mattress per man, and 15 days to kill. Only here you never really kill time. You wrestle it, choke it, stomp on it and grind your heels. But there is always more. "Breakfast at 7 a.m.," he said, "and then you just lie around. Lunch comes in at 11. Then you just lie around until dinner at 4. The guards don't even come in. They slip the food through a slot."

You want to know how time passes in jail? Wait for the slot to open. That's how time passes. You can try to sleep. But the lights are always on, even at night. You can make a phone call — one every other day, with the guards standing by. You can shower. Except the water in this cell was scalding. "So hot," Skiles said, "you couldn't stand under it. You stood to the side and splashed it on you." After a few days he asked a guard about it. The guard grinned.

"This ain't no hotel, boy," he said.

How far this was from the cheers, the halftime bands, the court at Michigan State where Scott Skiles could run as fast as his legs would take him. He was arguably the best college guard in the country this season, a brilliant shooter, a deft passer, a live grenade in green sneakers. But here in the cell he had just enough room to do push-ups in the corner near the toilet.

"I felt like a caged animal," he said. "I'm so active. And now I couldn't even walk around. Guys had their mattresses on the floor. You couldn't walk without bumping into someone."

He rolled his neck, as if stiffening at the thought of the cell. "But," he said, "I know that's part of the punishment. It's not supposed to be a place where you can go out and play ball. It wasn't supposed to be fun. I knew that."

Skiles was free now. He was sitting in an atrium lobby of a Holiday Inn coffee shop. He had done all 15 days, done what was expected. It was the longest he had gone since the second grade without touching a basketball. On his third day in jail, Skiles and his cell mates were watching a game on the black-and-white TV — one allowed per cell — when CBS ran a clip of his amazing behind-the-back pass against Georgetown. "Hey, man, you're on there!" one of the inmates said. Skiles doesn't remember answering. All he remembers is the feeling — seeing himself on tape, while the concrete and the bars and the stale air reminded him it was still days, days, before freedom — and the feeling was lousy. Terrible. Embarrassing. The worst of his life.

And thousands of people think he got off like a baby.

I made a mistake," Skiles said when asked about the drunken-driving arrest that led to the jail sentence. "One of the rules of probation was not being in a public place that served alcohol. For nine months I never violated that."

He leaned forward. He hadn't told this story to many people, certainly not to reporters. He was going to get it right. "One night," he said, "I was out with friends, we were playing pool, and they said, 'We're going to this club called B'Zar.' I said, 'I can't go in there.'

"They didn't pressure me. But I ended up going. For nine months I had been paranoid of even going into a restaurant that served liquor. I guess that one night I was tired of being the guy who couldn't go anywhere.

"So I went in. I know that's no excuse. I should've just stuck it out for three more months and it all would have been over. It's not that I forgot. It's just, you know, you're 20, 21 years old, you don't know what anything's about. I still don't know. . . . "

He paused. His short blond hair was stringy and disheveled, and his face was set in that clenched jaw pose, the same face he uses when driving down the lane or whipping the ball over his shoulder or sinking a last-second shot. It is an angry face, or so it seems, even when he is not angry. Had he been blessed with an angel's countenance, a Magic Johnson smile, Dale Murphy dimples, maybe people would have been kinder. Felt sorry for him. But they saw his pale skin and his gunfire eyes and the veins that bulged in his neck and they just figured this kid was guilty of everything he was accused of, and probably more. He received the probation when he pleaded guilty to a marijuana possession charge, following an arrest in which police charged him with having marijuana and cocaine.

Letters came in when Skiles was allowed to play for MSU after the drunken-driving arrest. Editorials were written. Angry. Horrified. People in his hometown spit at his name. The media hounded him. Fans in foreign arenas were downright cruel, as if they had some blood claim to vengeance, waving signs, hurling curses and shaking bags of sugar that suggested cocaine. "Guilty!" they said.

But guilty of what? The night he left that club, Skiles got in his car, drove "about 50 yards" and was stopped by police and charged with drunken driving. That clinched a jail sentence: not for drunken driving but for violating probation. There are suggestions that the police knew very well whom they were stopping. Skiles won't rehash them. What's the point?

"I could've taken a cab," he said, "and everything would have been different. Why didn't I? I remember there was a cab right there on the corner and I said to myself, 'I should just jump in that.' My friend's house, where I was staying, was only two blocks away. Two blocks. Why didn't I just take a cab? But I didn't want to leave my car there. So I got in and I was arrested about 50 yards later. . . ."

He shrugged. "People have visions of me swerving all over a four-lane highway. But that's not the way it was."

Two blocks.

Fifteen days.

In the jail cell, Skiles would drape his undershirt over his eyes to try to escape. But sleep came hard. The shirt smelled, because he had to wear the same one for a week at a time. On Mother's Day, he tried to call home. His mother was in church. His father answered. Skiles said hello, then hung up quickly so the guard would think he hadn't gotten through. Didn't work. The guard heard him. He had used up his one call.

People who figure 15 days in jail is nothing have never spent 15 minutes there. For a guy with a nowhere life and a nowhere job, it's a dull change of a dull pace. For a college student who puts miles on his sneakers every day, it's torture. Time becomes a leech on the mind, and it doesn't take long before you feel the life forces draining.

"When I woke up the first morning in there it was so hot, I was covered with sweat, and I remember thinking, 'Oh, boy, it's true. I'm really in here,' " Skiles said. "I said to myself, 'No way I'm gonna make it through

15 days.' "

Skiles blew out a lung full of air. He talked about waking up each morning with a day count on his brain. About talking to his mother through the visitors' glass, and hearing the guard say his 10 minutes were up. About seeing that church wedding through the barred window and feeling helpless, paralyzed. Imprisoned. His voice was flat. These were answers to questions, that's all.

"Look," he said. "I don't want anybody feeling sorry for me because I had to spend time in there. That's not why I'm telling you this. I know the law. I know what I did and I'm sorry for it. It was probably good for me to sit in there for 15 days. I will never drink and drive again, I'll tell you that. I never, ever want to go back there."

Isn't that what jail is supposed to accomplish?

But you pay and sometimes you keep paying. Skiles is NBA material, and the draft is June 17. For other players, it's the pot of gold. Yet when Skiles spoke of it, he did in a somber voice, an old voice. He was a first-team All-America, an honor that should lock you as a top pick, yes? But jail. Always jail. What will it do to his future? He doesn't know.

"Let's face it," he said, frowning. "Any team that makes me a first-round selection has a public relations problem right away, right from day one. 'Why did you pick him?' people will say. 'What about his trouble?' You know that. I know it. People who say (that) this won't affect my chances don't know what they're talking about."

He rested his elbows on the table. He didn't look at anything, just up, then down. "You know," he said suddenly, "I think that anyone who sits down and talks to me realizes I'm not an alcoholic, realizes, you know, I don't have a drug problem. . . . Maybe you can't tell that from just sitting down with someone, but you can get a pretty good idea, can't you? But teams aren't even taking time to interview me. That's why I'm getting the impression they're not really interested in me, at least not in saying, 'If Scott Skiles were available by this pick he'd be our first choice.'

"Don't get me wrong. I'm ready to play. But, I don't know. A few years ago if you'd have told me I couldn't play in the pros it would have killed me. Now, with all the stuff I've been through, it's not live or die with me anymore. It's not gonna kill me if I can't."

As he talked, this kid — and remember he is but 22; how grown-up were you at that age? — this kid who led his team to within two games of the Final Four, who blistered opponents, who probably dreamed of the NBA draft, say, only forever, this kid who was always on fire when it came to basketball, appeared suddenly weary and uninspired, like a schoolboy awaiting a detention hall.

It was impossible to listen to him and not sense a loss.

When he got out of jail, Skiles drove to Indianapolis to see a friend who was graduating from college. That evening, they went to a supermarket, and Skiles, who was ready to slip out through his own rib cage for a chance to play basketball, spotted a man and his two kids playing on a nearby court. "I'll be back in a bit," Skiles said to his friend.

He walked to the court. The man did not know who he was. Nor did his kids. "I've just been dying to shoot some baskets," Skiles said. "Do you mind if I shoot with you?"

The family said OK. Skiles picked up the ball, threw up a shot, then the kids rebounded and threw up their own, then he got the rebound and dribbled out and shot, and so on. A nowhere court. A department store basketball. "It felt so good," Skiles said. For those few moments, away from everything but the pure joy of the dribble dance, gravity was the only thing keeping the ball and the shooter from sailing off into joyous space.

This is where we should leave Scott Skiles. Anonymous on a basketball court, the thumping of a ball in sync with his heartbeat. Enough already of the snide jokes, the spitting when his name is mentioned, the letters to him recommending Alcoholics Anonymous. Enough of the self-righteous posture and show-no-mercy lectures. Have you never known anyone to get in a car after a couple of drinks? Jail is in his past, as indelibly as an ink stain on your best shirt. For a couple of mistakes. For being belligerent. OK. He did all that. Enough already.

"People don't realize I'm intelligent enough to know I let them down," said Skiles, who will return to MSU this summer to complete work on his degree. "I know I let them down. People in my hometown. People in East Lansing. That's harder on me than anything else.

"It was just a mistake, a foolish mistake, and I'll regret it until . . . until the day people forget about it. Until it's not printed next to my name in the newspaper. Until I stop getting letters about being in trouble."

He looked the questioner in the eye. "Maybe 10 years from now, if for some reason my name should still be in print, there'll only be something good after it. But for quite a while, I'm sure it won't be that way. I don't think there's anything I can do about that. I wish there was. . . ."

He got up from the table. In his jeans and polo shirt and clean-shaven face, he seemed far too young for such a conversation. But it was over. He said thanks and he left the Holiday Inn, walking out through the double glass doors. He did not see the people at the counter who turned to stare at him. And it was just as well.

What is behind Scott Skiles and what is ahead of him matter little compared to what is inside him. And what is inside him, for a long time, will be churning and chawing and eating him up. He has learned his lesson. Enough already. Let him be.

HAS CALIFORNIA CHANGED WACKY ONE? BLEEP, NO

May 25

Oh, he's a knucklehead all right. The Wacky One. Your buddy and mine. Joaquin Andujar.

You remember Joaquin from last October, when he single-handedly trashed the World Series, the umpires, and most likely the rest of his career by throwing a tantrum in Game 7? Take it away, Joaquin. Go nuts.

Put on a show. And what did it get him? A one-way ticket, a new league and a new uniform — green and yellow, with an "A" on the cap. He was shipped out, traded to Oakland, a place where good quiet men such as Al Davis, Reggie Jackson and Billy Martin had all tried to make a buck.

Good company, I figured. But deep down I knew we hadn't heard the last of the Wacky One. He would be back.

I had knocked Joaquin last October, and I never regretted it. Not really. What can you say about a guy who spits at reporters all year, then calls a press conference at the World Series to tell the media how much he likes them? No one really knew what was boiling beneath the skin of that self-proclaimed "One Tough Dominican." But I remember a moment in that St. Louis clubhouse when Joaquin told a group of writers: "You ask any of my teammates. They love me. Just ask them." I looked around, and it seemed as if all the Cardinals were quietly moving their chairs as far away as possible.

I knew right then that Joaquin wasn't playing on the same board as the rest of us.

But OK, I figured. Bury the hatchet. The A's had hit the beach here in Detroit on Friday, and a visit with the Wacky One seemed like a good idea. Andujar, a 20-game winner the last two years, had already quietly built a 4-2 record. Maybe, I thought, those California winds, the amber sunsets, and the splash of the Pacific breakers had cooled his hot blood. And maybe not. You never know with a knucklehead.

I walked into the Oakland clubhouse. And there he was. I recognized him immediately by the cut of his profile, that sharp nose, the jutting chin, the brooding eyes. He was dressed in a polo shirt and turquoise jeans, as tight as a teenager's, and he didn't look happy.

"You tell me one pitcher who throws faster than me, man!" he was yelling. "Tell me one!"

Obviously I had walked in on something.

"One?" said teammate Dusty Baker. "OK. There's one." He pointed to

Jose Rijo.

"You bleeping crazy man. Can he throw 98?"

"When do you throw 98?"

"Never in my life," said Joaquin.

It was a strange scene. Several Oakland players sat by their lockers laughing. Ricky Peters, Tony Phillips, Dave Kingman. Andujar circled like a hawk, they swung back and opened fire.

"You are a bleeping bleep," he said to Peters.

"No man, you're a bleep," Peters answered.

"You tell lies behind my back," Andujar said. "You are a bleeping bleep bleep. Don't bleep me."

"Bleep," said Peters.

"Ah, bleep," said Andujar.

Then it started coming from every locker. Too fast to record verbatim. Allow me to paraphrase.

ANDUJAR: "Stay the bleep away from me. I am warning you, you bleep."

TEAMMATE: "Who the bleep are you talking to?"

ANDUJAR: "Don't bleep with me. You are bleep."

TEAMMATE: "You don't bleep with me I don't bleep with you. You bleep."

ANDUJAR: "Don't bleep with me."

After a few minutes of this, Andujar stormed into the trainer's room, then came back out. Peters had a bat in his hand, and I wasn't crazy about the way he was squeezing it.

Andujar finally dropped into his locker, across the room from the seething mob. I eased over, giving him a few minutes to let the smoke clear. It didn't seem like the time for the heart-to-heart chat I had hoped to have. But what the heck?

I asked anyhow.

"I don't talk in the clubhouse," he said.

I could have pressed it, I guess. Told him I had a plane to catch, or a sick relative. But why risk it? The man could have a weapon.

Besides, I had seen enough. The wild man lives. Forget that mellow rubbish. You can't kill a knucklehead by sending him west. Uh-uh. This breed knows how to survive.

I headed for safer ground. Maybe next time Joaquin rolls through we'll have that heart-to-heart. Until then, he remains a hot-tempered mystery. Even his teammates, obviously, don't know what to make of him as he pulls on his new green and yellow uniform.

But they can tell you what the "A" stands for.

BIAS' DEATH AFFECTS US BECAUSE HE WAS PART OF US

June 27

WIMBLEDON, England — Forget the dateline; this column is not about tennis. Sometimes you can't help writing about home — even when you're far away — and the moment the phone call came to my London hotel room, I knew this was one of those times.

Medical tests confirmed it: Len Bias died of drugs.

Cocaine.

I had waited a week hoping it wouldn't be true: Wasn't he the Boston Celtics' top draft pick? Wasn't he about to become rich? Didn't he have the world in his very large hands?

Yes. And it made no difference. Sometime around 6 a.m. last Thursday, most likely for the first time in his life, Len Bias, 22, put the drug "everybody's doing" into his body and it returned the favor by sending him into convulsions, sending his heart and his brain to a dark forever, killing him quickly, so that even the doctors who tried to save him could do nothing.

Cocaine.

He dies, we die. Nobody knows why it happened. But somewhere in the corpse they buried Monday is a vein of a world we helped create.

Didn't you know Len Bias? Sure you did. He was the kid down your street with the basketball, the high school star your town came out to see.

He was the kid who was besieged by grinning recruiters, by promises that life would be grand if only he went to their school — until he came to his high school coach one day in tears.

"Nobody says hello to me anymore," he cried. "They just want to know where I'm going."

This was Len Bias. Didn't you know him?

He was a star at Maryland. An All-America forward with a torso like a building and legs like rocket launchers. What a leaper! What a soft shot!

So he became popular. Big man on campus. Enough that he could be surly when he wanted, he could duck the media when he wanted. The well was deep enough. Everybody loves a star.

Didn't you know him?

He was the kid who once told a reporter: "I want people to see Maryland and say, 'That's the school where Len Bias graduated from.'" Only now we learn Bias failed all of his classes last semester, and the team's academic counselor quit because she said the coach didn't care enough about academics.

Didn't you know him? Haven't you heard this story before?

This was Len Bias. This was a big-time college athlete — idolized, shielded and pampered as long as he excelled on the court. Only this one tried cocaine in his dorm one morning and it killed him.

And now it's his death that moves us. But why? Death can await anyone who walks down a drug-lined street. Here is the tougher question: What brings them there? What is it about sports and winning that leads young men to an orgy of insanity, to dance with the worst type of human leeches, to kiss drugs that they don't need?

What is it? Len Bias was reportedly not a drug user. "His body was a temple to him," a teammate said. So what suddenly prompted him to try cocaine, just as his star had reached its zenith?

Was it celebration? Then there is a sickness in how we celebrate. Peer pressure? Then there is a sickness in how we impress each other. Fun? Was it just for fun? That may be the sickest idea of all.

Bias' was not the first body to react fatally to drugs. His was simply one of the most famous. So now there are detectives running around the Maryland campus and teammates hiding, and accusations against the coach, and a dorm room that was mysteriously swept clean, and a grand jury hearing, and an ugly well of questions.

And what will it get us? What will it get his family? Only if the next Len Bias thinks twice about drugs will any good have come out of this.

Maybe the publicity will do that. Maybe not. The societal trends that led Bias to cocaine still are out there. Someone sold him the stuff, or gave it to him, maybe even a friend, because he figured it was OK. And now Bias is dead.

It is terribly senseless. It is brutal. I'm writing this in a London hotel room — with the world's most famous tennis tournament a few miles away — because I can't shake it from my head.

He dies. We die. Every one of us, just a little. What can you do, except take the image of Len Bias' marvelous body being placed in the cold earth Monday, an empty shell, and paste it on the front wall of every American brain?

You may never have met Len Bias, may never have seen him play, or taken the flash of his smile.

But did you know him? Sure you did. We all did. And the next one of us who starts up with drugs spits at everything he died for.

FOR BORIS, IT WAS A SHOT HEARD 'ROUND THE WORLD

July 7

WIMBLEDON, England — Oh, God, what a shot! The ball was a yellow blur coming down the line. Boris Becker dived for it and heard a slapping noise as he belly-flopped on the grass.

Then nothing.

"I was waiting for it to go past my ear," he would say. Instead he looked up and realized the noise had been Ivan Lendl's shot whacking the net. And now the ball was dropping innocently onto Becker's side.

Glory calling.

Becker, like the movie soldier you thought was dead, lifted suddenly to one knee and, barely balanced, swiped that ball across the net past Lendl — and into the instant-replay archives of every TV station in the universe.

Wimbledon was his. Hail, the Boy King!

Yes, officially there were a few more points to win. But the angels were singing and a royal light came from the sky, and for Lendl to come back against that kind of kismet would not only have been impossible, it might have killed him.

"What did you think when he made that shot?" Lendl was asked after losing the Wimbledon final in straight sets, 6-4, 6-3, 7-5.

"What could I think?" Lendl said, shrugging. "If I had a little more luck, the ball wouldn't have tipped the net anyway."

He had no luck. He had no chance. Boris Becker is the toughest thing to hit grass since the Toro 2000. And when he is serving well — as he was Sunday, in the most famous tennis match of the year — you might as well pack it up. "Boom Boom," they call him? "Boom Boom" he is.

"You like it here, yes?" someone asked him.

"It is my court, I think," Becker said. "When I walk on Centre Court, my skin, it feels pricks. . . . "

"Goose bumps?" someone offered.

"Yeah, yeah," he said. "Goose bumps."

Well, there were a few of those in this match. True, most points were over with the serve or the service return. But in the third set, things came to life. Because here was blond-haired Becker — only 18, the defending champion — up, 2-0, in sets and virtually daring Lendl, the No. 1 player in the world, to win one from him.

Lendl had three chances. Set point at 5-4, 40-0. Becker saved it all three times. He came to the net and poked winners to the open court.

The sharks were nibbling at Lendl's feet. He lost that game, fell victim to The Shot in the 12th game and — one point after that — sent a Becker serve into the net. That ended it. The line was cut, and the cheerless Czech splashed into the water, live feed for the critics once again.

"Is Becker the best in the world now?" someone asked Lendl afterward.

"To be the best in the world you have to play very well over 12 months," he said cooly.

True. And true, in between Wimbledon triumphs, Becker has won just two minor tournaments — while Lendl took the U.S. Open and the French. Yes, Lendl is, numerically, still No. 1. So you expect more class than he showed Sunday. After losing, he walked off the court alone — the tradition is both players exit together — rather than watch Becker pose for photos.

But enough on him. Catch this. Please. When they handed Becker the gold Wimbledon trophy, he leaned over to shake the Duchess of Kent's hand and the trophy's top fell off. The thing was what, 50, 60 years old? Glazed with ghostly tradition? And here it was, rolling across the grass. And what did Becker do?

He laughed like crazy. Laughed the laugh of someone too young to worry about embarrassment. In this age of grim, robot-like champions, that may have been the most reassuring moment of the year.

"What did the Duchess say after you picked up the trophy?" Becker was asked.

"She said it was probably my ambition to win Wimbledon four or five times like Borg."

"And what did you say?"

"I said, 'See you in three years, then.'"

L ovely. Thank heaven for someone with both a racket and a sense of humor. Lendl has been lacking the latter his entire career, and it has cost him — and his sport. Tennis quietly said a danke schoen for Becker's arrival last year. Now it's a double danke.

Most kids his age are washing their first cars and working at the supermarket. Yet Becker — who is a national hero in West Germany — already seems more controlled than John McEnroe, more pleasant than Jimmy Connors, and more interesting than a court full of Swedes.

"What do you think of Becker as a person?" Lendl was asked just before he left.

"I know him only as a player," he said. "I don't know the man — the young man, the boy, whatever you want to call him. Call him champion, yes?"

Becker serving, Becker laughing, Becker bouncing off the grass. Call him champion, yes. With a win for the books, and a shot for the ages.

Sure, Carl Lewis Is Still Wonderful – Just Ask Him

July 9

MOSCOW — Beautiful. Here was Carl Lewis sitting in the crowd at Lenin Stadium wearing gold-rimmed sunglasses, white pants and a tiger-skin shirt that came down to his knees. A human billboard. And he leaned back, surrounded by a small entourage, ignoring everybody.

Carl likes this; ignoring what he considers "other people" while doing everything he can to attract their attention. Back in 1984, that meant winning four gold medals at the Olympics, and appearing on the cover of Time magazine twice in three weeks, and paying an agent who said things such as "Carl will be bigger than Michael Jackson." Only the joke was on Lewis. Because when the Games ended, America pulled in its welcome mat. He couldn't get a single U.S. endorsement deal, while Olympic darlings such as Mary Lou Retton couldn't get enough.

People chided Lewis for passing his last three Olympic attempts at Bob Beamon's long jump record. And for seeming too . . . pre-packaged. Then rumors started that he might be gay, that he might take steroids, that he got too high on looking in the mirror — and the corporate types flipped their briefcases shut and went south.

Not that you blame them. Lewis was seen, at various times, wearing orange-and-black tights, lip gloss, a new wave Grace Jones haircut, white sunglasses, puffed sleeve shirts and eyebrow pencil. You stick your product on that.

So Lewis went on winning races and losing points. And now, here he was, in Moscow of all places — where he'll run tonight in the 100 meters at the Goodwill Games — 25 years old, half-faded from America's memory, maybe the biggest commercial flop in recent sports history, and you had to wonder whether the guy had any regrets about the whole thing.

Nah.

"Look, let's go through history here," he said, sitting at a small table inside the stadium corridor. "Heroes, or leaders, I mean, how many are really represented fairly throughout their careers? Take Jesse Owens, a big inspiration. Everybody says Jesse is a great man. But Jesse had to race horses to make money, OK?"

Ah. You see. That's the kind of stuff that gets him in trouble. Don't mix Jesse and horses, Carl. Come on. But then, ah, well. Lewis has long had a penchant for sticking his foot in his mouth — both of which move at the same speed. That's his problem.

That and an ego that can't fit in the door.

H ere is the gospel according to Carl on the 1984 Olympics: "The one death fall of those Games was that everybody was so concerned about money. . . . Everyone felt everyone had to take advantage. I don't have to take advantage of anything. I love to compete. Money isn't a major issue to me. I don't have to run out and jump on every little corporate dollar I can find."

Right. This comes from a man whose agent once said, "We want Carl to be associated with one company, like Bob Hope with Texaco." A guy who was peddling his own TV special before the torch was lit in LA. Remember when Lewis was photographed for Newsweek in front of his small mansion in Houston, while his virgin-white Samoyed looked on? Inside the house was his collection of Waterford crystal. The BMW was in the garage. And all this was before the Olympics.

True, he "loves to compete." As long as the price is right. There were stories that Lewis turned down $100,000 for a single meet once. And you might remember, when he was drafted late by the Dallas Cowboys for a possible football future, he said no way, no way, unless they were willing to pay $1 million a year. Then, let's talk.

And he wonders why McDonald's doesn't call back.

A ren't you disappointed in the way you're perceived?" I asked him. "I'll tell you this," he said, "people come to me every day, tons of people, and 90 percent who mention the Olympics say, 'Boy, it was so wrong the way the press treated you. We just saw you win and it was great for America.' So I don't think it's the people. I think it's the representation."

"You mean the press?" I said.

"Well, suit yourself," he said, laughing.

Natch. When the going gets tough, the tough blame the media. Otherwise angelic guys such as Joaquin Andujar, Ralph Sampson and Larry Holmes have recently realized that their only problem is evil reporters. Lewis, with typical speed, reached the tape on that one a while ago.

"The whole world watched on TV (the Olympics) and they saw me compete and compete well, and then they turned around and heard, 'This guy's an evil person.' They were confused.

"People can say anything. I can say you're mentally retarded, right? (Well, he can say it.) And maybe people will pick it up and it will spread. That's what happened to me. Some athlete says, 'I think Carl's on steroids.'

And people wrote it with no substantiation.

"But, hey, I don't have any bitterness towards anyone. Whatever other athletes do is their business, whatever the press does is their business, because I'm enjoying my life. Everyone prints rumors from people who are losing to me. . . . So, that's the whole thing."

Got that?

Now, yes, they still are losing to Lewis in most everything he tries. He hasn't lost a long jump competition since 1981. He rarely loses in the 100 or 200 meters, and his form and fluid movement are simply remarkable. So, much to the dismay of his fellow athletes — most of whom would love to see Carl get his tail waxed — Lewis remains, in track and field, king of the hill. "I am still the No. 1 athlete in the world," he said.

Humility doesn't come in his size.

Then again, there's this business of no world records next to his name; not in the long jump, the 100 or the 200. During 1984, Lewis said he would concentrate on four gold medals and go for records in 1985. In 1985, he suffered a few injuries and set his sights on 1986. Now he says, "I'm being a little passive. Maybe the records will come next year, maybe the year after."

Well, you can only watch a guy run straight ahead so many times before you want something . . . more. History, maybe.

But Lewis runs when he wants, jumps when he wants, pushes when he wants, and he'll be the first to tell you that's what matters.

He blames his lack of corporate hookups on "too much commitment time" demanded by the companies. "They want you for 40, 50 days a year," he said, scowling. Yeah. What a drag. And at such low rates. What's Michael Jackson getting, $12 million?

"My life," Lewis said, "is 100 years. Or whatever. My life wasn't the 1984 Olympic Games. It ends the day I die, which could be whenever, maybe 50 years from now. It's easy to look back and say, 'He made a mistake.' But we didn't know what was going to happen. I got more publicity before the Olympics than any athlete ever got after them."

"Including yourself," I reminded him.

"Well, actually," he said, "I got lots of publicity after the Olympics. It's just that most of it was negative."

Hey! He made a joke.

So what do you make of Carl Lewis now? How anyone could win four gold medals in the biggest sports event of the decade and still come out smelling bad is a pretty neat accomplishment. On the scale of laid eggs, you'd have to call that an omelet's worth.

But it doesn't seem to have fazed him. He still separates himself from the rest of the athletic world, still plugs his singing and acting as if someone cares, still dresses like some meta-sexual mannequin in a Greenwich Village window. Still runs and jumps. Fast and far. Still blames someone else.

I have this hope for Lewis. This is my hope: That at the end of the day, when he washes off the makeup and hangs up the furs and puts the Gucci boots in the closet, and it's just he, alone in his room, that he looks over his majestic physical self and his glorious potential and realizes it's too great a gift for him to ruin by being a dork. But this is just a hope.

"When you are a leader, of course," he said, wrapping up his little talk, "you stand out, and that sets you up for a barrage. People now are saying, 'Oh, Carl, you're not worth anything after the Games.' But I'm probably more well-known now than I was during or after LA. I'm still competing, I made a movie that'll be out soon. I'm bigger, in terms of people knowing me, than I was before.

"I know this. In 20 or 30 years from now, people won't remember some of the other athletes. But they'll look back and remember my performances."

Then again, maybe we won't.

FUN WITH TED TURNER, THE GOODWILL GURU

July 13

MOSCOW — See Ted run. See Ted run to Russia. See Ted shell out $35 million, put his arm around a Soviet official, and raise a vodka glass to their new sports festival.

"To Mr. Turner!" toasts the Russian.

"To my Commie buddy!" says Ted.

See Ted tour. See Ted tour Moscow. See Ted stop at Lenin's tomb, go inside, view the embalmed body, and come back out.

"What do you think?" someone asks.

"He looks good," Ted says. "A little pale, maybe. . . ."

See Ted Turner — R.E. (Ted) Turner, entrepreneur, millionaire, ugly American, busted millionaire. Is there anyone on the planet quite like him?

At last audit he was more than a billion dollars in debt — yet here he is Friday on a Russian cruise boat, his shirt rumpled, his pepper hair mussed, and he's shaking hands with top-ranking Soviets and laughing like a schoolkid.

Today marks the midway point of Turner's latest brainchild, the Goodwill Games, a two-week sports competition between East and West — most notably the United States and Russia — that was created, according to Turner, to promote friendship between the superpowers, while being aired on his superstation — cable TV's WTBS.

It's losing a fortune. People aren't watching enough back home. Stadiums are half-filled. Americans are calling Russians names. And nothing fazes him.

Nothing at all.

"What will you say," a Russian reporter inquired, "if you go back to America and people ask if you are now a Communist?"

"I will say, 'Nyet,'" said Ted.

See Ted laugh.

There are things in life you can't do and things in life you can do, and just when you figure out which is which, along comes Ted Turner. How does he do it?

Here is a born troublemaker, a guy who burned down his fraternity's homecoming float, a guy who's loud enough to be heard in the next room, a guy who took over his father's billboard company at age 24 and now, at 47, owns the Atlanta Braves, the Atlanta Hawks, WTBS, CNN, more interest payments than several Third World countries, and the MGM film library. You want to see "The Wizard of Oz," "Gone With The Wind," "Ben-Hur"?

See Ted.

He is, as Bill Murray might put it, a knucklehead. The uncle who is too loud at Thanksgiving, the slob who gets blitzed at the office Christmas party. His clothes are perpetually rumpled, his conversation just a play-by-play of his brain waves.

Then again, he is shrewd enough to build a failing TV station into a satellite cable channel. Sportsman enough to defend the 1977 America's Cup. Success is a cake with a lot of recipes, and Ted Turner, who is, above all else, no dummy, has apparently found one that's 100 parts chutzpah. It is not just anyone who gets America and Russia to play in his sandbox.

"How did you pull this off?" someone asks of the Goodwill Games.

"I came over here and suggested it," he said. "At first they looked at me like a nut. A do-gooder. But now we're friends. We've gone hunting together. They kissed me — on the lips. I don't even kiss my kids that way."

"Why are you doing it?" asked someone else.

"We've got to trust one another," he said. "If the U.S. and the USSR blow each other up with nuclear weapons, we blow up everybody on the planet. That means Bermuda, the Bahamas, Jamaica, Switzerland, Sweden, India, Ceylon, or whatever they call it — they call it something else now, I don't know.

"And what right do we have to decide the fate of mankind? All our history, all our culture, the artwork, the literature. And what have we done with the opportunity? Get ready to blow ourselves up! And not just ourselves! What about the elephants? And if you think about it, you know, a nuclear war, and what it can do and. . . ."

The elephants?

Well. Hmm. Is he serious? Who knows? He thinks it, he says it. He likes it, he buys it. Turner is tuned to his own frequency. Robert Wussler, executive vice-president of WTBS, tells this story: The two of them were crossing the street in New York City once and Ted was in the middle of a thought, gesturing wildly, not paying attention, and a car up and hit him. Ted rolled onto the hood, somersaulted off, and hit the ground running, without so much as interrupting his sentence.

You don't believe it, right? Then again, maybe you do.

Especially if you've had the chance to watch Ted in action for the last few days here. To have heard him say, "Howdy, darlin'!" to a Russian washerwoman, seen him wear topsider shoes to formal ceremonies, watched him borrow a pink sports coat and a purple tie to slip over his yellow golf shirt before awarding a medal to Edwin Moses.

All of which is funny; none of which makes up for his oversights. And there have been plenty here. From the start, these Goodwill Games have been marred by confusion, protests, complaining and general chaos — but they've looked OK on the screen. Like a made-for-TV movie set, the event has been largely a front with only the barest support behind it.

True, the opening ceremonies were spectacular. But the women's 50-meter freestyle swim — the Games' very first event — saw the gun go off before the swimmers were even set. The same thing happened in the men's version a few minutes later.

Many track and field athletes had little or no idea whom they were racing against and, in some cases, where and when. "We were dropped off at the hotel and told nothing about schedules, rules, times, nothing," said Steve Scott, the American miler.

Carl Lewis accused the Soviets of being cheaters. The Soviet officials accused American journalists of being irresponsible. Communication has been simply awful. Access between press and athletes has been scattershot.

And Ted? On Friday, Ted was on the boat rolling up the Moscow River, shaking hands with guests from India, from China, from Ethiopia.

"Can we have a picture?" asked a group of Soviet press officers.

"Da," said Turner, using the Russian word for yes. He grinned.

"Da, da," he said suddenly.

He grinned again.

"Da da da da da da. . . ." he started singing.

So life can be a dream, sh-boom, sh-boom. The word is that Turner will lose $20 million on these Games. He had once figured to make that much in profit. But what's a few mill to a man who once was $2 billion in the hole?

"Aren't you worried about how much you owe?" he was asked.

"It's just a matter of zeros," he said.

Not everyone can take debt that calmly. But then not everyone tries to take over CBS, buys and sells MGM, and has been quoted as saying his life's dream is to be "Alexander the Great — ride in on a white horse and save the world."

Is he rich or poor? Philanthropist or egomaniac? How do you figure it out? Not by watching him. He is, in appearance, half Rhett Butler, half Rodney Dangerfield. He is, in action, half tyke, half tycoon.

He is, in words, uh, well. . . .

"My son bought a cat here," Ted said the other day. "Now we've got a Commie cat. It purrs just like an American cat. The squirrels over here are just like American squirrels. They eat nuts."

Huh?

"The opening ceremonies here had the largest fireworks display on the planet," Ted said. "They seeded the clouds so it wouldn't rain. They can do that, you know. They did it for the Olympics. I told 'em, 'That's great. You don't even need God over here.' "

Huh?

"You know Lenin, he was everything to these people," Ted said. "He was George Washington and Jesus Christ rolled up into one. Really. . . . "

Everybody sing.

Da da da da da.

And on he goes. See Ted run. For better or worse, broke or more broke, his Goodwill Games are in full swing, and, barring a complete transportation breakdown — which is entirely possible here — they should wrap up next weekend as a complete event.

That in itself is an accomplishment. Bringing East and West into the same stadium — even if all the best American athletes weren't here — is still something the Olympic Games haven't been able to do in the last two tries. Like certain Beverly Hills dinner parties, the big trick here is getting the right guests to show up. So what if the soup is cold?

"I love my country very much," said Ted. "And I love all people. We're all brothers and sisters and we better start acting that way before we blow ourselves to kingdom come."

What do you do with a guy who says that, then slips on a crimson pullover and says to the Russian sports minister, "Look, I'm wearing my red sweater. Ha, ha."

Maybe he's out to save the world. Maybe not. You figure at the very least, Ted Turner, for all his insanity, his southern drawl, his sneaker-chic and his sudden lapses into existentialist philosophy, is just having some fun.

And when he hits 90, and he's on the porch in Georgia, rocking in his chair, he'll be able to say, "Yeah, there I was on this cruise boat shaking hands with these Soviet big shots and I had 30 banks chasing my butt and half the world's media on my case and I had caviar in one hand and vodka in the other. . . .

"And you know what?" he'll say. "I had a blast."

Not to mention the elephants.

MOOKZI OOZMASH ...
DON'T BUST MY HEAD

July 15

MOSCOW — So there I was, racing through downtown Moscow in an illegal car, with a frantic U.S. wrestler in the backseat, and a frantic Russian translator in the front, and visions of a quick death dancing in my head.

But let's back up a minute. . . .

As some of you know, I do a morning sports radio bit on WLLZ (98.7-FM). And on Monday, I had this idea. Why not get Andre Metzger — a Grand Rapids native, and one of America's best amateur wrestlers — to talk live from Moscow?

I thought it would be fun. Especially because that night he would face the USSR's Arsen Fedzayev — considered the best amateur wrestler in the world — for the gold medal in the Goodwill Games. Andre said he would do it, and I was grateful.

Did I mention that Andre once broke a man's neck while wrestling? I should mention that.

See, here was the problem. Within an hour of the phone call, Andre would be due to weigh in for his match. You can't be late for your weigh-in.

"We'll have a cab waiting," I promised.

We did the show. And a cab was waiting. Except it wasn't a real cab. Instead, I later found out, it was just some guy who was changing his oil when our translator — whom I'll call Katrina — asked whether he wanted to make some money.

It was also Katrina who told the driver, in Russian, where we wanted to go. Let's just say Katrina is not a wrestling fan.

Did I mention that Andre once split a man's ankle in half? I should mention that.

Anyhow, we drove along the streets of Moscow for 15 minutes. Not good, because we should have been to the sports hall in 10.

"This doesn't look familiar," Andre noted.

"No, it doesn't," I said.

I turned to Katrina. "Druzhba Hall, right?"

"Druzhba?" she said. Her face went pale. "OOH. . . . moozi GLISH!"

Now I have no idea what that meant. But I can tell you what it felt like. Remember those college board exams at 8 a.m. Saturday? And you wake up and the alarm clock says 7:59?

That is what it felt like.

"Are we . . . going to . . . the WRONG PLACE?" Andre asked.

"Mokzi, oozmash. . . . OOH!" Katrina said.

We were going to the wrong place. The wrong direction. It was 5 o'clock. Rushin hour. If Andre was not on a scale by 5:30, he'd forfeit. No gold medal. No meeting Fedzayev. And we were 25 minutes away.

Did I mention Andre once broke a man's face while wrestling? I should mention that.

The car spun around. Katrina put her hand on her forehand. A bad sign.

"Tell him to go faster," I yelled.

"He can't," Katrina said. "He get ticket."

"The hell with ticket," I said. I saw the headlines: "Detroit Columnist Costs U.S. Medal." . . . "Metzger To Writer: Your Fault, You Die. . . ."

"Faster," I yelled. "But the police," Katrina said. "Forget them," I screamed. "Tell the driver we'll pay 10 more rubles." She translated. He grinned. He hit the gas.

Then a policeman pulled us over.

By now Andre was banging the door with his fists. "Why did I do this!" he bellowed in anguish. I think it was anguish. I was too busy shaking.

The policeman asked for papers. It was then Katrina told me that playing taxi was illegal in Russia. I had a sudden hatred for FM radio. Andre was moaning. The driver was pale. When the policeman finally let him go, I had to offer 20 more rubles to get him to turn the key. It was 5:22.

Did I mention that Andre once broke a guy's thumbs? I should mention that.

I think it's up here!" Katrina yelled.

"Why did I DO THIS?" Andre yelled.

"Ten more rubles!" I yelled, being American.

Let's sum this up. We were riding in an illegal cab, a top U.S. wrestler was about to miss his biggest match, the translator was crying, I was writing my own obituary, the driver was figuring, what, he was up to at least 100 rubles?

And it was 5:30.

The car reached the Druzhba gates. Before it even stopped, Metzger was out and running. Katrina was 20 steps behind, in high heels, screaming. I gave the driver everything I had.

Well, OK. Here is the epilogue. Metzger made the weigh-in. Barely. Katrina cried for 10 minutes. I was out of rubles. We walked back.

And that night Metzger wrestled Fedzayev, and he lost, 8-2. I don't think the ride had any effect. This Russian was good. But afterward, I apologized, and Metzger shrugged it off, nicely.

"Forget it," he said. "It was no big deal."

And I guess I believe him.

Then again, he knows where I work.

SOVIET DOES THE SAME JOB, BUT IN A SEPARATE WORLD

July 16

MOSCOW — He was I and I was he.

He wrote about sports. I wrote about sports. He lived by deadlines. So did I. We were close in age, we both carried notebooks. If not for an accident of birth, we might have been on the same newspaper somewhere, desk to desk.

Instead we sat silently across a wooden table in a Moscow restaurant, until a female translator came by and threw a rope between our worlds.

"Ask him his name," I said.

"Kak vas zovut?"

"Vladamir," she came back. "And yours?"

I told him. We shook hands.

He said he wrote for Soviet Sports, a large daily newspaper. And he asked me whom I worked for. He said he'd been covering sports for eight years. And he asked me how long I had done it. Our questions filtered slowly through the translator, and we waited for the words to come home.

"He would like to know how you write your stories," the translator said.

"By computer," I said. "We have an ATEX system throughout our office. And him?"

She asked the question. He made a writing motion with his hand.

"He uses the pen and paper, of course," the translator said.

A waiter brought coffee. We both reached into our pockets to pay, and we laughed.

It was not hard to tell us apart. Like most of his Soviet colleagues, Vladamir wore a dark sports coat, a tie and brown shoes. I had on jeans, a cotton shirt and white Reebok sneakers.

But the more he talked, the more I heard myself. His first journalism job was at a small newspaper in the Ural mountains near Siberia. I began at a free weekly newspaper in suburban New York. We had both gotten into the business by accident; I was a musician, he had been a poet. "He wrote verse," the translator explained. "He says it was nothing special."

He should have heard my songs.

He sympathized when I complained about crowded locker rooms, and athletes ruined by success. I knew the feeling when he told of writing a long story, only to be told the paper had no space.

"What does your desk look like?" I asked.

He smiled when he heard the translation. "It is very messy."

My kind of guy.

He lit a cigaret. I took out a piece of gum. There was a point there, when the translator was buzzing and the words were almost simultaneous, that it felt as if we were colleagues in some Hyatt Regency bar after a night game.

But it did not last.

"I travel quite a bit," I said. "Does he?"

"Yes, very much," came the translation. "He has been to Bulgaria and Poland and Romania."

"How about the West?" I asked.

"No," came the answer. "He . . . has not."

There was an awkward pause. We both took quick sips of our coffee, but it was more out of embarrassment than anything else.

There is probably a match here for every one of us back home, someone who laughs at the same ironies, who dreams the same dreams. But the line that separates us is straight and hard as steel. The difference between yes, you can, and no, you can't.

"What if he wrote something critical of the government?" I asked.

"Well, he would not do this," came the answer.

"Does he aspire to other jobs?" I asked.

"He will stay in this one," came the answer. "Here, you see, it is not so easy to change."

We talked for a few minutes more. He told me his salary, which was about $4,800 a year. He asked about mine. I lied.

We exchanged business cards. I pointed to my phone number; I don't know why.

"Tell him I hope he will come to America one day, and he will stay with me."

She translated. His eyes widened for a second, then he opened his hands in front of him — body talk for surrender.

"Yes," came the answer. "Maybe I will."

No he won't.

The lights in the room flicked on, meaning the place was closing. A heavyset waitress took away our cups. We both got up to go, and made a feeble attempt to communicate without the translator.

"Sank yu," he said.

"Spacebo," I replied.

And that was it. He crushed out his cigaret and went to join his Soviet colleagues. There were a thousand more things I wanted to tell him. There was nothing I could say.

In another world, we were the same man, and that was I walking off in his brown shoes. But this is this world, where freedom is still a crapshoot, and at that moment, I think we both realized who'd gotten the luckier roll.

Jogging Some Nerves Around Kremlin Wall

July 17

MOSCOW — So I wanted to jog around the Kremlin. What's the big deal? I mean, you gotta jog somewhere, right?

"You're insane," a colleague said.

"Hope you like Siberia," another said.

"Boys, boys," I said, slipping on my running shoes, "the Kremlin is just a big building. Buildings are meant to be jogged around."

They shook their heads.

"Nice working with you," one said.

"Can I have your bags?" another said.

This was overreaction. Wasn't it overreaction? No matter. I had to do it. I was leaving the USSR the next morning, and for the last 11 nights I had seen that red star atop the Kremlin from my hotel window, calling to me like a lighthouse calls to sailors. "Jog me," it whispered. "Jog me now."

I had to do it.

"You're really going?" they said.

"Life is but a run," I said, bending over into a hamstring stretch.

What could happen? Really, what could happen? It's not as if I was hiding concealed weapons. I wore those shortie-shorts and an old sweatshirt. Nor did I plan to jog the hallways.

I just wanted to get inside that massive castle-like wall and circle the grounds. Maybe wave as I loped past a cabinet meeting window. Then curl around to the Kremlin parking lot, and, you know, see whether they numbered the spaces with yellow spray paint, like: RESERVED: A. GROMYKO.

Maybe they had a lunch truck outside the front entrance. And as I scooted past Gorbachev in the middle of a hot dog, he'd nod and say, "Nice pace. Try to keep your arms lower."

OK. Did I expect too much? Well. OK. But I meant no harm. And out the hotel door I went, at an amazingly average pace. . . .

I started across the street. SHRIIEEK. A whistle. A policeman waved me back. Don't cross the street. Use the tunnel under it.

OK. Use the tunnel. I came out and headed into Red Square. SHRIIEEK. A whistle. Another policeman. Stay within the white lines.

OK. I can do that.

Across Red Square and down toward the wall. Up to an entrance I jogged, a good mellow pace, and I nodded as I started past the guard.

SHRIIEEK.

He threw his arms in front of me. Grabbed my press pass. Shook his head and reached for his walkie-talkie.

Maybe another entrance, I figured.

SHRIIEEK. That was the other entrance.

This went on three or four more times. A whistle, a stern look. A couple of "mooshki, ushki, dreshki . . ." warnings.

I was bouncing off the wall in a circle, every 200 yards, like a kid playing Duck Duck Goose. Only the wall went on around two corners, and past a park, and another corner. It was as if they had walled in Kennedy Airport.

Anyhow, soon the problem became less their wall than mine. I should mention that I am not much of a jogger.

I reached something like my 14th entrance about the same time as a black limousine. The guards pushed me aside — they touched me, which should at least be a technical foul, or something — and marched over to the car.

And then I saw it.

About 20 feet away. An entrance with no guard. What could happen? Really, what could happen?

I was through it like destiny.

My flesh tingled. I was inside the wall. What a feeling! My mind began to race, my eyes became motor-driven Instamatics. Take it all down, I said to myself. Everything. The White House might want to debrief you. Take it all down.

And I did. And here is what I saw. Here is what I can tell you about the Kremlin.

It is yellow.

That is all I got to see before a guard grabbed me and threw me out. OK. So it's not much. Hey. I got in. Let somebody else set up camp.

Geez.

Actually, I wasn't in, per se.

Actually, I was about what you call halfway in.

Actually, I had jogged into the trash pickup.

I walked back around, no longer feeling mellow. I reached the line of people waiting for the official Kremlin tour. What the hell? It was my last day. I slipped in, and soon I was at the gate.

And a guard grabbed me.

"Ve trusak nelzia," he said, directing me to the street. "Ve trusak nelzia."

Which means, "no shorts allowed."

So that was the problem.

POKER-FACED TWAY FINDS TREASURE IN HIS SANDBOX

August 12

OLEDO — He was jumping up and down in the sand like a kid. Bob Tway? Jumping up and down? All golf season long he had been Mr. Deadpan, the analyst, the troubleshooter, the Swiss watchmaker on a grass workbench.

What had they called him? The Poker-Faced Kid? And now he was jumping up and down, waving his fists and kicking up sand, until the sea of people lining the 18th green at Inverness was cheering and jumping with him, and some people were crying, they were so overwhelmed.

And soon he was crying, too.

"How do you feel?" asked a TV reporter who grabbed him as he came off that final hole.

"I feel. . . . I feel great. . . ." he said, a tear rolling down his right cheek.

Only a minute earlier he had made the shot of his life, a 25-foot wedge from the right bunker, that lifted to the green in a spray of sand and rolled like destiny to the pin.

And went kerplop.

It's twue, it's Tway! He had won the PGA Championship. He had won his first major title. He had beaten Greg Norman, the superstar heir apparent whom everyone had been talking about all month. He had done it with one shot from the sand. One incredible shot.

"Were you confident you could make it?" someone asked him afterward.

"I wasn't even trying to make it," he said. "I was just trying to get it close. I'm not that good."

But on this day, he was good enough. The Oklahoma golfer — who, despite his 27 years, still looks like Chip from "My Three Sons" — had started where he left off Sunday, when the final round was postponed because of rain. He was four strokes behind Norman — who was 11 under — and Norman had looked unbeatable.

But on Monday, Norman seemed to be set on playing to Tway's level, and in the end, playing just a shade beneath it. So his lead went from four strokes to two strokes and then one stroke and then no strokes. The two leaders were tied from the 14th on.

Tway played — what else? — steady golf, with often magnificent approach shots and only acceptable putts. Several times he had chances to leave Norman behind with birdies, but the ball rolled past or came up short.

So when they lined up their approach shots on 18, the final hole, the thick crowd was still whispering, "Norman." And when Tway hit the bunker, they figured the "Shark" was smelling blood.

Not this day. Norman had a 20-foot chip to the pin, a tough shot at best. But before he got the chance, Tway made that magical wedge, knocking his ball from the sand to the superlative.

And Norman knew it was over.

"What did you say when his shot went in?" someone asked Norman afterward.

"I said, 'Oh, s—!' " he answered honestly.

It twue. It's Tway.

Norman missed the chip. He shook Tway's hand. Tway's wife ran out and hugged him. He pulled off his visor and waved it high, and the personality was peeled out from under the perfection. No more analyst. No more watchmaker.

"Way to go, Bobby!" someone yelled.

"Tway! All the way!"

"All right, Bob!"

He smiled. He cried. "You've always been so unemotional," someone pointed out.

"I guess . . . I am . . . pretty serious," he said, stopping twice to catch his composure. "But right now, I'm the happiest person in the world."

So the PGA is over, with a new champion. And not the one many expected. Norman took his loss well, and his accomplishments are not at all diminished — as some may suggest — by finishing second at yet another major tournament. It only means that more than anyone else, Norman belongs at the top of the golfing world.

And Tway belongs alongside him. Remember that this win is only the capper on a spectacular year, in which Tway has 13 top-10 finishes and four tour victories.

The Masters returned us Jack Nicklaus, the U.S. Open revitalized Ray Floyd, the British hailed Norman and now the PGA celebrates Bob Tway. The, uh, excitable Bob Tway.

"You were really thrilled," someone said.

"Oh my," he said. "That shot may never happen again in my career!"

He held the trophy, his wife held roses, and the Monday sun was setting as on a weekend on this, a richly satisfying golf season. One with drama at every Grand Slam corner, and now, four worthy champions: two veterans, one new superstar, and a poker-faced kid, jumping in the sand.

LIONS' MR. ROGERS IS ALWAYS NEIGHBORLY

September 5

Well, gosh darn it, what are we talking about here? This is a football coach? Darryl Rogers, the guy in the blue shorts and the bony legs and the voice that sometimes sounds disturbingly like Kermit the Frog's?

Come on. Jiminy Crickets! He looks like the same guy they brought in here last year — the guy who never coached an NFL game in his life. OK. Skinny and green you can understand at that point. But he has had a year to learn the ropes, this Rogers guy. Where's the muscle-flexing? Where's the cursing? Where's the new deep voice, the swagger, the strut, the Lombardi quotations, the iron jaw, the "I'm-in-charge" bark that sends terror down a rookie's spine?

Where's the. . . .

Where. . . .

Where are you going, Darryl?

"Over here," he said, walking to the far end of his office to start an interview. "I never sit behind a desk when I'm talking to someone. Makes them feel uncomfortable, so I don't do it. Let's just sit in these chairs here across from one another. Now, then. What are we going to talk about?"

Uh. . . .

Well, let's start with last season. Rogers arrived from Arizona State, still damp from the college showers. Everything was new. NFL schedules. NFL personnel. NFL pressure. When reporters cornered Rogers early on, he'd simply shrug and say things like, "I don't know. I'm new around here."

People had a hard time believing an NFL coach could be so unassuming, so goodness-gracious. Or so naive.

"Was that just an act?" he was asked in his office last week.

"Not really," he said. "We honestly didn't know a lot of things when we got started last year. ('We' being Rogers' way of saying 'I.') Then when we got into it, we found out we knew more than we thought we did. Then again, when we got further into it, we found the things we thought we knew, we didn't always know."

What all that translates to, basically, is the Lions' 1985 season: Beat the teams no one expects you to beat — Miami, San Francisco, the New York Jets, Dallas — then crumble like corn flakes against such chest-beaters as Tampa Bay and Indianapolis.

Where was the sense in that 7-9 record? Where was the pattern? Who were the "real" Lions? The team that showed up at the Silverdome? Or the team that took its plane tickets and compiled one of the worst road records in the NFL?

With the 1986 season about to begin, it is clear the so-called experts believe the real Lions were the ones that whimpered, not the ones that roared. They are predicting mediocre results for Detroit, at best. Fourth place in the NFC Central.

To which Rogers replies:

"I can understand that position. It's logical, when you look at our numbers from last season.

"Hey. We don't have any great offensive statistics. We don't have any great defensive statistics. We don't have an all-pro player. We don't have anyone we can hang our hat on since Billy Sims retired. Let's face it. We're sitting here with a team of a lot of just no-name people."

Great. Glad to hear it. Thanks for coming by and brightening Detroit's day. And what, pray tell, Darryl Rogers, do you expect to do with a team like that?

"Oh, I expect to win," he said, quite naturally. "Every time we go out there."

Confused? It is understandable. The genius who coined the phrase, "Grin, it'll make people wonder," never met Darryl Rogers. Or he might have written: "Don't react at all. It'll drive 'em crazy."

Rogers is, at 51, so laid-back he challenges gravity. After victories he is calm, analytical, liable to crack a joke. After losses he is calm, analytical, liable to crack a joke.

So it's no surprise he can predict big things from a football team most everyone already is writing off, and do so without a megaphone or a brass band.

"I have just always been this way," he said, shrugging. "You don't need to scream at people to get things done. Anyhow, it won't work, unless you're a screamer. Intimidating people won't work, unless you're an intimidator. The only thing that will work for you is to be the way you are naturally. So I am.

"When I was younger, as a quarterback in college (a brief stint at Fresno State), I tried being something I wasn't. I thought it would make me lead the other guys better. Finally one of them came up to me and said, 'Darryl. Stop it. Just be yourself, OK?' He was right."

Since then, Rogers has been so true to his nature it is hard to even picture him any other way. You can, for example, imagine — and let's emphasize the word imagine here — coaches like the Chicago Bears' Mike Ditka soulfully drunk in a Rush Street tavern. Or Don Shula so angry that smoke comes out of his ears, instead of just his nostrils.

But Rogers? Singing in the rain? Posing as a drill sergeant? Crooning a nightclub number? Nah. It doesn't work. Even his misbehaving has to make sense.

"Did you ever get in fights when you were younger?" he was asked.

"Oh, sure," he said.

"Really? When?"

"When we played football."

"What over?"

"The ball, mostly," he said.

O K. This much Rogers will admit about last year. He was impressed by the specimens. College bulk is one thing. But you talk NFL, you talk behemoth, ugly, mean, strong, fast. And those are the guys you cut. "At first I couldn't get over how fast these guys were, how powerful," he said. "It's a whole different breed."

It took Rogers a little while before he adjusted his standards upward. When players he recognized from college became available, he quickly found he needed a second opinion. A typical conversation would go like this:

ROGERS: How about this guy? I remember him.

ASSISTANT: But look at his times.

ROGERS: Really? These are his times? But he was so fast in college.

ASSISTANT: Look at his strength.

ROGERS: Really? These are his numbers? But he was –.

ASSISTANT: He's no good, coach.

ROGERS: But he was a good player in –.

ASSISTANT: Coach, he's no good.

ROGERS: Well. . . . I'll be darned.

The "I'll be darned" is a direct quote, by the way. Rogers uses foul language about as often as he uses a triple-reverse.

Rogers knows personnel much better now, he said. "I was looking at our kickoff team from last year, and I realize eight of those guys are not even with us anymore. And at the time, I thought they were good."

But then, there were players he just shook his head at in awe last season. James Lofton of the Packers. Walter Payton of the Bears.

"You know, in college, you very rarely match personnel to personnel," Rogers said. "You match system to system. In the pros, there are times when their guy is just flat-out better than your guy. And you have to scramble so they don't keep taking advantage of it."

Rogers said the Lions made a mistake by acquiring certain players in the middle and end of last season. Without elaborating, he said, "We took some players out of desperation, and it turns out we weren't as desperate as that. We would never pick up those players again."

"How good was the team last year?" he was asked. "Was it good enough to beat all those top-ranked teams?"

"Well, let's say when we played them, we were good enough to beat them," he said. "That doesn't mean they were necessarily at their best. But that's not our responsibility. Our responsibility is to prepare our own team as best we can. And on those days, we played better."

"How about the teams the Lions lost to?" he was asked.

"Well, in my mind the two worst losses were the ones to Washington (24-3) and to Green Bay (43-10). We were completely controlled in those games."

"Whom do you blame for those losses?"

"After losses like that you tend to degrade everybody. In fact, after losses like that, you think about getting rid of your entire team."

He grinned.

"You can't do that, of course," he added.

And how about the 1986 Lions? Rogers thinks this year's team is "no doubt" better than last year's. But there still is no one big name — no Top Gun character he can point to.

"That's a big difference between us and a lot of teams," he said. "A guy you can really hang your hat on. A guy you know, no matter what happens, he's gonna come through for you. Most of the time that's not a lineman or any defensive player or even a running back. Most of the time, that's a quarterback."

"Does Chuck Long fit the bill as a 'guy you can hang your hat on'?" he was asked.

"We hope so," Rogers said. "We hope that's what he'll become."

In the meantime, Rogers is left with a continually sticky quarterback situation. Eric Hipple or Joe Ferguson? It's a repeat of last season's dilemma. But make no mistake. Rogers sees the selection as crucial for the team's chances — although he kept the decision his own until naming Hipple this week.

But then, that, too, is a Darryl Rogers pattern: Avoid controversy if you can. There were whispers about the way Rogers left Michigan State for Arizona State back in 1980 and whispers about the way he left Arizona State for the Lions last year. There was talk that Rogers was less than candid with his soon-to-be former employers. But Rogers — who acknowledges that he was never fired from a football job; he initiated all his changes — remains entirely non-plussed.

"I don't need to concern myself with what was said about what happened or what was written about what happened," he said, "because I know what happened."

Nothing, he said. At least nothing wrong or suspect. He said he had no jitters about coming back to Michigan last year because "Michigan State was a positive experience; so was Arizona State."

Gee whiz.

End of subject.

No controversy.

So here, football fans, is the man you are dealing with, the thin guy with the Haggar slacks and slightly bemused expression. In a nutshell, he is not much of a nut. In fact, his call letters could be NTFN — No Time For Nonsense.

One of the few things Rogers will not tolerate — and he tolerates a lot — is mental errors. "I won't be telling a player the same thing over and over," he said. "You get it wrong, you're gone."

Another pet peeve? Reporters who ask him how he feels after a loss. "How the heck am I supposed to feel?" he said, in astonishment. "Why would anybody care how I feel, anyhow? That doesn't change anything. It's just not important."

No Time For Nonsense.

Braggarts don't impress him. Loudmouths don't impress him. When asked why not, he replied, "I've seen a very big man brought down by a very small man with a gun."

He said it again, but when asked to elaborate, he shook his head. His answer was enough to answer the question. The rest, as he determined it, was not important. Not for now.

You get the feeling there are a lot more of those sentences inside Darryl Rogers — a lot of complexly wired parts inside that second-year coach's brain. But he keeps them to himself, because revealing them serves no purpose. He would just as soon shrug it all off with a self-deprecating remark and a squeaky laugh.

But Rogers is no foot-shuffling rube. He will answer almost any question, albeit safely. True, you are not likely to hear "Darrylisms," the way you might hear "Sparkyisms." But you won't find Rogers having to take back half the things he has said, either.

So here he is, in his second pro season. Where is the swagger, the strut, the iron jaw? They never were there. They never will be.

"Not every coach is like that," Rogers said, his voice rising into the range of that famous frog again. "Bill Walsh isn't that macho type. Don Coryell isn't that macho type. I don't think Tom Landry is that macho type.

"So I'm in good company, right?"

He smiled from the chair, a half-room away from his desk. The 1986 season will begin in two days. Jiminy Crickets! Holy Moley! How will he take it?

He'll take it as it comes.

BO SCHEMBECHLER WON'T BEAT HIS OWN DRUM

October 3

L et me give you a date," I say to Bo Schembechler, who is sitting in the big chair behind his desk.

He nods OK.

"Oct. 5, 1963," I say.

Nothing.

"Miami of Ohio beats Western Michigan, 27-19," I say.

Nothing.

"Well? Doesn't that mean anything to you?"

He looks confused.

"Bo, that was your first win as a head coach."

"Was it?" he says.

"Your first win, Bo."

He grins. "Oh, yeah," he says.

Oh, yeah? Well, what did you expect? He would jump out of the chair and start singing the Miami fight song? This is Bo Schembechler, remember, a guy who harps less on victories than losses. And besides, that first win was 23 years ago, when, as he points out, "I had more hair."

Today, it is true, there is less on top. But a lot more under the belt. Schembechler is one win away from 200 career victories, a milestone to most, a tombstone to some. But all he will say for public consumption is, "If we're lucky enough to win against Wisconsin Saturday, I'll be glad."

Yeah. And if Christie Brinkley phones, I'll take the call. Come on. He'll be more than glad — he'll be tickled blue. Because deep down, Bo revels in the wins, in the applause, the plaques on his wall, even the echoes of his own screaming. But what he lets show and what he doesn't let show. . . .

Well. For example, a few years ago, in practice, the Wolverines ran a pass play and a lineman came running by and Schembechler couldn't get out of his way and — boom! — down went the coach. "It hurt so damn much," he recalls, "I didn't want to get up. It was killing me. But I couldn't just lie there. They were all watching."

So he got up quickly, and he turned to his players, who were collectively holding their breath, and he made a face, a good mean face, and said, "Well, that probably would have killed an ordinary man."

Oh, yeah? Oh, yeah.

S o what you see and what you get are not always the same in Glenn (Bo) Schembechler, 57, the only son of an Ohio fire chief, who has managed, in his long coaching career, to set a few blazes of his own.

111

What's the record now, 199-55-7? Not too shabby, no?

What happens when the man a magazine once called "the most overrated coach in America" goes for his 200th win? Well, first understand that 200 college wins, even if you did them all in a row — even if you never lost — would take you nearly 19 years. Overrated?

So 23 years to get the big 200 is pretty damn impressive, and this from a man who, as soon as he arrived as head coach at Miami of Ohio — after working 10 years as an assistant at Ohio State, Northwestern, Bowling Green and Presbyterian — met his starting quarterback in the student union, a skinny fellow named Ernie Kellermann, and greeted him by barking, "THIS IS MY QUARTERBACK? THIS SCRAWNY GUY?" He then began to feel Kellermann's arms and shoulders, checking for muscle tone, and the kid just stood there being probed, as students passed by wondering what kind of place they had walked into.

"I had heard he was that kind of coach," recalls Kellermann, now a manufacturer's rep in Ohio. "I was kind of in awe of him. Finally, I said something in my defense and he laughed and stopped squeezing me. From then on we got along OK."

It was Kellermann who helped get Schembechler his first college win (after a loss and a tie). He remembers no special celebrations. Just the normal, "Let's go on to next week" attitude that is the linchpin of every good coach. But there were plenty of explosive moments, even back then. There was screaming. There was head slapping. There was a rainy-day loss to Dayton, when, on the last play of the game, half the players splashed into the sidelines, knocking Schembechler into a mud hole.

Bo delivered his post-game chew-out covered from head to toe in brown goop.

A nother date," I say.
    "OK," he says.
    "Oct. 4, 1975," I say.
"Mmmm."

"Michigan beats Missouri, 31-7."

"Oh, yeah, that was a big payback game for us. Missouri had kicked our tails in 1969. Worst loss we ever had."

"I know. But that was your 100th victory."

"Oh, yeah?" he says.

"Do you remember any celebration?"

"I don't think so. No."

"According to the newspapers from back then, the players dragged you into the showers with them."

"Really? You know, by God, I believe that's right. They did drag me into the showers."

He leans back, grinning.

"I'll be damned," he says.

There are now a few hundred anecdotes that follow Schembechler around like so many cans tied to the back of a newlywed's car. Some, like the one about his heart attack — suffered the night before the 1970 Rose Bowl — have to do with his tenacity. Others have to do with his poor bowl record. But most have to do with his temper.

Yes, he once angrily kicked a garbage can in the locker room that turned out to be made of concrete. Yes, he once threw chairs at Woody Hayes, his boss at Ohio State. But Woody threw them first. Yes, he screams, he throws tantrums, his eyes can be liquid fire. Rough. Tough. Gruff. Had enough?

Well. Remember this: College coaching is at least 50 percent inspiration, and you're not going to get too many linemen psyched to risk life and limb by coming on like Truman Capote.

"Are you as rough as people think?" I ask.

"Look," he says, "my image has been molded by the press from the time I came in, just from my background with Woody. They said I was volatile, I had a temper. And I do."

He allows a mischievous grin. "But sometimes I just do things to fuel that. Like this stuff about me not wanting to pass the ball. You know that's not as true as everyone thinks. But I figure, what the hell? Even if I throw 40 times, the one time I run it, they'll say you should have passed it. So I scream now and then just to have fun with it.

"It's at the point now where, when something happens that should cause me to get upset, particularly with the coaches, they all look at me to see what I'm gonna do."

But don't be fooled. The anger is part of the package. Like the brushfires started by forest rangers, it is a wildness with a purpose.

In the mid-'70s, Michigan and Ohio State, bitter rivals, were trying to recruit Art Schlichter as quarterback. Schembechler and an assistant, Jack Harbaugh — now head coach at Western Michigan and father of Bo's current quarterback, Jim Harbaugh — went down to the Schlichter home in Ohio. Schlichter's father sat in an easy chair across from Schembechler, who was sitting on the couch. Between them was a glass coffee table with several flower vases on it.

"Look, Bo," the senior Schlichter said, "let's get right down to business. Woody Hayes has assured Art that he will start next year as a freshman in their very first game."

Bo's eyes turned red. "Wait a minute. He has a junior quarterback, just like I do."

"He's going to make him a wide receiver," Mr. Schlichter said.

"Furthermore, Woody promises they'll throw at least 25 times a game. And he's going to let Art play basketball."

At this point, Bo leaned over and began banging the coffee table with his fist, so hard the vases began to shake. Harbaugh scrambled to try to keep them from falling.

"MR. SCHLICHTER, LET ME TELL YOU SOMETHING," Bo bellowed. "WHEN MY SEASON OPENS RICK LEACH IS GOING TO BE MY STARTING QUARTERBACK. IF YOU WANT YOUR SON TO COMPETE FOR THE POSITION, YOU SEND HIM TO MICHIGAN. IF NOT, YOU SEND HIM TO OHIO STATE."

He turned to Harbaugh, who was still trying to catch the vases. "JACK, GET MY COAT!"

They marched out the door. Harbaugh was shaking. He anticipated the worst ride of his life back to Ann Arbor. As they reached the car, Schembechler turned to him, and dug a soft elbow in his gut.

"Well," Bo said, "what do you think?"

He knew that tantrum was the only chance he had to get Schlichter. He didn't. "But at least," he says now, "I put on a good show."

Have you ever apologized to a player?" I ask him.

"Oh, sure," he says, erupting into a laugh. (Bo's laugh, like most of his emotions, is best described as an eruption.)

"Who?"

"Well, lots of them."

"Who?"

"Well, I apologized to (Jim) Brandstatter for kicking him in the butt (laugh) for messing up a punt in practice (harder laugh) when he wasn't the guy (explosive laugh) who did it.

"Aah ha haaa. . . . "

He collects himself. "Actually," he says, "I don't think I ever did apologize to him."

"Anybody else?"

"Sure. Lots."

"Who?"

"I don't know."

"You can't remember any specifics?"

"I don't know. There were hundreds."

Well, there was, after all, the day in 1973 when Schembechler had to call his players in and tell them they had been passed over by a Big Ten selection committee. They were not going to the Rose Bowl, despite their 10-0-1 record. Ohio State, which had the same record, was going instead.

"That's the most upset I've ever seen him," recalls Jack Harbaugh. "He was trying to tell the team, that's life, that's the way it goes, but there were tears streaming down his face. He was really crying.

"Heck, he had gone to Rose Bowls before. It was the team — that team, those guys who had done so much for him. It killed him that they weren't getting to go."

The times he chews out players, the times he makes them feel like water bugs, the times he makes them shake, those are the times when anger seethes inside his young men. Moments like that and the occasional compliment, the occasional joke, the occasional glimpse at the coach's underside — which is actually rather sensitive — are enough to cause countless players, from Kellermann, the scrawny first quarterback, to Jim Harbaugh, the current version, to volunteer the corniest of tributes.

"I love the guy like a father," they say.

So, on Saturday, Schembechler, who has been Michigan coach since 1969, goes for career win No. 200. Only eight other Division I coaches have done that. It is from this point on that numbers can become seductive, a siren call to immortality, to stay forever.

Schembechler, as usual, has a story for that.

"It was after Bear Bryant broke the record for most college wins by a football coach. We were coaching at the East-West Shrine Game. At the time I was being pursued by Texas A&M. I told Bear I wanted to talk to him about it. He came by my hotel room that night.

"Well, he walks in, sits down and says, 'Aren't you gonna offer me a drink?' I get him a drink. He says, 'Now, tell me about this job.' So I tell him.

"We talk about it for an hour, an hour and a half. Then he stops everything and says, 'Well, we talked enough about you. Now, —damn it, let's talk about my problems.'

"I said, 'What problems could you have? You're on top of the world, the winningest coach of all time.'

"He said, 'Bo, I don't want to go back to the office. I don't wanta call the office. I don't want to recruit one more son of a bitch. I wanna quit.'

"I said, 'Go ahead and quit then. What better time than now?'

"He says, 'Oh, no you don't. Let me tell you something. I got 47 people down there at Alabama. I hired them all, and when I quit, I promise you they'll all be out of a job. Some of them are pretty old. I can't do that.'

"Sure enough he went on and coached another year, but he really didn't want to. I don't think he really enjoyed himself the last 10 years. He was just going after that record. And when he got the record he still couldn't quit."

"What does that mean to you?" I ask.

"It means simply this. If you're gonna go for records, you better make damn sure you enjoy what you're doing. Or else you're making a colossal mistake."

want to ask him something. I want to catch him off-guard. I wait for the moment, then I fire away.

"Bo, answer me honestly. Are you the best college football coach in America right now?"

"No," he says, without missing a beat.

"Who's better?"

"Lots of guys."

"Like who?"

"I don't know. You pick 'em."

"I don't want to pick them."

"I don't know. The Joe Paternos, the Barry Switzers, the Tom Osbornes, the Jim Youngs, some lesser-known coaches in the South. I don't want to compare myself with them."

"Why not?"

"I just don't."

"Well, where would you say you stand relative to those coaches?"

He thinks about it for a second. "Just one of the guys," he says.

He leans back in his chair. He is happy with his answer. Happy with the image, with the dose of humility. He rubs his thinning hair, and his eyes look off for a moment. Then he leans forward suddenly.

"Don't get me wrong," he says. "I think I can beat any of those guys. Anytime."

Oh, yeah? Oh, yeah.

IT'LL BE BOSOX AND METS – I'D BETTER TAKE NOTE(S)

October 7

BOSTON — It is no secret that sports writers take a lot of notes. Some, I have heard, can even read them. Our baseball writer, John Lowe, takes meticulous notes, almost constantly. He keeps them organized and neat, and sometimes uses more than one color pen — not just because the first one exploded in his pocket, like mine always do.

Sometimes in May and June, I wonder why a baseball writer takes so many notes, and then I bite into another hot dog and forget about it. But every year around this time, I slap my head and say "ARRRGH!" Now I know why they take so many notes. Because inevitably, come October, you are sent to cover a playoff series between two teams that you know nothing about — except that they are much better than the team you cover, or else your team would be here, right? And then you wouldn't need any notes.

Right. So. There are notes and there are notes. John's notes, for example, could be bound and edited and sold in bookstores. In their original form. And I'd bet they'd sell. And then there are my notes.

My notes are to John's notes as bikini briefs are to a tuxedo. They are not quite John's notes. Actually, they could not even share the same loose-leaf as John's notes. They would be too embarrassed. If notes could talk, mine would say, "Yo! Get us outta here. Who's da stiff in da ballpoint?"

I don't show John my notes. If he comes by while I am making an entry, I quickly grab a hot dog and act casual until he goes away. Not that I make that many entries.

Anyhow, this morning, John is cruising. I'll bet, even as you read this, John is in his hotel room, sipping tea and reviewing his notes in preparation for tonight's Boston-California playoff opener, perhaps using the cross-check system he put together in August by last name, team, record against left-handers and farm club affiliation.

While I look for the pad with the taco stain.

Was it taco?

No. Wait.

Where the heck? . . .

Well. You see the problem. My plan was to have at least one page for each major league team, and that page could be built upon all season long. And I started out OK. The paper was crisp and new, and I wrote "NEW YORK METS" on the top line, and "BOSTON RED SOX" and the rest. It looked sharp. It looked together. It looked like something John might have on his desk. And then the orange juice spilled.

I'm not sure what morning that was. It was probably before the Swiss cheese croissant, but I'm not sure. One of the team's pages, I think it was Seattle's, I used to take down directions to a Memorial Day barbecue that I never attended. Which is just as well, because I probably would have spilled the sauce. Besides, John might have been there.

There were also plane reservations and phone numbers and a sudden call from some athlete who decided to do the interview after all, only I was out of paper. Except for, of course, my notes.

Besides, I like to eat at my desk.

Which leaves me looking at this:

NEW YORK METS: Look strong early. . . . Gooden? Can he repeat? . . . Carter, 4-for-5, May 3d. . . . 1-800-654-8000. . . . Cleaners, 10 Mile and Telegraph. . . . grtyply. . . . Hernandez, book? . . . CALL PETER IN SPAIN! . . . (Diet Coke stain). . . . xxxxyu. . . . CHECK! . . . Elsie's, 13 Mile Road. . . . MENDEL B-DAY, DEC. 4, LAWN MOWER, SEARS, 547-920. . . . Trouble at Houston bar. . . . (coffee stain). . . . Tues. 9 p.m. dinner, Jay, Ken. . . . ytrpppyt. . . . D. Strawberry .275. . . .

Those are my notes on the New York Mets. Based on this, I believe they will win the National League pennant.

I am not so optimistic about the California Angels. They have problems. For one thing, there is jelly on their page, and something green that could be fertilizer or toothpaste — the mint kind — or maybe something else. That is a bad sign. Besides, their bullpen is just average.

The Red Sox, on the other hand, have everything going for them, including Wade Boggs, Roger Clemens and several legible entries on their page: "Rce, Bylor, Armas, trn bt Fenway, rt-lft HR/RBI/. . . . McNamara t. Boyd. . . . rtyfzp!!!"

I am not sure what that means, but I have a good feeling about it. Which is why the Red Sox will win the pennant.

So there you have it. Mets over Houston. Red Sox over California. And I am taking my notes now and getting ready to go to Fenway Park and start another October baseball playoff. I feel confident in my preparation. Very confident. Sort of.

Besides, I have a plan. A foolproof plan. It is a plan that has worked before, and I feel certain it will work again.

I am going to find John and buy him a hot dog.

And I am going to beg.

WHERE WERE YOU DURING THIS INCREDIBLE GAME?

October 13

NEW YORK — The affair began when my hotel room door shut behind me. I can't tell you what time it was, but I can tell you what inning. The ninth inning. That's what the announcer said. "Top of the ninth. . . ." I felt in my pocket for the room key, tapped my shoulder bag and headed for the elevator. In my hand was one of those miniature TVs, a five-inch set with a one-inch screen, the kind people bring to the beach. I flicked it on. And although I didn't know it then, I had just put my grip on the greatest championship series baseball game ever played.

Or maybe it was the other way around.

What made me grab that thing? I hate electronic gadgets. I was meeting two fellow writers, Gene Guidi and Mike Downey, to catch a taxi to Shea Stadium, where the Mets were to lose to the Astros, 3-1, in the National League championship series, and I figured, why not? Bring it with you. Watch in the cab. See what happens.

What happens? What happened? Did you see that game? Can you ever forget it? From the moment the elevator doors opened, top of the ninth, with the Red Sox trailing, 5-2, and down three games to one in this best-of-seven series — surely a hopeless situation for a star-crossed team such as the Sox — the whole thing comes back to me in jump cuts, like a rock video. Here, there. This hit, that play. How long? Forty minutes? Fifty? An hour? Who knows? I remember being in the lobby when Boston put a man on base. And walking through the revolving doors just as Don Baylor — who hadn't hit a home run yet in the series — sent a ball into the seats.

"Hey, hey," I said, "a home run."

"You're kidding," said Guidi. "What's the score now, 5-4?"

"Yeah. Ninth inning."

"Humph."

We got in the backseat, all three of us, and I pushed the volume knob, so the voices were like miniature screams from the silver electronic box. The driver pulled out. We huddled together. Rich Gedman, the Boston catcher, was hit by a pitch and took first base.

The tying run.

Hit by a pitch? . . .

'm sure there are a million of these stories this morning. Where were you when the Red Sox played the Angels? Won't that be the question from now on? Where were you when Dave Henderson, sad-faced Dave

119

Henderson, playing only because Tony Armas had left the game, and who had inadvertently knocked Bobby Grich's high fly ball over the fence for a home run in the sixth inning — where were you when he came to bat with two out in the ninth and the Red Sox's season on the edge of his bat? Where were you?

We were in a taxi, bouncing along Third Avenue.

Strike one on Henderson.

"Jeez," I said. "Poor Red Sox."

"Man," said Guidi.

"Hmmph," said Downey.

Another strike on Henderson.

"Look out," I said.

"We're going to California."

"Yep."

So this was where the American League pennant would be decided. This pitch. Two strikes. The taxi hit a pothole and the little TV lurched in my hand.

"Watch this," said Downey. "He hits one into the seats."

"Yeah, right," I said.

"Yeah, right," said Guidi.

He hit one into the seats.

I will never forget it, because the picture kept buzzing in and out — what kind of reception do you expect in a cab, for Pete's sake? — but I saw the left fielder go back to the wall and could make out his stationary pose, an outfielder's surrender, and I said, "Holy bleep! He hit it out! Ho-hooo! He hit it out!"

"No!" Guidi said.

"Yes!" I said.

"Jesus."

"Told you."

"Unbelievable."

Unbelievable. The Red Sox lead, 6-5. My God, what a moment! Had the thing ended there it would have been great. But this game, and my love affair with that five-inch television with the one-inch screen, was, in the ninth inning, really just beginning.

You know how you can sometimes chart a baseball game by the stains on your program? Ketchup, third inning. Coffee, sixth. For the three of us, the greatest championship game ever was scored by clicks on a meter and landmarks out the window. When did California's Bob Boone hit that single in the bottom of the ninth? Was that the FDR Drive? And Ruppert Jones came in to pinch-run — 98th Street? 99th Street? When Joe Sambito took the mound for Boston — and we said, "Forget it, he stinks" — was that the Triborough Bridge? It was the Triborough, wasn't it? 10.50 on the meter?

"Hey, any of you guys got change?" the driver yelled, as we pulled to the toll booth. I didn't answer him. None of us did. A pitch was on its way.

"He hits a single!"

"Who hits a single?"

"Wilfong! Jones is gonna score! HOOO!"

"Ruppert Jones?"

"What's that make it?"

"It's tied. It's TIED!"

"Holy Jeez."

Look at that. The wind blew through the taxi window as we cruised through Queens and Steve Crawford took the mound for Boston on this tiny screen. I pulled on the antenna.

Crawford? A guy who hadn't pitched an inning in this series. He surrendered a single and intentionally walked a man, loading the bases with one out.

"I can't believe they're gonna lose it after all this."

"Typical Red Sox."

And then Crawford retired Doug DeCinces on a fly ball to right, and Grich broke his bat on a liner to Crawford's glove, and this game, which felt like an eternity, was going to extra innings. We pulled up to the curb alongside Shea. Guidi opened the door.

A sudden thought. How good were the batteries? This game might go all night.

What can you remember about the rest? Where were you? At a friend's? Stuck in your car? Late for supper, in a bar that you were supposed to leave an hour ago? In games like this, you lose track of time and space, and I can only tell you I was in a dreamy fog, locked into that tiny black and white picture, with my legs taking me through a press gate and an elevator and down the stadium steps and toward the field, but my eyes never leaving the one-inch screen.

"What's the score?" someone would scream when he saw me pass.

"Tied, 6-6, top of the 10th," I answered.

"Who's up?" someone would ask when I passed a food stand.

"California, bottom of 10th," I said.

"Whoo-ee!" someone would say.

Whoo-ee.

It was somewhere in the top of the 11th, when Gedman tapped a bunt single, loading the bases and bringing up Dave Henderson — who, as far as I was concerned, had crawled into the Red Sox pantheon back on the Triborough Bridge — that I completely gave up on my present. I became small. I crawled inside that set. Whoever passed, I ignored. Whoever screamed, I could not hear. My husk was somewhere in the hallway of Shea, next to a nachos stand. My soul was on the field in Anaheim.

I was there when Henderson lifted the ball to center field, bringing in the deciding run on a sacrifice. I was there when Brian Downing made that unbelievable catch on Ed Romero's fly ball — saving a sure run — then crashed into the wall. I was there in the bottom of the 11th when Calvin Schiraldi — who, the night before, had buried his head in a towel after blowing the game — came to the mound and shut down the Angels 1-2-3.

California had been one strike away from a pennant, and now Downing's foul pop was ending the thing. The final out. And Schiraldi came dancing off the mound into the arms of his teammates, who were suddenly going back to Boston after all. Weren't you there? Weren't you? What a game. What a bloody great game.

"Red Sox win," I said, to no one in particular. "Red Sox win."

T here was a sudden blast of organ music that brought me back to the here and now. I had lost Guidi and Downey somewhere along the way. I don't remember where.

I know this game was 3,000 miles away. I know watching it on a one-inch black and white screen is like trying to catch whales with a plastic bag. I know all that. But when the announcers said, "That's it from Anaheim Stadium. . . ." — which I heard only by pressing the speaker to my ear until it hurt — I felt as if I was watching a lover walk out the door. I felt alone.

The scoreboard in Shea's center field lit up, right above a cookie ad. It read BOS 7, CAL 6. That's it. Duly noted. The Mets' and Astros' players continued their warm-ups, unaffected. Ushers helped fans to their seats, then held out their hands for tips.

"WELCOME EVERYBODY," the Mets' announcer boomed. And as I clicked off the little TV, I realized, for the first time since entering the stadium, that another baseball game was going to start in a few minutes.

Lord, how could it possibly matter?

MOVE OVER, RON DARLING; IT'S TIME TO TRADE PLACES

October 23

BOSTON — Listen. I have a trade to propose: Me for Ron Darling. One for one.

Here's the deal. Darling, the New York Mets' heartthrob pitcher, gets everything I own. Everything I ever accomplished. Everything I ever laid my eyes, ears or hands on, including my first bicycle. And I get to be him for 24 hours.

That's all. Just one day. I do not jest. Everything in the kitty. For 24 hours.

Of course, I get to use those 24 hours any way I want. So if I accidentally spill some Dom Perignon on the carpet of his penthouse duplex in Manhattan, he can't be ticked off. Or if I blow one of the modeling assignments he has for the cover of, what, Gentlemen's Quarterly? Yeah. He can't get too mad over that, either. After all, it takes awhile to get used to being that good-looking.

But I am willing to learn.

Under the agreement, I get to speak French, just like Darling. I get to claim Hawaii as my birthplace. I get to be 6-feet-3, 195 pounds, and sport that two-day stubble that everyone finds so sexy these days. I get to win a World Series game, 6-2 — as he did Wednesday night — and be interviewed by every TV reporter in the free world. I get the Mercedes. I get to speak Mandarin Chinese.

Did I mention Yale?

Oh, yeah. Yale. I get to call Yale my alma mater, get to stroll down the ivy path — or is that Harvard? Wait. Well, what's the difference? — and when someone asks, "Did you really major in Southeast Asian history?" I get to shuffle my feet coyly and say, "Well, yeah, you know. . . . "

Your wife, Ron? The model from Ireland?

Part of the deal.

Now lest you think this a rash proposal, let me explain. I have been watching Darling, 26, since this World Series began. I knew about his academic background. I saw the brooding good looks.

Last week, in a crowd of reporters interviewing him at Shea Stadium, I noticed another crowd behind us in the stands. It was mostly young, attractive women screaming and waving pieces of paper. I believe they were phone numbers. Maybe they were stock tips.

Anyhow, the women kept screaming and waving and blowing kisses at my man here. It was then that I figured, "You know, this guy could use a break."

Oh. Your pitching arm, Ron. I get that, too.

True, it is hard to believe a man with Hawaiian skin tone, an Elvis pout and wavy black hair, who earns more than a half-million a year, has been linked with Madonna and Brooke Shields, played defensive back in a Harvard-Yale football game, chats with Norman Mailer, plans to study Russian, looks natural in charcoal gray silk suits, and was once chased down a Manhattan street by a pack of squealing teenage girls, should also be blessed with a 15-6 record and a big World Series win for the New York Mets.

But then, that is why I'm suggesting the trade. You don't give up the store to be Spike Owen.

Now, I know there might be difficulties in my 24 hours as a star pitcher. It cannot be easy when your manager keeps calling you "Darling." But I'll face that.

Did I mention the New York Times crossword puzzle? Darling has done that in eight minutes. I might take nine. Is that OK?

Listen, Ron. About your wife. Don't worry. I'll be so busy with the other things.

Besides, didn't you once say getting married to a gorgeous, long-limbed, redheaded model was not in your plans when you two met? "The last thing I wanted was to meet someone unbelievably special," I believe was the quote.

Ron. Kid. We all sympathize with that.

So why not take a day off? Ron Darling's Day Off. They'll probably make it into a movie. Meanwhile, you can have my typewriter and my files and there's even a free one-way Greyhound bus ticket in my top drawer, I think to Philadelphia, a little something special for you, Ron, as a bonus.

Don't worry. I will take good care of your existence. And you can mess up mine any way you like. Just don't expect a Mercedes. It's, uh, you know, in the shop. Yeah. That's where it is.

So let's do it. Make the trade. You can use the relaxation. And I am prepared for the tough times, the ugly side of being a World Series winner.

Your wife has been candid about what I might face. "Women sometimes push me out of the way to get Ronnie's autograph," she has moaned. "It can really be annoying."

Like I always say, Ron, life's a pitch.

METS TAKE SERIES WITH TYPICAL NEW YORK FLAIR

October 28

NEW YORK — The ball rose high over the outfield, farther and farther, and every New York fan swallowed his chewing gum waiting for the ball to reach its destiny. "GET OUT OF HERE YOU SON OF A–.

"YAAAAAAAAAAAAAAAH!" Forget it. Forget it all, Boston. The only thing missing in this very long, very late, very strange World Series had finally come to pass. Home runs for the home team. Ray Knight had hit one in the seventh inning. And now, here in the bottom of the eighth, as sure as an omen from the gods, Darryl Strawberry — who had suffered indignity like no other Met in this series — was watching his ball fall innocently over the right-center field wall, hearing the Sinatra music explode over the loudspeakers ("START SPREADING THE NEWS. . . ."), and as the fans in Shea Stadium blew their skulls open with noise, trotting slowly around the base paths as if he knew it all along, the end, the inevitable. . . .

The Mets were going to win the World Series, four games to three. Glory, glory, glory.

That's right. The Mets. The one-strike-away-from-elimination Mets, who had come back to win in spectacular fashion in Game 6 Saturday, turned around and did it again Monday night, winning, 8-5, taking every tendency, every warning signal, every negative sign and tossing it in the East River.

"When you were down 3-0 in the sixth, weren't you worried?" someone would ask Keith Hernandez, whose bases-loaded single in the sixth knocked in the Mets' first two runs.

"You know, I never was," he would say, champagne dripping from his hair. "I had this feeling all night. . . ." He pointed to his heart. "I had a feeling right here."

Right there. Where else?

Hadn't Boston's Bruce Hurst looked unbeatable against these Mets for the first five innings? "Forget Bruce Hurst," the Mets seemed to say. Hadn't Dave Henderson — always-the-hero Dave Henderson — come to bat with the tying run on base in the eighth? "Forget Dave Henderson," the Mets seemed to say. Hadn't Ron Darling, their own handsome hero, let them down in the second inning, surrendering three early runs to Boston, including two homers? "Forget that," the Mets seemed to say. "Darling? He's OK."

In classic New York fashion, the Mets arrived fashionably late for their own championship, their bats not showing up until the sixth inning. But oh, how they showed up! With all the aplomb of Bruce Springsteen bounding onstage, of Sinatra taking over Carnegie Hall.

"Just a matter of time," Strawberry would say afterward, and surely few words were ever as sweet coming out.

Every Met got a key hit. Didn't it seem that way? Hernandez and Mookie Wilson and Knight, who would win the Series MVP award, and . . . hell, before it was over, even Jesse Orosco, the relief pitcher, would drive in a run.

And finally, when Orosco put that last pitch past Marty Barrett — ironically, the best hitter in this Series — and struck him out swinging, and the earth moved, and the skies opened, and Orosco leaped halfway to the lights, lifting his legs, never wanting to come down. . . .

Well, if it's one thing you needn't tell New York, it's how to celebrate. "METS! METS! METS! . . ."

This was a show of strength in a city where only the strong survive. How many people figured it was over when Boston took a 3-0 lead into the final four innings? Well, perhaps not that many. Certainly not those who had watched this Series from the start. Both of these teams had been one out away from winter vacations at some point in the last few weeks. And at times, both seemed destined to win — and to lose.

In the end, sadly, it was Boston that lived up to its history.

Oh my, yes. Boston. The Red Sox had gone 180 degrees, from one end of the earth to the other. In the playoffs, they had been one strike away from going home losers and on Saturday night they were one strike away from going home winners, World Series winners, and now. . . .

Oh, my.

"Can you describe how you feel?" someone asked Barrett afterward.

"Well," he said, sighing, "what goes around comes around, I suppose." He grinned, but it was a sad grin. "I just didn't think it would come around this fast."

How tough is this for Boston — the team and the city? Very tough. Very, very tough. In baseball championships, the Red Sox are the kid at the end of the lunch line who waits until everybody else has gone, only to reach the front and see them all ahead of him again. How long had the Red Sox been without winning the World Series? Sixty-eight years?

They are at the end of the line again. Their dugout in that final inning was a study in agony. Calvin Schiraldi — who let the game get away — burying his head in a towel. Jim Rice — whose most consistent quote was "I've waited a long time for this" — staring at the ground. Dwight Evans — with Rice, the only man left from the 1975 team that lost Boston's last

126

Seventh Game — staring at the sky, perhaps trying to figure out why his team seems so cursed.

How else could it end for Boston? Tragedy seems to follow the Red Sox like a loyal dog. Didn't they have the tying run at second in the eighth inning with nobody out? Didn't they have Rich Gedman and Henderson and Don Baylor at the plate? Didn't they have the better starting pitcher? Didn't they grab the early lead? Weren't they supposed to benefit from Sunday's rain postponement? And didn't they lose anyhow?

Yes. Yes. Yes.

Let John McNamara call it "crap." If the Red Sox aren't jinxed, then the New York subways are safe at midnight.

And what of New York? Madness! The last glimpse of Shea saw four of the Mets sitting on the pitcher's mound, spraying champagne as the crowd chanted, "WE'RE NO. 1!"

Where do you begin? They had heroes all over their lineup Monday night. Strawberry coming back at last with the demoralizing home run, just minutes after Boston had closed the gap to one run. And Knight, with his seventh-inning home run. And Hernandez, and oh — what of pitcher Sid Fernandez?

Fernandez? Yes. "The unsung hero of this game," Gary Carter would yell. He was the second Hawaiian-born pitcher to take the mound for the Mets this night, but his 2⅓-inning, no-hit, four-strikeout performance in relief of Darling simply inspired his team to victory.

"SID!" someone screamed at him in the frenzied, soaking clubhouse afterward. "YOU'RE BIGGER THAN MAUI!"

And the Mets — favorites from Day 1 in this baseball season that is finally, finally over — are at long last, bigger than their expectations.

Moments after they won Game 6 Saturday night, Wilson ran into the clubhouse and encountered Strawberry with his hand held high.

"Miracles always happen!" Strawberry yelled, slapping Wilson's palm. "Miracles always happen!"

They have happened once again.

Mets. Mets. Mets.

The World Series is theirs.

TINY FRANKFORT GRIPPED BY FOOTBALL FRENZY

November 9

We landed at the small airport, rented a car, and drove through the darkness. It was late and it was cold. There was a McDonald's and a Burger King and then there was nothing.

"We take this road 30 miles to the traffic light," I said to Mary Schroeder, the photographer, who was driving.

"Which light is that?" she asked.

I looked at my notes.

"They only have one light," I said.

To tell you the truth, when you called to say you were coming out to do a story on us, I thought someone was playing a practical joke."
—Tim Klein, football coach, Frankfort High

Surely this was the end of the earth. Frankfort, Mich.? Population, what — 1,600? A car ferry used to run here across Lake Michigan, but it doesn't anymore, and the railroad is gone now, too. There's the Pet Frozen Foods plant and a Five-and-Ten, owned by the mayor, and a few small motels. And the high school.

We had come for the high school. This was the opening weekend of the high school football playoffs, and the idea was to see what a small town was like the day of the big game. Frankfort seemed perfect. It was obviously small, it had won its conference title six years in a row, and was playing Lake City Friday night in the first round of the Class D playoffs.

Perfect.

"Coffee?" asked the waitress.

"Yes, please."

"Eggs and bacon?"

"Over here."

"These people are up here from Detroit."

"Oh, really?"

"Gonna do a story about our team."

"Really?"

"Uh-huh."

"My."

"Who's gonna win the game tonight?"

"Oh, the Panthers, of course."

"Of course."

We were sitting in a booth inside Fav's Grill, a Formica joint where the football talk begins each morning before work. "Fav" — a grizzled fellow named Don Favreau — has a son who was once the school's star quarterback. Around us were several of the current players' fathers. Like most men in this town, they played for Frankfort at one time.

"How'd your kid sleep?" someone asked Jim Martin, whose son, Todd, is the Panthers' quarterback now.

"Better than me," the father said.

"Anybody hear the weather?" someone asked.

"Thirty percent chance of rain."

"Lake City doesn't throw much, do they?"

"Nuh-uh."

"Well, that's not good."

"Better than snow."

"Remember last year?"

Everyone nodded. Last year, it snowed the night before the playoff game. Six inches. The people of Frankfort got up early, brought shovels and snow blowers to the field, and went to work.

"That field was green by noon," someone said.

"We won, too," said someone else.

had a son who played here, and a nephew, and now I have friends whose grandchildren are playing. My dear, I've been watching these games for 40 years."

— **Elsie Gilbert, the town librarian**

The kids at Frankfort High School look, well, like high school kids — jeans, Reebok sneakers, combs in their pockets. On Friday the players all wear their football jerseys and if they have girlfriends, the girlfriends get to wear jerseys, too. Half the males in the high school are on the team. That is a lot of jerseys.

The hallways are a gallery of pep art: posters on the walls, little purple footballs taped to the lockers, purple and gold streamers hanging from the ceiling in neat lines.

During a study hall, a handful of players filled Tim Klein's classroom, and immediately set up a TV set and a VCR. Study hall on Friday means game films. The quarterback, Todd Martin, the starting center, Mike Nigh, a starting guard, Elwin Farnsworth, watched the Lake City highlights silently.

"What are you guys thinking about right now?" I asked them when the tape was over.

"My blocking assignments," said Elwin, the guard.

"Number 99 on Lake City," said Mike, the center.

"Winning," said Todd, the quarterback.

The last answer intrigued me. I asked Todd — a tall kid with a page-boy haircut and a shadow of a mustache — if being the quarterback of the only team in town gave him any special privileges.

"I have a pretty big scrapbook," he said, shrugging.

"Do people treat you differently?" I asked.

"Not really," he said. "Sometimes when I go to get groceries, it takes an hour. Everybody wants to talk about the game."

I *f the Detroit Lions were playing down the street, I'd still be watching Frankfort."*

— Sonny Nye, 46, sheet metal worker

We were sitting in Mike's Pastry Shop on Main Street just before lunch. Mike has a son on the team. His place, therefore, is a good spot to get a scouting report, or listen to the story about the playoff game a few years ago where the score changed four times in the last minute.

It is also — because it looks out onto the street — "a good place to watch for new cars in town," according to an old man in a cap and red plaid jacket, who did just that.

And in walked Sonny Nye.

Sonny Nye once played for Frankfort. He also coached the junior varsity in the days when they had to go door to door to recruit players. He is a name in this town, a big man with a bulging belly and a few teeth missing. He gets sheet metal work from the union halls, and has to go where they send him.

"What time you get in?" someone asked him.

"About 4:30 this morning," he said.

"Where were you coming from?" I asked.

"Flat Rock," he said. "Been doing work down there lately."

"You don't have to work today?"

"I took the day off," he said, grinning.

"To see the game?" I asked.

"Yeah," he said. "I wouldn't miss this."

Frankfort is in Benzie County, one of the poorest counties in the state. Unemployment can run as high as 30 percent up here. Most of Frankfort's economy is based on tourism, and most of that is in the summer. I knew that. Sonny Nye knew it better. He took the day off.

"Why is football so important?" I asked.

"That's the way it is here," he said. "It's a community thing. Everybody knows the kids. It's either your kid, or your brother's kid or your neighbor's kid.

"We all went through it. When you're growing up in this town, you can't wait to be a seventh-grader so you can get on the junior varsity. When you're a seventh-grader you can't wait to be a 10th-grader. When you're a 10th-grader you can't wait to be a senior. That's the way it works."

We took sips of our coffee and looked out the window.

"What if they told you no?" I asked. "What if they told you, 'Sorry, but if you take off today, you lose your job'?"

"I'd have to lose the job then," he said.

I*'m sorry, I won't be at the pep rally. I have a funeral."*
— **Elsie Gilbert**

This is what playoff Friday means in Frankfort. It means the art classes go outside in the morning and decorate the stands with purple and gold construction paper chains. It means the giant banner — "BEWARE! YOU ARE ENTERING PANTHER COUNTRY" — is hung on the side of the Pet Frozen Foods building in front of a spotlight.

It means the pep rally.

It began at 3 and it was packed — and not just with kids. Mothers, fathers, grandparents, charter boat captains, painters, electricians, the guy who owns the Amoco station, the school superintendent. The local radio station, WBNZ, was there and its sportscaster put on a Frankfort jersey and raised his hands and the place went wild. The cheerleaders wore yellow outfits and had purple paw prints painted on their faces.

"HEY YOU PANTHERS IN THE STANDS,
"STAND UP AND CLAP YOUR HANDS! . . ."

The cheers rang loud for a solid 20 minutes. No letup. No end to the drumming. The band blasted along and the freshmen and sophomores and juniors and seniors all got a chance to bust a gut screaming. That wasn't surprising. What was surprising was that everyone took part. Usually in high school there are pockets of kids who just will not participate, who find school spirit boring, who simply don't care.

I looked around. I didn't see a single one.

"WE SAY PURPLE! YOU SAY GOLD!
"PURPLE! GOLD! PURPLE! GOLD!" . . .

N*obody thought they'd miss the ferry boats. But they do."*
— **Jim Ricco**

After the pep rally the kids went home and the whole town seemed to close for an early dinner. With an hour to kill, Mary and I drove to the bay where the car ferry used to board. More than 100 jobs were lost when that closed down, a considerable amount in a town this small. Someone said that once, as many as seven ferries ran in these waters. But that was a long time ago.

The terminal building was boarded up, its white paint peeling. There was a string of railroad cars, now darkened with rust. One large ferry, called The City Of Milwaukee, still sat in the water. It was to be turned into a museum, but a legal battle fouled that up, and now it just sits there, a hulking reminder of better days.

We saw a small office open, something called Koch Asphalt, and we walked inside. There was a young man and an older woman behind two desks.

"Excuse me," I said to the man, introducing myself. "Was that one of the ferries they used to use?"

"Yeah," he said, "for a little while."

"When did it stop running?"

"Four or five years ago," he said.

We talked a little bit about the town. His name was Jim Ricco and, like most people there, he was surprised we came all the way from Detroit. He said he'd be at the game and I said maybe we'd see him there.

"Did you play football for Frankfort, too?" I asked.

"Sure did," he said. "Early '70s."

We drove away, past the rusting boxcars and the ferry. It was cold and quiet. I thought about something Sonny Nye had said about the young people needing to look elsewhere for work, and why the adults clung so to football.

How sad, I thought. The town was dying.

We were one win away from the Silverdome last year. I tell the kids I want this season to last two hours longer than the last one."
— **Tim Klein**

By 5:30, Tim Klein was already in the locker room, dressed in his coaching outfit: gray pants, purple shirt and white shoes. He is a trim man in his mid-30s who came here eight years ago planning to stay just a few seasons.

His current team is undefeated. Its goal is to make it to the Class D final, which is played Nov. 29 at the Silverdome in Pontiac. Friday night was Step 1.

"Are you nervous?" I asked him.

"Hell, yes," he said.

Only 195 students attend Frankfort High School. None of Klein's players is particularly big, or outlandishly gifted. But they have something, they take it seriously, and as 6 o'clock came around, they wandered in and they were dead silent.

They stripped out of their jeans and T-shirts and Reeboks and sat on the trainer's table, one at a time, as Klein taped their ankles. They placed Styrofoam pads over their thighs and plastic pads above their shoulders. They grew bigger. Thicker. Moment by moment. Little men turning to bigger men. One by one.

They walked out to the gymnasium and waited. Some lay on the stage.

132

Others just sat on the bleachers. A couple tossed a football back and forth. They didn't peek outside to see the people coming. They didn't go looking for their parents.

Suddenly the corner door opened and there stood a player from Lake City, in full uniform. The whole Frankfort team turned to look. The player — who clearly had been directed to the wrong door — let it close very softly. A few Frankfort players glanced back and forth at one another, and then it was quiet again.

N*othing left to do but do it, so let's. . . .*
— Final words between Klein and his players before the game

By 7:15, the field was mobbed. Cars and vans enveloped the area. If a store or gas station was left open in town, it was by accident. Everyone, it seemed, was there. Grandmothers wrapped in blankets and construction workers still in their boots and children in pink and blue winter jackets hanging from the railing. There was room for about 200 people to sit in the wooden bleachers and the rest stood along the field. The "rest" numbered at least 2,000, all the way around, sidelines and end zones, four and five deep. A couple of bikers hoisted each other on their shoulders for a better view. Several students climbed the side of the bleachers.

"The Star-Spangled Banner" was played and then, instead of sitting down, the fans ran on the field and formed a human tunnel nearly 50 yards long. This is how they welcome their team. One by one the Frankfort starters were introduced and ran through this tunnel, a tunnel of their families, friends, their town. How could you not give a kidney to win with so many eyes on you? One boy, a 260-pound sophomore named Bubba Banktson, ran through the tunnel with his eyes squinted closed and his mouth clenched in a roar and he looked frightening.

"F! . . . H! . . . S!" hollered the cheerleaders.

The band sounded a drum roll. The few people left sitting rose to their feet. So here was the moment, the kickoff, the culmination — and if there was ever a mystery to the frenzy of Friday night it was gone when the foot hit the ball. Football here is less a game than a birthright. These sons of Frankfort fathers do not play just because they are athletes.

They play because it is their turn.

Two hours later, Frankfort had won the game. It was a good win, 28-7. It had been close at halftime after a long pass with less than two minutes left had let Lake City close the gap to 13-7.

"Damn, we don't need that!" Sonny had screamed.

"COME ON FRANKFORT! GET TOUGH!" cried the fans.

No worries. Frankfort took control in the second half. By the end, a fullback named Scott Parsons would have 238 yards rushing, including a

64-yard touchdown. Todd Martin, the quarterback, would throw for a touchdown. The cheerleaders would be hugging one another. The fathers would be waving their purple hats.

When the final gun sounded, the fans ran on the field and made another tunnel, and the team charged through again. In the locker room the players celebrated by spilling cola on one another, until Klein told them to cut it out, and to remember they had more games yet to play.

After the game the kids and their families gathered at a designated house, the adults upstairs, the kids in the basement. There were ham sandwiches and potato chips and coffee and pop and everyone crammed around the TV set to watch the highlights on the local news. When the screen replayed Parsons' touchdown the living room crowd let out a whoop and Dell Parsons, the proud father, sat in the middle of it, his mouth half-opened in a smile.

"Way to go," someone said to him, raising a can of beer.

It was getting late. Mary and I said goodby. We drove the 30 miles to the airport, slept a few hours in a hotel, and by 9 o'clock Saturday morning we were landing back in Detroit.

And now, hundreds of miles away, I am still thinking about that Friday night. It was crazy and strange and maybe way out of proportion — I mean the whole town was into that football game — but there was something quietly right about it, too.

At one point during the game, Sonny Nye, the big man who was sacrificing his day's wages, found me on the sideline.

"You know," he said, yelling to be heard over the crowd, "a few years ago, I went to Tim and said, 'So, when are you going to leave us?' And he got all upset. He said, 'Why do you say that?' I said, 'Well, you're a young man, a good coach. You won't want to stay in a small town like this for very long. . . .'"

He tucked his hands deep in his pockets, and laughed.

"But now," he continued, "well, now I know he'll stay at least five or six more years. I'm sure of that."

And then he stopped. He didn't explain.

So I asked.

"How do you know that?" I said.

He pointed across the field to a skinny 12-year-old boy who was watching the game with wide eyes and a frozen smile.

"His son," Sonny said. "He wants to be quarterback."

WISH YOU WERE HERE —
I'M NOT JUST SAYING THAT

December 4

MEMO TO: OFFICE STAFF
FROM: HAWAIIAN CORRESPONDENTS
Dear Everybody,
Well, we just landed in Hawaii, and I must tell you, it's not all it's cracked up to be.

And I'm not just saying that.

For one thing, it's cold. I mean, it's really cold. Like I'm-still-wearing-my-winter-coat cold. Grass skirts? Ha! The people in this airport dress in scarves and gloves. And I'm not just saying that.

Where's the nonstop sunshine, you ask? That's what I ask. Do you know what I see when I look out the pane-glass windows? I see gray skies. Gray skies. Can you imagine?

I must admit, this is hardly what my colleague, Tommy George, and I counted on when we boarded the plane in Detroit this morning.

Not that we expected a vacation. I mean, we treated this Saturday's Michigan vs. Hawaii football game as we would any other crucial, news-breaking, deadline-beating assignment, which is why we packed the tennis rackets. But, I must admit — and I think Tommy will back me up on this, as soon as he comes off the plane — that I expected a little more, well, tropical environment.

I mean, look. That guy is drinking hot cocoa.

And I'm not just saying that.

Where are the pineapples? Where is Don Ho? Where are those women who greet you at the plane and put a lei around your neck and say, "Welcome to our tropical island paradise, you handsome stud" — or something like that. Where are they? I know we booked economy class, but come on.

There were no women to greet us at the airport. You know who greeted us? A middle-age airline representative who told us where to make our gate connections. In Hawaii? Where are we connecting to? Guam?

And there was no ukulele music, either.

And I'm not just saying that.

Now, I know some of you were a tad upset when Tommy and I got this assignment. Hey. I understand. Why should we get to go to sunny Hawaii, when you're stuck in a miserable Michigan winter, right? Under the circumstances, you reacted normally. I should have the spray paint cleaned

135

off my house by this afternoon.

Still, I wish you could be here to see this. You wouldn't envy us at all.

No surfboards. No sails. No scooters. And, on top of everything, I can't tell you how stupid I feel standing here in my Hawaiian shirt and my baggy shorts, holding a bottle of Coppertone, which I bought at the drugstore before I left, and. . . .

Hey. What the –?

It's snowing.

What a fraud!

That really cuts it. Snow? In the islands? You know, before I got here, everyone said, "Oh, you lucky so-and-so, you get to go to Hawaii." Actually, they said, "Oh, you slimeball rodent, I hope you die in midair." But they should see this. Snow. And everyone's rushing through the airport as if there's no tomorrow. And I might as well forget about a suntan. Fat chance. Look at how pale these people are.

Volcanoes? Ha! All I see are clouds. And beaches? Yeah, right. Beaches. Like that woman in the ski parka just came in from the beach, I suppose.

About the only good thing I can report is that the flight went quickly. I fell asleep as soon as we boarded and when I woke up we were landing here in Hawaii. It didn't feel like 12 hours.

Big deal.

And I'm not just saying that.

And I don't see any pina coladas.

So, lighten up, you guys. You're not missing a thing. This place is a joke. I bet their team plays in long sleeves. And to think I had to crawl on my hands and knees to the boss to tell him how crucial a game this was for Michigan.

When I get back, I'm giving that travel agent a piece of my mind, and same goes for my next-door neighbor, and if any of you makes wisecracks like, "Eat any papaya lately, you handsome American stud?" well, I can't be held responsible for my actions, because this is really ticking me off, it's a real downer, for me, and I'm sure for Tommy, too.

Isn't that right, Tommy? I mean, look around us. They're wearing snow boots, for heaven's s-.

What's that? . . .

Oh.

Tommy says relax. We're not in Hawaii yet.

This is Chicago.

Never mind.

PART OF US LIES WITHIN THE ARIZONA'S TORN STEEL

December 7

PEARL HARBOR, Hawaii — They never pulled the bodies from the USS Arizona. They tried a few times, but back then salvage equipment was too bulky, and besides, there was a war on, so they quit it, and then, later, there was talk about raising her altogether to get them out, but that was impossible because she was in pieces, several giant pieces of battleship lying on the harbor's floor. After a while, the families and the Navy and everybody just figured, enough, too much, let them rest in peace.

So they are still down there, all those young men who never finished that Sunday morning, buried in 38 feet of water, and the guide who leads the ferries out to the Arizona Memorial — a gleaming white mini-bridge suspended over the sunken warship, close enough to see fish swimming around her skeleton — refers to them as "the 1,102 men entombed in her hull," and tourists nod sadly and take snapshots.

Where are you today, America? Do you remember this Sunday, 45 years ago? Did a radio voice interrupt to tell you the unthinkable had happened, your country had been wounded, her very flesh cut by Japanese bombers, and she was now at war?

Where are you today? In church? Shoveling snow? At a restaurant ordering pancakes? It doesn't matter. Nor does your age or your memory. Part of you must be drawn to this harbor, along these sugar cane shores, where, on one side of Ford Island, the Utah lies in 50 feet of water, and, on the other side, a few feet from the memorial, the Arizona's gun turret No. 3, now rusted a muddy brown, pokes up out of the water, a structural last gasp of the horrors of war.

Did you know this? That oil still leaks from the Arizona's engine room, so when the sun hits just right, you can see a tiny slick rainbow floating gently above her?

The 1,102 men entombed in her hull.

Forty-five years today.

She is still bleeding.

We could see their faces," the old man was saying. "The bastards were grinning at us and shaking their fists and we could see their Japanese faces."

He folded his arms across his chest.

"That's how close those planes were. Yes, sir. We could see their faces and we were cursing at them and shooting at them but it didn't do no good.

137

They were too low. They were buzzing around us like bees around a hive and they were safe. They knew they were safe."

He paused, and he looked at me, and I looked back and nodded sheepishly. He had seemed, when I first saw him on the airplane to Hawaii, a ridiculous-looking man, someone out of a Woody Allen film, squat and wrinkled, with thick glasses and a cotton shirt and this hat — what was it? — a blue-and-white beret that suggested an Elks Lodge or a Mickey Mouse Club or something.

And then, as he got closer, I could read the letters stitched in that hat — "Pearl Harbor Survivor" — and a quick glance around the plane spotted several more, all men in their 60s, wearing the names of the ships they had served — USS Nevada, USS West Virginia, USS Honolulu.

They come back, every five years, the survivors. They pay for the hotel and the airfare and they come back, hundreds of men, like this man who said his name was Ralph McKinsey, a retired lumber worker and a gun loader on the USS New Orleans in 1941. He was putting up the flag that Sunday morning, he said, and then the planes came — "We thought they were ours at first, can you believe that?" — and within minutes there was hell on earth, and black billowing smoke, and he saw the Arizona "lift clear out of the water, 31,000 tons, when a bomb tore through six decks and exploded downwards, you understand, so she lifted out of the water and split in half and then sunk." The 1,102 men entombed in her hull.

It took nine minutes to sink.

To be in Pearl Harbor today is to be stitched into the very seam between past and present. This is, after all, Hawaii, land of honeymooners and sweepstakes prize-winners — "Aloha! Welcome to Paradise" reads one tourist brochure — and the university crowd is buzzing over Saturday's football game, and the tourist season is cranking up, and the shops along Waikiki are advertising Christmas sales.

But this morning, because it is Dec. 7, and it is the 45th year, the men in the blue and white hats will gather in the crater of an extinct volcano, a memorial cemetery known as Punchbowl, and sometime around 7:55 a.m., a squadron of planes will come out of the sun, precisely aligned, and then one will break away, as if shot down, to commemorate those who began dying at that very moment in 1941.

It is a movie to most of us, at least those of us under 50, something you might watch on a rainy afternoon with Kirk Douglas or Van Johnson frantically radioing Wickam Air Force Base and wondering why there is no answer. It is something we are told about, Pearl Harbor, rather than something we really remember.

And yet, there is something profoundly personal when you stand above the Arizona — a flag flying atop her severed mast, because the Navy still considers her in commission. She is an unlikely coffin, so close to shore, close enough for even the poorest swimmer to reach safety, and when you realize that, you realize just how little chance the skeletons below your feet really had.

No chance.

More than 2,400 men would die here that day, in an attack that lasted barely three hours. America would be pulled into war quickly, inescapably, and the war would last four more years and thousands more would perish, and it would end with explosions in Japan that wreaked far more hell than what was seen in this harbor.

And yet, while we have entered wars since then, there is something about Pearl Harbor that will not let go.

Five years ago, a survivor of the attack passed away, presumably of illness or natural causes. He had outlived the horror by 40 years. It did not matter. In his will, he had requested to be buried with his shipmates on the Arizona. His family came to the memorial and, in a simple ceremony, lowered an urn with his cremated remains into the rusting hull of the ship, where it remains.

"How old are you?" Ralph had asked me on the plane, and I told him, and he grabbed my hand and pulled me closer to him.

"Keep asking questions," he said. "My generation, they want to forget this already. Every five years, I come back to these things, and I ask about someone, and then I don't ask anymore because I find out he's passed away."

He looked around the plane and he sighed.

"We're old now," he said.

W here are you today, America? In the car? At the health club? In the kitchen with the radio blasting?

On the Arizona memorial Friday, another Pearl Harbor survivor walked slowly behind his wife. He was a big man, with a big belly, and although he once might have been quite strapping, his shoulders slumped now and his face was as sad as any I have ever seen. When his wife walked away, I approached and asked if he had indeed been here that day, and he nodded and I asked what he remembered most.

He said he had been on a ship on the other side of the island, and it was one of the few to actually get out moving in the water before the Japanese attack ended.

He pointed to an area just in front of the Arizona's remains. "We came right past here," he said, his voice weak and thin, "and a lot of these ships were already down or going down, but in the smoke you could hear the men screaming for us. They were cheering us, because at least we had our guns up, you see, at least we were in the water. And they figured, we would fight back. . . . "

He did not finish the thought. I did not ask him anything else. He stepped back behind his wife, and they walked into the room at the end of the memorial with the marble walls listing the names of all the dead, and after a few minutes he began nudging her toward the exit ramp as if he wanted to go, but she didn't want to go just yet.

It was very quiet, save for the rustling of the trees and the lapping of water against gun turret No. 3. It was a perfectly beautiful morning, much like that Sunday morning a long time ago, and, because the sun was clear and strong, soon you could spot the oil that still leaked from the engine room, and it formed a greasy rainbow atop the burial waters.

Where are you today, America?

You are right here.

"We should have brought flowers," said the wife, gazing out on the rusted flagpole, and her husband, who was crying openly now, only nodded yes, they should have.

OUR LONG WAIT IS NOTHING COMPARED TO LISA'S

December 15

You have been waiting for him. I have been waiting for him. It has become the thing to do here in Detroit.

"When, Chuck, when?" we ask.

"Soon, folks, soon," we are told.

His teammates have been waiting for him. His coaches have been waiting for him. All season long, they have watched with anticipation.

"When, Chuck, when?' they ask.

"Soon, men, soon," they are told.

Hasn't everyone been waiting? Yes, everyone has been waiting. We have waited 14 weeks for Chuck Long's first start — which comes tonight against the Bears. Fourteen weeks. Fourteen long, hard weeks. Waiting for Chuck. We are experts on the subject, right?

Wrong.

Lisa Wells is an expert. Lisa Wells is the expert. She has been waiting for Chuck for 13 years, since he was not only Long, but short.

"When, Chuck, when?" she would ask.

"Soon, Lisa, soon," she was told.

There is only one difference. One small but important difference. We are waiting for Chuck to become the Lions' full-time quarterback.

She is waiting to marry him.

Chuck and I have known each other since we were 10 years old," says Wells, 23, who is Long's fiancee. "I used to ride on the back of his bicycle back in Wheaton (Ill.). We played hide-and-seek in each other's backyards.

"We've been going together since junior high, so we both sort of knew we'd eventually marry. It's just . . . well, taken him a long time, I guess."

You might say that. The same girl for 13 years? At that rate, we'll all be retired by the time he chooses a receiver tonight.

"It's funny," Wells says, "my friends kid me about it, too. I know people who have met, gotten married, and had kids in less time.

"It's just that something always came up. Back in college Chuck wanted to finish the senior season. We figured we'd get engaged after that.

"But then there was a bowl game.

"After the bowl game, we figured we'd get engaged, but there were all these awards Chuck had to pick up."

She sighs.

"And then came the draft."

When, Chuck, when? It was not as if Long didn't want to marry her. It would be hard to imagine a truer mate. She'd walked with him to Little League games. Been his prom date. Taken bus rides to his college. She even forgave him for the time in high school when, as a freshman, he "gave her away" to the then-varsity quarterback.

"He says he only did it because he figured I'd rather ride in that guy's Camaro than on the back of his bike," Wells says.

He was wrong. Luckily.

So she waited. And waited and waited. And one day, after the bowl and the awards and the draft were over, they were sitting in her apartment and he pulled out a ring and popped the question and she started crying.

"Well? . . ." said Chuck.

She should have made him wait. You know. Cried for a couple of months, or something.

Instead, she said yes, and their wedding is set for June 6, 1987. It is not a Monday night. And I do not believe any Chicago Bears are invited.

"Chuck would have done it right after the season," she says, "but I always wanted to be a June bride. I figure, I've waited this long. . . ."

So all's well that ends well. Still, it must be amusing for Wells to hear Detroiters chant, "When, Chuck, when?" — as if they really know what it's like to wait for him.

Even now, he'll say "hut two!" before "I do."

"It's OK," she says, laughing. "Actually, I've sort of enjoyed his not playing up till now. He's home more, and there's less pressure. This week has been crazy. But I'm glad he's starting, because he's really wanted to get in there."

He'll get in there. And when the game is over, and all the lights and cameras and fans are gone, Wells will be there, as usual. Waiting.

I bring this all up for a lesson. If you watch the game tonight, and Chuck doesn't do so well, just remember. You haven't really been waiting that long. Not when you consider the alternative.

And when Chuck and Lisa walk down the aisle next June, should he suddenly, after 13 years, get cold feet, she can take a lesson from tonight's game as well.

Tackle him.

THE COACH AND THE QB:
BO, JIM HAVE SPECIAL BOND

December 28

PASADENA, Calif. — Death before this. That's what was racing through Jim Harbaugh's brain the first time he threw a pass in a Michigan practice. It wasn't a bad pass. Not for a nine-year-old. The problem was neither he nor the football was supposed to be there. Harbaugh was the son of a Wolverines assistant coach, Jack Harbaugh, and he was playing on the sidelines with the other coaches' sons, and his pass accidentally flew out into the middle of the big boys' practice ... and when he heard the whistle shriek there was only one question left to be answered.

Would he get out alive?

"GET ... THOSE ... DAMNED ... KIDS. ... " The voice was sizzling like onions on a grill, and Harbaugh can hear it even now. He does hear it now. Almost every day. The same voice.

Bo Schembechler's voice.

"GET ... THOSE ... DAMNED ... KIDS ... OFF ... THE ... FIELD ... RIGHT ... NOW! ... "

There might have been more said, but we'll never know. Because by that point, little Jimmy Harbaugh — the kid who would grow up to be Bo Schembechler's finest quarterback to date — was running for his life.

This is a story about a football player and a coach who are about to play their last game together, and if you never had a coach you may never understand it. What is it that ties the guy with the helmet to the guy with the whistle? Fear? Admiration? Love?

Love? You wouldn't have thought so the time Schembechler called Harbaugh "the worst quarterback I've had in 40 years," or when he threw him off the team in his sophomore year, or when he told him, as a freshman, he would "never play a down for Michigan" in his life.

You call that love?

But then again. ...

Well, you'll see.

Harbaugh: "To me Bo was bigger than life."
Schembechler: "Aw, Jim was an ornery kid."

Jim Harbaugh can barely remember a time he wasn't in awe of Bo Schembechler. Maybe in the crib. But from the moment he could pronounce the name, there was a tingle that went with it. He first became aware of Schembechler when Michigan used to roll into Iowa — where Jack Harbaugh was a coach — and smear the Hawkeyes by 50 points. He became more aware when his dad was hired as a Wolverines assistant and the family moved to Michigan. Bo would visit, and one time, he found Jim, then 10 years old, wrapped in a blanket, watching TV.

"What are you doing watching TV?" Schembechler growled. "Why aren't you doing something productive?"

What could Harbaugh do? He grabbed a book and pretended to read.

Today Jim Harbaugh is a completed version, senior quarterback, 23 years old, affable, mischievous, with a look that falls somewhere between Richard Gere and Dennis the Menace. He has been on the cover of magazines. Been televised by the major networks. Get him talking about an opponent and he sounds like a sergeant. But get him talking about his coach, and soon comes this glazed-eye look, like a child staring at a big rock-candy mountain, and when he really gets going he sounds almost religious.

"I'm starting to realize now I'm playing for a living legend," he says. "No matter what I do the rest of my life people will ask me, what was it like to play for Bo Schembechler. I'll always have that."

And if that sounds a little, well, enthusiastic, remember that this was a kid whose fourth-grade show-and-tell project was a film titled "A Week In The Life Of Bo Schembechler." A kid who used to play in his underwear down in the basement, imagining he was a star at Michigan. "Jim Harbaugh's having a great day today," he would say into a make-believe microphone. "Yes," he would add, now playing the color commentator, "I think he's going to win the Heisman Trophy."

He finished third in the voting for the Heisman Trophy this year. He holds most of the important U-M passing records.

Not bad for a guy who never figured to be here.

Schembechler: "Jim Harbaugh didn't need Michigan to have a great career. Jim Harbaugh was a highly recruited quarterback out of high school."
Harbaugh: "I had like two schools recruiting me."

It was his senior year in high school, he was living in California, and as he walked across the street to the Stanford football stadium, Jim Harbaugh figured his future might be determined in the next hour. He was dressed in a nice sweater, his hair neatly combed, loafers on his feet. Did he look grown up? He wanted to look grown up, because he was going to see Bo Schembechler, who was coaching in the East-West Shrine Game. He hadn't seen him since the family moved from Michigan two years earlier.

"They weren't even recruiting me," Harbaugh recalls. "I got a few things in the mail, but, you know, no phone calls, nothing.

"So I went to see Bo after practice and he was nice to me, real cordial. He said they hadn't seen any film on me, they didn't really know anything about me. He talked a little about the quarterback situation at Michigan and then he started to talk about my parents, and that was it. I got the feeling he was just being nice to me, but there wasn't really any interest."

Harbaugh walked back to high school, got out of his nice clothes, and sighed. There was no question he dreamed of playing at Michigan. And there was no question he had no chance. Or so he thought.

According to Schembechler, this was all part of the strategy. "I knew Jim wanted to come here," the coach says now, leaning back in the big chair in his U-M office. "Of course some of these kids figure just because I know mom and dad they're gonna get a scholarship. That's just not true. I don't do that for anybody. But in his case, we had planned to offer him a scholarship before I ever went out there."

"Why did you wait so long then?" he is asked.

His voice deepens. "If Jim Harbaugh was going to come to Michigan, then Jim Harbaugh was going to wait for me."

Well, he waited. Right up to the last weekend of recruiting. Wisconsin had wanted Harbaugh badly. Arizona had expressed legitimate interest. Yet on the last possible weekend, the kid was flown into Ann Arbor, walked into Schembechler's office — the same office where he had romped as a child — and the coach said simply, "We want you to come here," and although he didn't answer right away, Harbaugh walked out knowing he was hooked.

Not long after, he called Schembechler to accept. And that was that. So understated was the whole process that after Harbaugh said, "I'm coming," and after Schembechler said, "Good," the kid was compelled to ask one more question.

"Uh, Bo," he said, "that is a full scholarship, isn't it?"

Schembechler cracked up.

Schembechler: "I never had any off-the-field problems with Jim."
Harbaugh: "He threw me off the team twice."

This will be Jim Harbaugh's first and last Rose Bowl. He led the Wolverines to a Fiesta Bowl victory last season over Nebraska. He could be the first U-M quarterback to win two bowl games. Impressive, no? Especially considering the way he began his football career at Michigan. Which is to say, in the dumper.

"It was the very first meeting of the freshmen," he says. "I was out somewhere and I lost track of the time. Oh, man. I popped my head in five or 10 minutes late and Bo just exploded. 'WHERE HAVE YOU BEEN?' he said. I just froze. I couldn't get a word out. 'WHERE HAVE YOU BEEN?' he said again. I mumbled something. I was petrified. He was screaming at me in front of all these guys I had never even met before. He goes, 'You of all people! I can't believe you! Your dad's a coach! I'm gonna call him tonight!' He was enraged. He stormed around. Then he said, 'YOU'LL NEVER PLAY A DOWN OF FOOTBALL HERE! NEVER!' "

Welcome to Michigan.

It would prove to be only one of a dozen times Harbaugh was told he would never play. Such is the method of Schembechler — whose most common profile is with his mouth in mid-scream. But in Harbaugh's case, Schembechler's outbursts were more deliberate than you might think.

"The consensus about Jimmy," Schembechler says now, "is that he would have been a problem to coach at quarterback. He was too stubborn, too cocky, and his temper was out of control. I remember seeing him as a freshman get up after a guy took a late hit at him and throw the ball right at the guy's face. You can't do that and be quarterback. You have to control your emotions."

Schembechler smiles. "The other thing was, the other coaches around here seemed to think he played better when I stayed on his case."

He never got off.

Harbaugh: "I used to think, 'My whole life will be ruined if I don't play football here.' "

Schembechler: "I was a little surprised at how Jim hung on every word I said."

Harbaugh saw little action his first two years. He thought he had a pretty good freshman spring, but whenever an assistant coach would compliment him, Schembechler would bark, "Leave him alone, I'm coaching him." Then he'd turn to Harbaugh and say, "You've done nothing here." Once, after a few mishaps, the coach called him "the worst quarterback I've had in 40 years of coaching."

"I walked away thinking, 'That can't be true, can it?' " Harbaugh recalls. "But what if it is? Forty years? God!" In February of his sophomore year, 1984, he and a few buddies went out after watching the Olympics and they got into trouble. They had a few beers. A screen was ripped from a dormitory. Words were exchanged with students. One football player shoved a student and the others turned and got out of there. Harbaugh was actually guilty of nothing but being along for the ride, but the next day Schembechler called him into his office.

"YOU'RE OFF THE TEAM!" he began.

Harbaugh swallowed. "What?" he said.

"IS YOUR NAME JAMES JOSEPH HARBAUGH?" Bo screamed.

"Yes. . . ." Harbaugh squeaked.

The coach slammed down a police report. "This is your name on this report! Assault and battery! Drunk and disorderly conduct! Damaging school property!"

"Bo, I didn't do any of that!" Harbaugh said.

"IT'S IN THE REPORT!" the coach screamed, his face within inches.

"WELL I DIDN'T DO IT!" Harbaugh screamed back. It was the first time he retaliated so strongly. Schembechler stared at him for a long time, then said, "Well you better clear it up."

He did. He was reinstated. The weeks passed. Spring practice arrived. Harbaugh played well, won the starting job, and when it was over, Schembechler called him in.

"He told me I played great, that I was his starting quarterback, that he expected great things out of me," Harbaugh says. "I left there feeling 10 feet tall.

"And the very next day he calls me in and says, "Forget everything I said yesterday! None of that is true today. You'll probably never play here again!' "

What had happened? The night before, Schembechler had gotten a call from a dorm director charging Harbaugh with breaking a fire alarm, and with being guilty of the earlier charges to which he had pleaded innocent. Once again, the charge would be proved false and he would be reinstated. But he never forgot the 24-hour roller-coaster ride. "It was the lowest and highest I have ever been."

And he would never get that high or low again.

Harbaugh: "How is he different than me? He has so much more charisma."

Schembechler: "How is he different than me? He's a better athlete."

Harbaugh broke his arm his junior year against Michigan State. His first season as a starter ended after five games.

Schembechler went to the hospital that night. "I told Jim there's nothing he can do, just rehab it, stay up on the books, we'll see if we can get it ready for spring. And as I'm walking away, you know what he says?

"He says, 'You won't forget about me, coach, will you?' "

Schembechler laughs. "You won't forget about me," he repeats, "that's the kind of kid he is."

Know this. For all the macho that comes with football, there is still some genuine emotion wrapped into the Michigan program. Schembechler stalking the sidelines, harping at his players, breaking their spirit and building it back, is the sort of thing the older guys return and thank him for later. There are a lot of ways to grow up. Football can be one of them.

Especially when you are the son of a coach.

So it was that Harbaugh returned in his third season more mature, more confident, less abrasive. And smarter. A week before the opener, against Notre Dame, he had a bad practice (he was playing with a jammed finger) and Schembechler, as usual, flew into a rage.

"He called the team together," Harbaugh recalls, "and he said, 'Don't be surprised if (Chris) Zurbrugg is the starter when we open against Notre Dame. I'm leaning that way. Your quarterback is a *prima donna!* He's done nothing since he's been here! He hasn't won a *damned thing* since he's been here and I'm going with Zurbrugg!'

"I left that practice a shell of a man. I said, 'Why is he doing this?' I didn't need that type of motivation anymore. I kept my mouth shut, but I never forgot it."

What had happened was inevitable. Schembechler would later sense it, and would never threaten to replace his quarterback again. What had happened was this:

Jim Harbaugh had outgrown the strategy.

And from that point on, Schembechler trusted him more and more with the offense. Harbaugh, of course, started the Notre Dame game, and every game since. His scrambling style and strong arm allowed for a more wide-open attack. He chopped down all sorts of passing records. The Wolverines came into the annual Ohio State game last season with an 8-1-1 record, and on the sidelines just before it started, Harbaugh broke with tradition; he approached his coach.

"Bo," he said, "whenever you need a play, whenever this game gets critical, just make sure the ball is in my hands."

Schembechler never forgot that. To this day, the tone of his voice changes when he remembers the fourth-quarter pass Harbaugh threw in the teeth of a blitz — the touchdown pass that sealed the 27-17 victory.

And a year later, the two teams played again, and this time Michigan fell behind, 14-3, in the second quarter. And Schembechler grabbed Harbaugh, who had given him the finest passing season of any quarterback he'd ever had, and the coach who was always known for his tough defense and conservative offense said, "Damn it! I don't care what we do! We just gotta *outscore them!*"

That's how far he had come with Jim Harbaugh. Outscore them.

They did. Michigan 26, Ohio State 24.

After the game, Schembechler took Harbaugh aside. They were going to the Rose Bowl. How far had they come since Harbaugh was a short-haired kid running around Schembechler's office, or a teenager baby-sitting Schembechler's son, or a high school senior dressing up in a sweater and loafers to try to get Bo to recruit him?

"Do you know how proud you've made your father today?" Schembechler said. "To be a coach and have a son who's done what you've done? God. He's so proud of you. .... "

He paused.

"And I am, too."

Harbaugh: "I'd like to get all the quarterbacks he's ever had together and

148

take him out to dinner."
Schembechler: "I'd go."

The California sun is warm and relaxing — clearly the reward for a good season. One more game. One more tug of the helmet. You don't know what you've got till it's gone, but you start to realize it a few days before.

"I'm really going to be sad when the Rose Bowl is over," Harbaugh says, "knowing I'll never play again under Bo. I mean, these have been the best five years of my life."

The best? The insults? The degradation? The anger, the turmoil? The best?

The best.

"I know it sounds strange, but I always wanted to impress the coaches. To have them think I'm a hard worker and a good kid. Why? I don't know. I guess it's because my father is a coach, and it goes back to a day when I was 10 years old and he told me I would never amount to anything. Ever since then I've been trying to prove him wrong.

"It's funny now. I hear Bo yelling at freshmen, 'You'll never play a down for Michigan.' The other day, he told the entire second-team offensive line they'd never play a down while he was there. *The whole line!*"

He laughs and crosses his arms behind his head. "I just crack up at that," he says.

Someone asks how he'd like to be remembered by Schembechler. He thinks about it for a moment.

"I guess I'd like him to say I was a competitor, a hard worker, a 'Michigan man' . . . and a friend. That would be the ultimate. That would be the kicker. If he said I was a good friend. Yeah. I'd be psyched."

And there it is, the completion of the circle. Idol, hero, mentor, tormentor enemy, teacher, friend.

He wants to be his friend.

"You know, he reams you out, but sometimes lately when it's happened, I'm thinking, 'God, this is what it's all about.' Me and Bo, we're fighting together, we're both on the same sideline, we both want the same thing. And I say to myself, 'You know, I'm gonna miss this.'"

And so, says Schembechler, will he. He has seen other special quarterbacks come and go. Dennis Franklin. Rick Leach. John Wangler. "But I am going to miss this kid a lot," he says. "He is the best passing quarterback I've ever had. And I've never felt as confident with anybody out there as I do with him. I know I yelled at him, I was on his case. But remember, I've known this kid since he was this big. I knew exactly who I was dealing with and what I was doing."

"And did he turn out the way you figured?" someone asks.

He grins.

"Better than I ever expected."

149

1987

TONY GALBREATH WIELDS CAMERA IN A SUPER WAY

January 25

COSTA MESA, Calif. — The Giants were in their designated seats. Tony Galbreath's seat was empty. He would not be available for interviews this day. He had taken the big leap, stepped off the silver screen of the Super Bowl. Like the hero in the "Purple Rose of Cairo," he was walking through real life now.

With a video camera.

"Look at all these people!" Galbreath said, eyeing a mob of reporters around teammate Phil McConkey. "This is no good. Excuse me. . . . Excuse me. . . ."

With each "excuse me" he yanked another reporter out of the way, until he was through the crowd, then in front of the crowd, his large frame dwarfing those alongside him. Tony Galbreath, the New York Giants' running back, with a video camera on his shoulder. A Hitachi Cam-n-Cord with a microphone the size of a baby dill pickle.

"NOW THEN, MR. McCONKEY!" he said, leaving no doubt whose question would be answered next. "WITH ALL THESE PEOPLE WATCHING YOU IN THE SUPER BOWL, DID YOU EVER DREAM YOU'D BE HERE?"

Phil McConkey grinned the way he would never grin at a real reporter. He answered the way he would never answer a real reporter. He made a face.

"NYYYAAAAAGHH. . . ."

Gotcha.

Things have come full circle. Once, the players were the story. Now, a player is getting the story. On film. From the inside. Tony Galbreath. The Hitachi Cam-n-Corder with the baby dill microphone.

It was a gimmick thought up by CBS officials. A Super Bowl diary. Pick a player on each team. Let him go all the places they cannot, tape rolling. At day's end, he gives them the tapes, they take what they can use and give them back. Galbreath gets to keep the camera. That is his payment. The camera and the tapes. All the tapes.

"MR. JOE MORRIS! STAND ON THE TABLE! STAND UP ON THE TABLE!"

"Oh, maaaan," Morris said.

"UP ON THE TABLE, MR. MORRIS. COME ON!"

Some players might have pooh-poohed the idea. Captured a few moments, kept the camera. Not Galbreath. He had taken it into the locker room. He had taken it into the hotel rooms. He had taken it seriously.

Almost everywhere he went last week, the camera went with him, resting straight on his broad shoulders. He was the soldier as war correspondent, the mirror that is held up to a mirror, held up to a mirror, held up to a mirror. . . . He was a player filming his own Super Bowl week.

"What have you captured?" he was asked Tuesday.

"I got some guys mooning the camera in the locker room," he said. "CBS won't be able to use that, of course."

"What did you capture?" he was asked Wednesday.

"I got some guys singing," he said. "They won't be able to use it, 'cause there was some, you know, not-so-great language."

What will they be able to use? Who knows? Who cares? This is Tony Galbreath's first Super Bowl. He will be 33 Thursday. He may never be here again. He was a star with New Orleans in the late '70s, then was traded to Minnesota and eventually to the Giants. Now, he is mostly a pass-catching specialist. He is no longer one of the big names. But he has the camera. He is keeping the tapes.

"I got it all in here," he said, tapping the Hitachi. "I am going to be like Richard Nixon. I will have all the tapes, the inside story, and everybody is gonna want to get them.

"I ain't gonna let 'em have 'em, either. This is just for me and my teammates."

He walked into the hallway, camera on shoulder. People stared at his black sweat suit and sunglasses. He saw them only through a one-inch viewfinder.

"Let's check out the defense," he said, entering its designated interview room. He spotted Jim Burt and stuck the camera in his face. Burt grinned. Galbreath found linebacker Carl Banks, who was already being interviewed. Banks started laughing in midsentence. Galbreath went up to cornerback Mark Collins.

"MISTER COLLINS!" Galbreath bellowed.

"HI, MOM!" Collins said.

On Tuesday, Galbreath caught several teammates in the showers. On Wednesday, he sneaked in on Mark Bavaro, the silent tight end, and got him to laugh and wave at the camera, something no legitimate reporter has done. On Thursday, Galbreath lined up five players in a make-believe game show and fired questions at them. "WHICH NEW YORK GIANT HAS THE BIGGEST NOSE?" The players slapped at make-believe buzzers, each trying to be the quickest to answer. "Bobby Johnson has the biggest nose!" "Maurice Carthon has the biggest nose!"

No reporters saw that. Or the serious moments recorded when the players were alone, realizing this was just among themselves. Galbreath

154

saw it. Galbreath was part of it. The film rolled. Rolled and rolled.

He has it all. What do we have? For all the hype, all the reports, the countless newspaper clippings and 10-second sound bites of the seven-day insanity known as Super Bowl week, what do we really know? Does any of us have the players mooning the camera? No. None of us does.

The fact is, what plays itself out in front of the world's media each January is mostly a series of well-calculated answers to predictable questions. A player says he is working hard. It is written he is working hard. A coach says his team is ready. It is written. There are no mooning stories. None.

"MR. BOBBY JOHNSON, YOU ARE THE BEST RECEIVER ON THE GIANTS TEAM –."

"I am?"

"YES YOU ARE, AND I WANT TO KNOW HOW YOU FEEL ABOUT PLAYING IN THE SUPER BOWL AND HAVING 100 MILLION PEOPLE WATCHING EVERY TIME SOME GUY KNOCKS YOUR BUTT OFF."

"Damn, Tony! Nobody gonna knock my butt off. Damn!"

"OK. THANK YOU!"

So here we are, Super Bowl day. This is what we have come to. A sport that was once reported by radio, and now the players have their own cameras, and they are filming the filming.

It is crazy, yes? It makes no sense? Well. This is a week in which reporters lined up like cattle outside a Southern California stadium until the gates were opened and the players made available. This was a week in which someone asked John Elway: "What is your favorite opera?" On one day, Lawrence Taylor said he was threatened with a $5,000 fine, but no one knows who threatened him, and on another day Vance Johnson talked about his artwork and his earrings and his Grace Jones hair. There are big plans to dump Gatorade on a coach's head. And this morning there are people running through hotels with their faces painted blue and orange, and they are talking about a football game that will be aired around the world, including Thailand, Saudi Arabia and Iceland, and did you know the halftime show will feature 100 years of Hollywood?

"What do you think of all this?" a reporter asked Galbreath Wednesday from behind a TV camera.

"What do you think of all this?" Galbreath answered, spinning around so that his camera pointed right back.

A mirror to a mirror. A camera talking to a camera. Super Bowl week. All is well.

IF I'VE GOT 47 BAGS OF NUTS, I MUST BE DOWN UNDER

January 30

FREMANTLE, Australia — I am very far away. I am as far away as you can get. I am so far away, if I went any farther I would get closer.

I am Down Under.

"Why are you standing on your head?" says a voice. "Are you all right?"

"Just getting my bearings," I say.

How far away am I? This is how far. Remember when you were a kid and you said, "If I dig a hole right beneath my feet and I keep digging and digging I will end up in China"? Wrong. You will end up here, next to me, standing on your head in an Australian hotel room, which I hope will stop spinning soon.

I am Down Under.

I would like to tell you how I got here. It was a great trip. Ha! I lied. You want to know the truth? It would have been easier to dig a hole beneath my feet and keep digging and digging.

I am here for the America's Cup final. A boat race. That is a good reason to come across the world, don't you think? A boat race? I thought about that all the way down, starting with the very pleasant first leg of the flight, which lasted only 16 hours.

Let me say this. I have never seen two movies, one TV show and a short subject in a single day before. Not even on a rainy vacation day. I saw all that on the first leg of the plane trip. Two movies, a TV show and a short. And dinner, and breakfast, and a snack, and peanuts. The beverage cart? Forty-seven times. I saw it 47 times. That has to be some kind of record.

Then we ran out of fuel.

Headwinds. The pilot said the headwinds had sapped the fuel. We would not make Sydney. "Brisbane," the pilot said.

And we landed in Brisbane, which was not where we were supposed to land, but which is better than landing on one of those little islands where they eat you. I guess.

S ure you're all right?" asks the voice.

"No problem," I say. "Why are you on the ceiling like that? You'll get dizzy."

I would like to say landing in Sydney was the end to a long but exhilarating trip. I cannot say it. I can say this. What time is it?

Here is the problem. Somewhere on the way to this America's Cup competition, we cross a cute little imaginary line whose single purpose is to drive the traveler completely insane: our friend, the international date line. I do not know who thought this thing up. I would like to strangle him, and stomp on his wristwatch.

Once you cross the international date line, today is yesterday, or yesterday is today. Tomorrow is another day. Which I have always said, but never meant, until now.

So as we landed in Sydney, the pilot told us that it was "11:40 in the morning, Wednesday," except that we had left on Monday, and no one could account for Tuesday, and besides, Sydney was on different time than Brisbane, and the rest of Australia was only 13 hours different from America.

And here came the beverage cart.

Did I tell you it was summer here? It is summer here. And they drive on the left. I hit the turn signal in my car, the windshield wipers come on.

But wait. Let's finish with the plane. Sixteen hours was not enough. Nor was the one-hour jump to Sydney, or the two hours in the transfer lounge. Next we would fly five hours to Perth.

"Will there be another movie?" I asked.

"No," the stewardess said. "It is too short a flight for a movie."

Five hours. Too short for a movie.

And here came the beverage cart.

Maybe you should eat something," the voice says.

"Yes," I say, "I could go for dinner."

"But it is 6 a.m.," comes the voice.

"Oh, yeah," I say.

This is a slight problem. I will admit it. I wake up, it is the middle of the night. I go to sleep, everyone goes for lunch.

I cannot help it. My body is Down Under, my brain is up over. People here go north to get warm. I have always gone south. They have bigger money than we. It is worth less. They drive on the left. Today is tomorrow. Catch a wave and they're sitting on the bottom of the world.

A boat race. I am here for a boat race. The America's Cup. The final will begin Saturday, which for us is today or last Monday, I'm not sure.

I must find out. I must be ready for that race. I must know a Kookaburra from a kola nut. I must know the Stars from the Stripes.

"First you must come down from your head," the voice says.

"I know," I say. "I am getting the hang of it. I am starting to adjust. Look. Over there. What a beautiful sunset."

"That's the moon," the voice says.

157

DENNIS CONNER KNOWS WHERE NICE GUYS FINISH

February 4

FREMANTLE, Australia — You hear lots of things said here about Dennis Conner, but you do not hear anyone say he's a nice guy. That's usually a safe expression, no? "He's a nice guy." Especially when people don't know what else to say. But descriptions of Dennis Conner go from "dedicated" to "ruthless' to "an absolute bastard." People skip "nice guy," frankly, because he isn't one.

But here is your next hero, America, Dennis Conner, 43, the drapery king from San Diego, plump and tan and looking like your Uncle Sid on his vacation to Miami Beach. All he needs is the Instamatic around his neck and the black socks. This is a sports star? Well, remember, this is yacht racing, the America's Cup. Everything is relative. The Australian press has actually nicknamed him "Big Bad Dennis," which goes to show you what becomes of a country where they don't have an NHL team. One caller told a television station Tuesday he would shoot Conner rather than let him take the America's Cup back home.

"DENNIS DOES IT IN STYLE!" a headline read after Conner's Stars & Stripes took a 3-0 lead in this best-of-seven America's Cup final against Kookaburra III. "HIS HANDS ARE ON THE CUP!' And indeed, by the time you read this, Conner might have recaptured the ugliest trophy ever to travel 12,000 miles. But then, this isn't about aesthetics. Dennis was the guy who lost the thing back in 1983. This is about revenge.

"Do you feel confident?" Conner was asked after his initial blowout victory Saturday over Kookaburra III.

"We have three more races to win," he said, grimly.

"Do you feel confident now?" he was asked after the second blowout Sunday.

"We have two more races to win," he said.

"Do you feel confident yet?" he was asked after the blowout Monday.

"We have one more race t-."

You get the idea. This is a man with one thing on his mind. Win that damn Cup back. Everything else can die and rot.

Tuesday, the day before Race 4, Conner was being shuffled around a press conference called to announce the signing of two new syndicate sponsors, Polaroid and Sprint. He'll show for this kind of stuff. Sponsors are money. Money is success. Here's a guy who spent $4 million and used four boats when losing the Cup in 1983. He has spent $15 million and five boats to try to win it back.

158

Not that Conner grew up rich. His father was a fisherman for a long time. But Dennis hung around yacht clubs and made friends with a lot of rich people, and he has certainly learned how to hobnob — he has the silliest, paste-on smile this side of a Herbalife salesman — and he was doing some hobnobbing Tuesday when an ordinary Joe sneaked into the circle.

"Hey, Dennis," the guy said, "will you still sail in the next Cup in 1990?"

Conner recognized the man as a nobody. His face tightened like a snare drum. "I plan to," he said, coldly.

"You know," the guy continued, "you're the same age as me, and it just seems a long time to stay with one thing–."

"I enjoy what I do," Conner snapped, "that's the difference. That's the difference between me and you. I enjoy what I do."

Ooh. No fun. But then, this is the guy who many think took the fun out of yacht racing altogether. Develop. Design. Improve. The 1980 America's Cup, which Conner won aboard Freedom, signaled the end of the good ol' boy, hoist-the-sails, hoist-the-martini stuff that made Ted Turner a legend. Remember when Turner showed up half-smashed for his victory press conference in 1977? None of that for Conner. He was already thinking about the next defense.

And when he lost that in 1983 to the winged-keeled Australia II — the first time the Cup left the United States since its inception 132 years earlier — an obsession was born. Conner showed up for the post-race press conference, fought off tears several times, then left without taking questions. Someone reported seeing him wandering outside the yacht club aimlessly, as if not sure where he was going. That is inaccurate. He knew where he was going. He was going to war.

D ennis isn't a bad guy," said Jack Sutphen, the veteran yacht man who helped select the Stars & Stripes crew. "He's just feels everybody should be as dedicated as him. If he sails six days a week and meets every night with sail people or designers, well, he expects that kind of effort in return."

Which can't be easy. Conner's crew went through a year and a half of grueling training in Hawaii — if "grueling" is possible in Hawaii — under security so tight, Conner controlled all photographs and occasionally even air space. The Stars & Stripes dock here has been nicknamed "The Compound" for its military-like restrictions on access. But this, too, is vintage Conner.

Those who know him say that despite his skill behind the wheel, which is as good as it comes, his most haunting demon is preparation.

By most accounts, Conner is happy only when everything is perfect before he hits water. Stars & Stripes led on every leg of the first three finals races here, as complete a thrashing as you can imagine. It is merely status quo for the skipper.

Asked whether he feels any pressure here, he said, "Pressure is defending a 132-year-old winning streak with a slow boat." Get it? The slow boat was the enemy. Weakness was the enemy. Conner is certain he will win if he holds all the cards. Opponents complain he hires the best talent and puts them on his second boat — just so the enemy can't use them. That's not courage. That's management. That's Conner.

If fact, for all his excellence on the water, the record will show that the one time Conner really had to mix it up for all the chips, he sat in it. We're talking about the last race of the 1983 America's Cup, when, with a 57-second lead on the fifth leg, he failed to cover Australia II and went searching for more breeze. He never found it. Australia II did. But why was he looking? Many think Conner was so psyched out by the winged keel of his competitor's boat that he thought even a 57-second lead wasn't enough, when it probably was. He was out of kilter. He knew at the start his boat was second best. His knowledge that it could happen might have forced the very outcome he dreaded.

"This time," Conner said a few days ago, "I know if we sail correctly and don't make mistakes, we can win."

Translation: I have the faster boat. Let's race.

So he is on top again, even though he won't admit it. But then, Conner now seems to say only what serves him. Those who watched him in 1983 see a different man here in Australia. He has been accessible at organized media events, and seems to smile as often as he breathes. But it is a calculated smile, with calculated answers, as if someone were cuing him. And perhaps someone is. After all, Conner is wooing big bucks into yachting now. The Budweiser spinnaker he hoisted after winning Race 1 was a harbinger of corporate things to come — all with Conner's blessing, and, occasionally, his begging.

But corporate money creates blandness, and Conner tiptoes around controversy as if he were spying on a rival sailmaker. Even the ridiculous will not get a rise. At a post-race press conference Monday, someone asked about rumors that Kookaburra III and Stars & Stripes — which both use Digital computers — had discovered each other's codes and were stealing secrets. Kookaburra skipper Iain Murray simply laughed. Conner, ever the smoothie, answered, "We're, uh, very pleased to have Digital on our team."

End of statement.

He is robotic at times, reacting like a wind-up politician. Yet the man who turns even car rides into competitive games — "Betcha a dollar we reach that building within 30 seconds" — retains a private ability to slice a visitor into pieces. His eyes can go freezer-cold. When people on the street try to get his attention, he often glides past them as if they are invisible. His voice is thin and at times unsteady, yet he can whip on someone like a stiletto.

No nice guy here. "He lives to sail" is the typical left-handed Conner compliment. Even his crew members joke that they have to take shifts talking sailing with him, so singular is his interest. But when pressed, few, if any, will confess to really knowing the guy. Even Jon Wright, who has sailed with Conner in 1980, 1983 and 1987 America's Cups, simply shrugs when asked to explain. He mentions intensity, aloofness, preoccupation with success.

"Dennis is Dennis," he said.

So here is your cover of Time magazine, the People interview, the Esquire profile subject. Next hero, America, Dennis Conner, a self-confessed "not very good-looking high school kid who found out that sailing was something I could be the best in." Pudgy, self-conscious, zinc cream on his lips making him look as if he just came up from a box of powder doughnuts — and now an entire country refers to him as Big Bad Dennis because of the way he sails? Imagine that. He is living a nerd's daydream, all the accolades he missed as a kid being showered on him in middle age.

"I came here to win the Cup," he will say. "This is like a dream come true." The words will look right in print. The stories will be complimentary.

He is missing heart, but he doesn't need heart. He is missing warmth, but warmth is a luxury. He has lived for one goal the last three years, and by the time you read this, he might be celebrating its arrival, downing his drink and laughing with all the right people. The victory will be earned, the smile will be fixed like an open curtain. But no nice guy here. You remember where nice guys finish?

So does he.

AUSTRALIANS TEACH US A LESSON IN LOSING

February 8

FREMANTLE, Australia — Now the waves can come and swallow this town again. For a few glorious days it was hanging ten on the world, the yachts were racing, the cameras whirring, but now that's over and the crowds are thin and you can get a table easily in the good steak houses, even the ones near the water.

Sail la vie, Australia. It's America's Cup again. Did you even watch this crazy thing on cable TV after midnight? Four boat races — all for a silver trophy most of us never even heard of until it was lost? Did you watch? Doesn't matter. Dennis Conner and his Stars & Stripes crew and the San Diego Yacht Club big shots are flying home the Cup even as this is being written, en route to a ticker-tape parade through the streets of, naturally, New York City, where, as we all know, yachting is a very popular sport.

And here in Fremantle they're watching the nest egg float out to sea. Having the America's Cup was a transfusion of life to this place; millions of dollars poured in, the stores and the hotels got a face-lift, it became a stop on the map — and as Ft. Lauderdale or Atlantic City or Cape Cod can tell you, being a stop on the map can keep you alive.

Gone now. And if anyone had good reason to be surly and bitter and downright depressed about Stars & Stripes' 4-0 sweep over Kookaburra III, it would be the Australians here who just got boxed out of a future. But on Wednesday night, after that final victory, the celebration for the conquering visitors was wild and loud and honest. The Aussies were singing and cheering and hailing the Americans deep into the harbor night, when the winds grew cold and their voices carried around the corners and bounced off the street lamps.

We are leaving now, the press corps, and in our memory suitcases some of us are packing a great and historical American victory. But I am taking home the way in which the Australians lost. I hope I never forget it.

Remember that this was a wipeout, total humiliation, the Australian boat never leading at a single leg mark of the four races. When Conner lost the Cup in 1983, four races to three, he mumbled through a post-race remark, near tears, then departed the press conference without taking questions. This time, naturally, he stayed for the whole thing. So did Iain Murray, the Kookaburra III leader who said he will not skipper a boat again, and therefore will almost certainly remain known for the rest of his life as "the man who lost the Cup."

Murray was quiet but gracious. And then, just as Conner was asked

162

how it felt to win, something terribly fitting occurred. Murray's dog, Cliff, somehow found his way to the stage — how he got in is the kind of thing they don't bother to explain here — and once he found his owner, poked his head over his shoulder and licked him affectionately in front of the whole media-stuffed room. And Murray, as if it were the most natural thing in the world, simply petted him back, even as Conner was wondering aloud why everyone was suddenly laughing. "Upstaged by a dog!" Conner finally exclaimed. Not the dog, Dennis. The compassion.

This thing was war to Conner and a sporting event to the Aussies, and maybe that's why they lost it. They didn't cover every angle, every possible substance for the boat bottom, every type of sail and keel design and wind pattern. They won in 1983 by catching the Americans with their technology down, introducing the winged keel, but that won't happen again. Who knows whether Australia or anyone will ever take the Cup away from the United States now that it is a race of better mousetraps?

The fact is, until Conner lost it in 1983, almost no one in the United States besides boating enthusiasts knew what the America's Cup was. "Losing in 1983," an insider told me, "was the best thing that could have happened to American yacht racing." Sure. Conner led a $15 million cavalry-like charge to get the thing back — "Steal our Cup, will ya?" — and corporate sponsors, who always act like dumb horses to a bugle, have now jumped on the bandwagon for the next one. Polaroid. Sprint. Pepsi. Budweiser. More sponsorship money hooked up with American yachting these past two weeks than it has probably seen in 10 years. Bing, bang, boom. It smells like Big Time now. I guarantee you the next America's Cup will be like covering the Super Bowl.

None of which helps the Australians. They held the Cup for just three years, after it sat 132 straight years in the United States. Ah, but what a celebrated three years! Here there is no Super Bowl, no World Series, no 50 other sports and 85 cable channels to detract the attention. Winning the America's Cup was something not forgotten in the next week's newspapers. It may have been like Leon Spinks' heavyweight title — enjoy it while you can — but it made national heroes of Alan Bond, the financier behind Australia II, and John Bertrand, the skipper. The Cup itself was constantly visited in the trophy room of the Royal Perth Yacht Club.

Yet when the designated parties turned it over Friday on the docks of the Swan River — with both crews and 5,000 guests present — they could only repeat how thoroughly Conner had earned it, and how they were sure it was going back to worthy hands. The roar from the crowd for Conner was impressive, as was the compliment from Prime Minister Robert Hawke on how 'graciously" Conner had accepted his defeat in 1983.

Nice words. Flimsy facts. Conner never even showed up for the Cup presentation ceremony that year, nor for a later White House reception for both crews. He showed for Friday's bash, however, without any socks and in a wrinkled suit that looked as if he'd just pulled it from below deck. No one wants to hear this. Tough. The man is a single-minded sailor, a master organizer and a hollow person. Never was that more clear than when he fumbled through his speech Friday in what should have been a shining moment.

By comparison, the Australians were embarrassingly sporting. The press hailed Conner's triumphant comeback — even though he himself barely addressed it — and the people in Fremantle clamored around the bus that carried his crew, just hoping for a chance to say, "Well done."

So dominating was Stars & Stripes that one of the Kookaburra crew compared going out for Race 4 to the soldiers at Gallipoli marching senselessly into the enemy fire. Yet, less than two hours after that race, three of the Kookaburra guys were at the Stars & Stripes dock, congratulating their peers, toasting them with beer. "Hey, these are our mates," said Kookaburra grinder Rick Goodrich. That was first. That was enough.

Sail la vie. What can they do? Fremantle, which was struggling before the Cup came down under, may become a white elephant now. The shops and the restaurants may be in trouble. There's no red letter date, no month on the calendar to circle, no government aid to expect. The silver history is gone from the Royal Perth Yacht Club trophy case, on its way now to San Diego. And. . .? And not a sour word heard. What's done is done, what's won is won.

There was a billboard we noticed when we first drove into town before the races. It hung on the railway station fence. "Keep Dreaming, Dennis," it read in big letters.

The day after the victory, we passed the station again. The sign was still there, but the makers had changed it. Across the corner, in the same professional lettering of "Keep Dreaming, Dennis" they had added, "Dreams Really Do Come True." No spray paint. No foul words. Just a verbal slap on the back; nice job, good days, no worries.

Dreams do come true; what they don't do is last. We are leaving, flying away, and Fremantle is already blowing south in the memory. There was victory here, yes, but something even rarer. Sportsmanship. Good and true. Too bad there's no trophy case for that. Australia says it was honored to have the America's Cup even for three years. It should be the other way around.

EISENREICH'S POTENTIAL BATTLES HIS PROBLEM

February 15

S T. CLOUD, Minn. — They treated him like a freak, and he never deserved that. "The things I do, I've done all my life," says Jim Eisenreich. But people just saw what they saw, a center fielder suddenly twitching and gasping for breath, bending at the waist, not sure he would ever find air again. Just like that it could happen. In the middle of the game. And he would call time out and run off the field, scared and embarrassed. He was suffering from a disease, he says, Tourette Syndrome, but he didn't know it then, and his club, the Minnesota Twins, didn't believe it. And what did fans do? They laughed. They taunted. They greeted him with cries of "Shake for us, Eisenreich! Dance for us, Eisenreich! . . ."

Until finally, he quit.

He hasn't played in nearly three years.

Now he is coming back.

"What time is it?" he asks, sitting on a living room couch. His face is unshaven, his eyes sleepy-looking, his mouth a crooked line.

"Three twenty," comes the answer.

"At four o'clock, I gotta work out." He sniffs. His foot taps. "As long as we're done by four, because I gotta work out."

This is a story about trying again, and again and again, because when you dream of playing baseball, you don't just stop. You don't just live at home and sleep late and play on an amateur team where you stand out so much it's a joke — then go to a bar and watch your old club on TV. You don't do that. Not when you're still good enough to play. And Jim Eisenreich was always good enough, damn good, maybe great. "A future All-Star," one baseball owner called him. But when the problems started they put him in the hospital and they sent him to shrinks and then came the medication and the hypnotists and the faith healers and the headlines and enough — the spirit and the flesh can only take so much. "I felt," he now admits, "like an idiot."

So he quit, and the game forgot him, but he never forgot the game. Three seasons passed. Then last fall, the Kansas City Royals picked him up for the waiver price of a dollar. One hundred pennies. And because of that, and because he cannot sit anymore while the dream rots away, Eisenreich, 27, will get on a plane for Florida next week, and that alone will take more courage than most of us can imagine.

Spring training is about to start. He is walking back to the door.

Hello, nightmare. It's Jim again.

T *hey would sit in back of the classroom, they had their little stopwatches, that's what really used to get me, the stopwatches, and they'd be timing me, seeing how long I'd be doing every little movement. I used to get so mad at them when they watched me at school like that. I'd ask the teacher to (let me) go to the bathroom and leave for a while.*"

"*You'd just leave? Walk out?*"

"*Yeah. I didn't like those little stopwatches.*"

Jimmy Eisenreich began showing symptoms of his problem around five or six. "Hyperactive," they called him. He was nervous, agitated, he would twitch, hum, sniff — all symptoms associated with Tourette Syndrome, a neurological disorder that affects more than 100,000 Americans, although no one in St. Cloud diagnosed it as such.

People there really didn't know what he had. One day, during a Little League game, Cliff Eisenreich pulled his son aside and said, "What are you doing out there? Why are you making those faces?"

The boy started to cry.

That began a childhood of testing, of doctors, of hospitals. One place sent field people to observe him during elementary school. They sat in the back of the room and timed his movements with stopwatches. He knew they were there. So did the other kids. Sometimes he would whirl around and stare at them, just stare, with all the piercing anger of a child ashamed.

As he grew older, the things he did became a given — to others as well as himself. Social life was difficult. He rarely dated; he is unmarried. Ah, but sports. There was his salvation. It may seem a cruel joke that so much athletic talent lay inside such a troubled shell, but it was there, and young Eisenreich saw it as a way out. "As long as I was better at sports, I didn't care what all the people said."

He was better. Occasionally his symptoms would act up during games, but never would they affect his play. Baseball. Hockey. Soccer. "He was the greatest athlete I have ever seen," marvels his brother, Charlie, a major league prospect himself. "He could pick up a tennis racket and beat you at tennis, and it might be the first time he played."

Baseball was his dream, however, and for a while he was riding the rainbow. Promise? Is that a strong enough word? Eisenreich was a college star at St. Cloud State, then joined the Twins' organization and jumped from Class A to the majors in a single spring, 1982.

On fire. He was on fire. He finished that spring training with a .293 average. Great arm. Good speed. Could hit anything. Class A to the major leagues? And suddenly the shy kid from St. Cloud was flying north as Minnesota's starting center fielder.

"A star," the Twins people predicted.

He was 22.

166

Maybe I figured something bad had to happen to me, because all this good stuff had happened."

"Is that the way things have always happened in your life? Something bad counters something good?"

"In a way. Sort of. . . ."

The first incident people remember came against the Red Sox in Boston in May 1982. Eisenreich was clearly having problems in center field — twitching, labored breathing — and the Fenway bleacher crowd, showing typical kindness, jumped all over him. "What's the dance, Eisenreich?" someone screamed. "Shake, Eisenreich! Shake!" It was cruel and unforgivable — "They chopped him to little pieces," says Twins physician Dr. Leonard Michienzi — but of more concern to Eisenreich was air, which he suddenly could not bring down his throat. He bent over. His face was contorted. The game disappeared, the crowd disappeared. "I was hyperventilating, I couldn't stop," he says. When he reached that point where survival surpasses emotion, he did what made sense — called time and ran off the field.

The incident made headlines. Then it happened again, and again. Four straight games. Finally, in Milwaukee, Eisenreich went from the outfield to the hospital. He was treated there with Inderal, a drug prescribed by Michienzi. "He called it a 'guaranteed miracle cure,'" Eisenreich says, clearly angry. "It made me so jumpy, they had to give me two shots to try and put me out, and they still couldn't."

The whispers started. What's wrong with Jimmy? No one said Tourette. In fact, Michienzi, the Twins' team doctor of 20 years, ruled out Tourette early, largely because Eisenreich did not exhibit the sudden barking sounds or hallucinations often seen with the illness. Their diagnosis? Agoraphobia. Fear of open places.

Stage fright syndrome.

"That's just wrong," Eisenreich says. "That stage fright stuff, everybody jumped on that, and they don't even know me. The things I do can happen to me anywhere, in church, or in my room. The crowds don't bother me. Anyhow, if it was stage fright, how come the biggest crowds in 1982 were the first few weeks, and I didn't have any problems then?"

No one knew. What's wrong with Jimmy? All they knew was this was not normal. Eisenreich was put on the disabled list, and at the Twins' suggestion, was admitted to St. Mary's hospital in the Twin Cities.

They kept him there three weeks.

Were you ever afraid for your safety during a game?"

"I used to be. . . . I used to think one of these times I'm just gonna pass out and be gone."

167

"Did that ever happen, you passing out?"
"No, never. I never passed out."
"It scares you, though, when it happens."
"It used to. I was out of control. . . . I mean, it used to. But that stuff's behind me now."

In the hospital, Eisenreich lay in a bed, giving blood, undergoing tests. It was late spring, the beautiful season. He was in a climate-controlled psychiatric wing, with no idea of what was wrong.

"I'd get up every morning, they'd take my blood pressure, and I'd eat breakfast with people who didn't know what was going on, really sick people. It was all psychiatric stuff. I said, 'Jeez, I'm not nuts. There's something wrong with me. Why don't you fix it?' "

The psychiatrists pummeled him with questions. He felt like the Jack Nicholson character in "One Flew Over The Cuckoo's Nest." But the Twins maintained the problem was in Eisenreich's mind.

"Have you ever considered committing suicide?" a nurse asked him once. "Suicide?" He shakes his head at the memory. "I almost committed murder with that one."

The tests continued. No results. He went home until September. When he rejoined the team, he started a game at the Metrodome and his family and friends came to see him. Everything was fine for the first inning. Then it began again. The agitation. The movements. By the third inning it was very bad, and Eisenreich was bending over at the waist, looking for breath. They stopped the game. He came out.

A few days later, his season ended. Ironically, his talent had refused to be affected — he finished with a .303 average. That got him another trip to the hospital. Three more weeks.

He kept his anger inside. He wanted to listen, wanted to be a good soldier, because baseball is a sport that emphasizes good soldiers. "But I hadn't even played since the last time," he says. "I read the papers. I knew what was being said about me. I knew it was stupid. I felt like an idiot."

Who first diagnosed you as having Tourette Syndrome?"
"You mean the doctor?"
"Yes."
"His last name was Abouzah, or something. I can't spell it."
"He was the only one?"
". . . Uh-huh."
"When was that?"
"In 1982."
"Have you seen him since?"
"Nope."
"Did the Twins know about the diagnosis?"

168

"Yeah, but they didn't believe him or something."
"You do, though."
"Yeah. He wrote a book on Tourette's."
"This Abouzah guy? He wrote a book?"
"That's what he said."

Spring training the following year was the start of the freak show. Eisenreich was now off-limits to the media. In the clubhouse, reporters would glance over and, upon seeing him, their eyes would drop. Some of his teammates reacted the same way. Baseball, after all, celebrates the practical joker, or the strong silent type, but a guy whose problem is being scared of crowds? Doesn't fit.

What could he do? He couldn't tell the people who called him "the stage fright guy" that the nightmare struck just as often when he was alone, that when he drove to the ballpark he always took the back roads, that he "never wanted to be on the highway driving, because it could just start up, like at 2 in the morning, and I'd have to pull off the road."

What could he do? He endured that spring of solitude. And yet, like flowers growing on a mine field, his baseball skill was undaunted. He hit .400, and headed north again as the starting center fielder.

"He's got it licked now," the Twins people said.

He lasted two games.

T*his one guy they sent me to, he said the cause of my problem, he was sure, had something to do with my birth. Like when I'm born I'm sure I'm gonna remember coming out of my mom."*
"That's what he expected you to remember?"
"Yep. . . . Whoo. . . . I wanted to get away from him as fast as I could."
"Was he a doctor?"
"I don't know what he was."

When Eisenreich came home that spring — he had quit, after two games, saying he "didn't want to go through it again" — even his family didn't know how to react. "It was quiet the first day," says Charlie Eisenreich. "Finally Jim said, 'Well, aren't you even going to talk to me?' "

Eisenreich had given up on pro baseball, at least for the moment. But the Twins had not given up on him. Not with his potential. He's so good, he's so talented. What's wrong with Jimmy? Michienzi, the Twins' doctor, still maintained the problem was agoraphobia. He recommended specialists who recommended specialists. It became a circus. Therapists, psychologists, hypnotists, biofeedback people. What's wrong with Jimmy? The answer was a chance for fame, and the "faith healers" — as Eisenreich calls them — contacted the Twins every day claiming to have the solution. Some wound up treating him.

"They all had their little gadgets," he recalls, with an annoyed chuckle.

"They'd all dim the lights, all had recliners so you could sit back. They'd either talk or put on a tape. All they'd say was, 'Relax . . . relax.' That was fine. I was sitting in a chair. Anyone can relax sitting in a chair."

Not surprisingly, none really helped. Eisenreich was embarrassed. He became cynical. People would call up his house, claiming to want to cure him, claiming they had the answer. "Oh yeah?" he would sneer. "How come I never heard of you before?"

End of conversation.

He kept going, kept visiting these useless people, because of the good soldier part, because he wanted to play, because he needed the job.

For a while it seemed like a moot point. He was scared and weary and at odds with the Twins' doctors. Think of what he had already gone through! He really didn't know what he had, he didn't want to believe it was a stage fright syndrome, and he had almost no one to talk to. "Sometimes," says his brother, Charlie, "I wished the Twins would have hired me as a bench-warmer just so I could be there when Jim came into the dugout. I've been with him when we're driving and he starts to get excited. I can just yell, 'STOP! STOP IT!' and he calms down. He just needs somebody like that."

But there was nobody like that, and he had to make a decision. Play or stay away? What could he do? Dancers dance, painters paint, and baseball players play baseball.

Jim Eisenreich agreed to one more attempt in 1984.

I *never knew what everybody was so afraid of. . . . "*
This time the Twins protected Eisenreich like a boy in a bubble. No questions from reporters. No hassles from teammates. He had another good spring. A silent spring. By this point he was taking Haldol — a drug used to combat Tourette — without the Twins' knowledge. With his good numbers, it seemed the problem had abated. Twins owner Calvin Griffith predicted Eisenreich "will be an All-Star one day."

Not that day. Not that year. He was the Twins' first batter of 1984, the leadoff hitter, playing in center field, but they took him out of the lineup after the second game — "We were going on the road and I think they didn't want the crowds to ridicule me" — and shortly thereafter, the problems began again.

He lasted until April 26. There was talk about him acting drowsy, falling asleep in the dugout. He denies it. He went on the disabled list until May 18 and realized, upon returning, that the future was not grim — the future was gone. "They had Kirby Puckett by that point in center. I knew they wouldn't move him. I wouldn't, either.

"They used me in right field for one game. Then, a couple days later they asked me to go on the minor leagues. I said I didn't want to because I could play up here. Then they asked me to go on the voluntary retired list. I didn't want to do that because I needed the job. Then they said OK, we'll pay you until the end of the year if you go on the retired list."

That is how Eisenreich's major league career came to its apparent end. That is his story, anyhow.

Michienzi has a different version. He claims the Twins wanted Eisenreich off the Haldol, which, at first, the player vigorously denied taking. "(Manager) Billy Gardner came up to me one day," Michienzi says, "and he said, 'You been watching batting practice? The kid keeps falling asleep in the dugout, and every ball in batting practice he thinks he's pulling to left field is barely getting over third base.'

"So we had a meeting with Jim, we discussed the fact that he wasn't behaving like a man on Xanax (the drug Michienzi had actually prescribed). Jim said, 'That's all I'm taking.' So we said, 'Would you sign a paper allowing us to test for any other drugs?' He said, 'I can't do that.' We said, 'Why not if you're not taking Haldols?' He said, 'Well, I'm taking them.'

"He lied about it. If he's taking Haldol he can't play baseball. It's that simple. It affects the nervous system. It dulls the reflexes. If he got hit in the head with a wild pitch while he was on Haldol, your ass is sued."

Sympathy had turned to anger. Trust had deteriorated. Either Eisenreich felt he knew better than the doctors, or he did not want to risk the nightmare again without Haldol. "I think just being in a major league outfield is enough to bring on his problems," says Michienzi.

Whatever. On June 4, 1984, Jim Eisenreich voluntarily retired from the Twins. In three years he had played 48 games.

He has not played major league baseball since.

So what would you tell people?"
   "I don't know.... That I did have trouble, but I could still play. I could always play. I made it once, you know. ..."

Back in the living room of his parents' house, Eisenreich rises, getting ready for his workout. He is not unusually big — 5-feet-11, 180 — but his muscular torso is evident even beneath his cotton jersey. He lifts his glove.

"I'm ready."

He sniffs. He is still taking Haldol — but in a smaller, regulated dosage, once a night — and he says it has checked the problem. He is still clearly nervous talking with reporters, his foot tapping, his voice unsteady. But he is talking. He says he wants people to know his side of the story. Despite only one doctor's opinion — a man whose name he cannot fully remember — Eisenreich holds firm to the fact that he has Tourette Syndrome, and that he has it under control.

"If I don't make it now, it'll be because of my baseball talent, not my other problems," he says.

Either way, Kansas City thinks he is worth a dollar gamble — mostly because of Bob Hegman, a former college teammate of Eisenreich's, and now the Royals' administrative assistant for scouting and player development. Hegman never forgot how overpowering Eisenreich was in college. When he discovered Eisenreich had finally been granted his release by the Twins — late last year — Hegman went to his boss, John Schuerholz, KC's general manager.

"Nobody else was talking about Jim," Hegman says. "Most people had forgotten about him. But he's got unbelievable talent, All-Star talent. He can run, throw, hit, hit for power. Everything."

So the Royals claimed him for the waiver price of one dollar, and they have given him a one-year minor league contract. In the past three years, he has worked in an archery shop and as a part-time house painter. The only baseball he played was at the amateur level with a local St. Cloud team — where he was so superior he often hit better than .600. "Realistically I would say this is his last chance in the major leagues," Hegman says. "If it works out, that'll be great, that'll be fantastic."

"What are the odds?" he is asked.

He sighs. "At this point, to be honest, he has to play his way back to being a prospect."

Four o'clock. The scene has changed. In the cavernous echo of the St. Cloud State athletic facility, Eisenreich throws a ball to a player across the floor. He does the warm-up dance. Catch the ball, pose, look to the side, rock back, throw, follow through. His arm is strong, and his throws have that familiar big-league zip. Here, in the gym, the tics and the twitches and the disturbing sense that something is wrong are temporarily gone. He does not look uneasy. He looks like a baseball player.

"What if this doesn't work out?" he is asked. "What will you do?"

"I think I've pretty much accepted that this is the way I am," he says, the words coming slowly. "If I ever lose it, great. That'll be great if it goes away. But ... you know. ..."

And on he goes. The problem is Tourette, he says. No it isn't, says Michienzi. He can still play, he says. No way, says most of baseball. He can handle the medication, he says. It could get him killed, says someone else.

There should be some sort of guarantee here, some sort of payback. There should be some way that Jim Eisenreich gets out of baseball all he has had to endure from it for three years and 48 games and a lifetime's worth of hospital stays. He goes to spring training next week, back to the nightmare, a potential All-Star trying to be a prospect, and there should be some kind of happy ending, don't you think? Some safe bet that he will make it this time?

"How you doing, Jimmy?" asks a passing player.

"Fine," he says, sniffing.

TRAM AND LOU: IT'S BEEN NICE WORKING WITH YOU

March 8

LAKELAND, Fla. — When will they write the last Alan Trammell/Lou Whitaker story? Four years from now? Five? Ten? And what will it say? Probably some syrupy prose about the longest-running keystone combo in baseball, Trammell, the boyish California shortstop, Whitaker, the brooding-but-gifted second baseman, and what great partners they were on the field and off the field and how sad it is to see them breaking up and walking into the sunset arm in arm and. . . .

Well. OK. What's baseball without a little schmaltz? So that's what the story will say. Here is what it should say. It should say what the two players themselves will say — at least what they will likely say — when the moment comes to say goodby. Which is this:

"Nice working with you."

"See ya."

Now don't get me wrong. They are indeed a magical duo, Trammell and Whitaker. What's that scoreboard phrase they flash at Tiger Stadium? "Tram To Lou For Two!" Yes. Why not? Their movement on the crack of a bat is beautiful fury, a sort of Mexican hat dance around second base in which singles die and come back as double plays.

For 10 seasons now, Trammell and Whitaker have been in glorious sync, the same positions, the same infield, the same Tigers uniforms. And when they begin the 1987 campaign for real next month, they will be in the history books as well — the longest-running shortstop-second base act ever. And they still perform as if set to music.

But when the game ends, the music ends. And this may surprise. Nice working with you. For the off-field Trammell/Whitaker relationship is not a movie-of-the-week.

"Have you ever had Lou and his family to your house for dinner?" Trammell was asked Thursday after a spring workout.

"No," he said, mulling it over, "I guess we haven't."

"Well, has he ever had you and your family over for dinner?"

"Nope. Never has."

"How often do you and Trammell talk in the off-season?" someone later asked Whitaker.

"We don't, really," he said.

"Isn't that kind of strange, for all the time you put in together?"

"Shoot," he said, grinning. "It's a business."

ow, this is true. It is a business. So are the movies. And that same curious discovery that Fred and Ginger dance that way only for the cameras is at work here with these two. On the baseball stage, Trammell and Whitaker could not be any closer without wearing each other's clothes. They began their pro careers with the same minor league team. They were called up by the Tigers on the same day, and played in the same first game. They share adjacent positions, adjacent lockers, the same agent, for a while they shared the same room. They even did a guest-starring bit together on the "Magnum P.I." TV series.

And yet they are curiously distant. The other day someone suggested to Trammell that for all they had been through, he and Whitaker were little more than two guys at the office whose desks had been next to one another for 10 years. "Exactly!" Trammell said, grinning. "Exactly! I couldn't have said it better. You described it perfectly."

This, of course, is vintage Trammell. What time is it? It's enthusiasm time! He is fan and player rolled into one body, a gimme-the-ball guy, a guy who ended his first major league radio interview by yelling "Go Rebels!" — a message to his minor league buddies. He may have less pure baseball ability than Whitaker — "I think so, anyhow," he said — yet his passion seems to run twice as deep.

Whitaker, meanwhile, is an enigmatic mix, a warm smile on a cool soul, reluctant to talk, resistant to team spirit. His passions run deep also — deep inside. There are few who claim to know him well (Chet Lemon, the center fielder who, like Whitaker, is a Jehovah's Witness, is an exception) and yet he is a natural, an All-Star, the best at his position today, and likely the best to ever wear a Tigers uniform.

"Like I said, it's a business," Whitaker answered, when asked about the closeness between him and his shortstop. "I'm sure a lot of people in big business, they just do their job . . . Tram and I don't do the same thing off the field. Maybe they'll be a team get-together and I'll show up for a few minutes, but I'm not gonna sit in the room and party all night. I don't do that. I never did, not when I met Tram, not before, not after."

There was, however, a time when they were closer. In fact, the more years pass, the further they seem to drift. In their early days of Instructional League ball, Trammell and Whitaker would pal around with Lance Parrish and Dave Rozema. Trammell remembers a pellet gun Parrish used to have, and how they'd beat the boredom by firing at the Florida lizards. "One shot apiece," he said, laughing.

"In those days Lou and I talked a lot, mostly about baseball. Then, of course, we roomed together our first four years. The routine was pretty similar. We'd get up, go get something to eat. I'd read the newspaper and tell Lou who was doing what and where. He'd listen, but he wouldn't say much." Added Whitaker: "Maybe once or twice we talked about something personal. But I can't remember it."

Trammell married first. He began to grow closer to other Tigers players, most notably infielder Tom Brookens and his wife, Christa. Then Whitaker married. The two stopped rooming together. In the winter of 1983, Whitaker embraced his new religion.

"When we came back in 1984, instead of just talking shop the first thing he said was, 'Did you know I was a Jehovah's Witness now?' " Trammell recalled. "I said, 'No, I didn't.' He told me about it.

"He changed his life, basically. He used to smoke cigarets, he stopped doing that. We used to have a beer together after the games. Now he almost never drinks. I would say the religion thing put a bit of distance between us. But I don't care what someone does off the field. That's his business."

These days, the pair will shake hands at the end of each season, and generally not speak to each other until they return for spring training. From April to October they will dress in the clubhouse, side by side, harmoniously — "I can't recall one serious fight with him in 10 years," Trammell said — and yet very few words will be exchanged. On plane trips, Whitaker will usually sit up front with Lemon, while Trammell is in the back playing cards.

"Do you miss not being closer?" Trammell was asked. "Would you rather you and he talked more?"

"Not really," he said, shaking his head, "because Lou's been that way since the day I met him. It's not my job to go and change somebody. He's always been quiet. Always."

The next question, of course, is what difference does it make? None. At least none on the field. It is as if all the two don't know about each other's regular life is made up for by a sixth sense on the diamond. They are so well choreographed, neither can remember the last time the other got in his way.

"That's one of the little things you get by working together so much," Whitaker explained. "You don't see us stepping on each other, or bumping into each other. Like when Tram is directly behind second base, making a throw, I'm never blocking his way. Or if he's gonna make the play himself, I'm never in the way of the bag."

Trammell nodded at Whitaker's explanations. He admits he barely looks at his partner anymore before throwing to him. "It's a little careless, I guess. But I just know where he's gonna be."

Their double plays are a tribute to economy of movement. A stop, a flip, a rocket to first. How many, after all, have they practiced? Maybe 10,000?

175

20,000? So tuned is each to their private frequency that both confess a need to wake up when a substitute partner is out there. "It's not the same," said Trammell.

How could it be? It's a wonder these two aren't fused at the hip. Look at these numbers: .281 and .281. That's Trammell's career batting average — and Whitaker's career batting average. How about these? Career games played: Trammell 1,289, Whitaker 1,283. Career hits: Trammell 1,300, Whitaker 1,320. Career RBIs: Trammell 504, Whitaker 522.

Their service in the major leagues is identical. Their team history is identical, from the lowest level of the minors. Their numbers are only one digit apart (Whitaker wears "1," Trammell "3"), and that is only because Phil Mankowski was wearing No. 2 when they showed up — and now, in honor of Charlie Gehringer, that number is retired.

No wonder they work together like the insides of a German clock. And, when cajoled, each will admit they probably are the best tandem out there today. And they are still young. And who knows what lies ahead? How many more double plays, more dances, more highlight films?

And yet. . . .

"What if Alan Trammell had never been around?" Whitaker was asked. "Wouldn't your career have been different?"

"Nuh-uh," he said, shrugging, pointing to the shortstop's locker. "The next guy would be right there, where he is. And I would be here. That's all.

"And it's the same for Tram."

So here comes history, the 1987 baseball season. And Tiger Stadium fans should be aware of what they are getting a chance to watch, even if it's not movie-of-the-week material.

"It's true," Trammell said, rubbing a fist though his hair, "we've kinda separated over the years, Lou and I. We very seldom do anything together off the field. But there's a special feeling when we get on the field. It's like eye contact. We don't even talk. We just look at each other. And that relationship, well, there aren't too many of those around. . . . "

When will they write the last Trammell/Whitaker story? What will it say? That they parted in a sudden splash of emotion? Or that they simply cleaned out their desks and shook hands? Nice working with you.

Who knows?

"Will you guys keep up?" Trammell was asked. "When this is all over, will you stay in touch?"

"Oh . . . uh, yes, I think we will, I think I will," he said. "At least once or twice a year. . . . I don't know. I would think so. . . ."

"What do you think?" Whitaker was asked. "Will you guys keep up?"

He looked at his knees, then his glove.

"That's a tough question."

LANCE PARRISH FEELS BETRAYED BY 'FAMILY'

March 15

This whole thing has been like a movie — 'The Negotiation of Lance Parrish.' It's ridiculous. This is not how I wanted my name in the papers. . . ."
— Lance Parrish, after signing with Philadelphia

CLEARWATER, Fla. — He pulled the new uniform over his broad shoulders and tugged on the zipper. Up came the pants around his waist, and the red belt went through the loops.

"It fits," he mumbled.

"Pinstripes," said an observer. "Nice. You look like an inmate."

"Yeah?" He smirked at the irony.

And out he went, into the Florida sunshine, into a strange stadium and a strange team and a strange league. A small group of fans applauded him, people who had never applauded Lance Parrish before, and a blond-haired kid in a Phillies helmet and Phillies jacket held out an autograph ball that barely fit in his hand.

"Mr. Parrish?" he said. "Pleeeease."

He's somebody else's hero now. Some other city. Some other park. Two years of trying to stay with the Tigers have resulted in his signing with another team — only the second major free agent to do so this year. His little saga has made headlines for months. It is a story with many implications. But before Detroit writes him off as a traitor, and before fellow players canonize him as a martyr, and before baseball lawyers make him Exhibit A in their "collusion" file, know this: None of that really mattered to Lance Parrish.

How can a guy who turned down a guaranteed $1.2 million from Detroit — a team he knew and loved — settle for a guaranteed $800,000 with a team he knows almost nothing about?

Listen.

For the last few years I felt I might have been playing below the pay scale for a catcher like myself. But because I had signed a contract, I was determined to honor it. I figured the Tigers would take care of me when the contract was over.

"To be honest, I felt very . . . let down . . . by their attempts to sign a new one. I'd done everything they asked of me. . . . I was naive. I felt like I had such a good relationship with the Tigers that they would do what was fair. And it wasn't even close.

"I understand they were concerned about my back (which made him sit out more than two months of last season). But I made concessions to that. Originally I wanted a three-year contract. When I realized it would not have been a good business decision for them to sign me for three years, what with my back, I resigned myself to a one-year contract. I was willing to prove I could play healthy. I would take a chance if they would. But I was not going to sign a one-year contract for less than I was worth.

"That's what they wanted. The week after they made their last offer in November ($1 million, one year, a raise of $150,000), that was the point where money stopped being the premier issue. That's when I started really taking this thing personally. . . . "

As Lance Parrish talked, he slowly pounded a bat into the bullpen grass. He would say he was happy now. It was obvious he was not. Other free agents in this winter of discontent may have been trying to make a statement to the owners. But Parrish — who has ended up doing just that — tumbled into the role out of hurt and resentment.

"People aren't going to understand this," he said, "but I thought of the Tigers as my family. They raised me in baseball. And in the end . . ."

He paused.

"What?" someone asked. "You felt betrayed? What?"

He nodded.

"That's exactly how I felt. Betrayed."

It is impossible to say whether the Tigers were right or wrong in their final offer — one year at $1.2 million with a second-year option at the same rate. A healthy Parrish is certainly comparable to the Mets' Gary Carter, who earns $2 million a year — but that figure is called "a reference point" by agents and "a mistake of the past" by owners.

This much you can say: The Tigers blew their chance with Parrish as much with their treatment as with their figures. Here was a guy who came up through their farm system, who felt like a son in their organization, an All-Star, a cleanup hitter, a 30-year-old team leader who gave them 10 honorable big-league seasons, and when contract time came he was handled like just another customer in the deli. Tigers officials delayed, as is their custom. They kept the offers low, as is their custom. Their communication with him was minimal, as is their custom. Sometimes these tactics work.

And sometimes they do not.

"What is it that you wanted from the Tigers, really?" Parrish was asked. "Besides the dollar figure? What was it you wanted that you didn't get?"

"I wanted them to talk to me!" he said, the exasperation gushing out. "I wanted them to be honest with me and try and work something out. If it was the back problem, OK, I think we could have structured a contract around that. Whatever. But I didn't even hear from them between November and after Christmas! I was owed better treatment than that. What I'm trying to tell you is, we've been trying to work something out with the Detroit Tigers for two years!"

Parrish was finishing a six-year contract with Detroit. He wanted the new one to reflect the time he'd put in. He wanted the negotiations to reflect that, too. He wanted, quite simply, to feel wanted. But of course, he let his agent, Tom Reich, do the negotiations. And the Tigers kept it strictly business. Claiming his back was too big of a question mark, and that Reich was clogging communication efforts, Detroit GM Bill Lajoie made no real moves for Parrish until the last possible day — the $1.2 million offer. It's a common ploy by the Tigers; a last-minute deal snagged Kirk Gibson one year earlier.

But by that point, Parrish was seething. He turned the Tigers down. He was out in the void.

In the next day's aftermath, many blamed Reich. It was said he wanted the catcher to sign elsewhere so he could break the alleged owners' "collusion" — as much for his ego as for his client's bank account.

"That's just wrong," said Parrish. "He's been taking a bad rap through all of this. I honestly felt that if I became a free agent, I would be able to do better than what the Tigers offered me. But they (the owners) have changed the system. They're obviously putting the screws to everybody."

Parrish found the Phillies to be the only interested party. And they were interested only at lower rates than the Tigers. Why? Here is one theory: Because that way, one owner isn't outbidding another, which is how free agency got to be so ridiculously expensive in the first place.

If Parrish signed, the Phillies could always tell the Tigers: "Don't blame us for stealing him. He came here for less money." Get it? As long as the new club offers less, free agency exists in theory, but it is always less lucrative than the alternative, staying put.

The players' union, of course, charged the owners with conspiring on this — and thus kidnapping a free market.

And Lance Parrish was suddenly prime evidence.

"Of course we initially demanded the kind of money from Philadelphia that we wanted from the Tigers," he said, when asked how he could ultimately sign for a lower figure. "But you can demand all you want. I had received word from Bill Giles (the Phillies' president) that his offer was the best he could do given the way everything was in baseball today.

"I wasn't happy with the position I was put in. But there was an obligation to do something for other players. Since no other free agents were moving, I felt I had to make every effort to be the guy who did."

So in the end — after some bizarre bickering over a clause entailing his right to sue baseball — Parrish agreed to one year at $800,000, plus $200,000 if his back did not cause serious absence before the All-Star break. He said he considered returning to the Tigers on May 1 and "was not too proud to do it if I had no other choice."

But any other choice was preferable. It was a matter of principle. It was a matter of pride. How could he sign for less money? Simple. In his mind, the Tigers owed him more. They owed him for 10 years. He would rather start anew with Philadelphia — at a lower salary — than give in to the Tigers.

"It cost me," he said. "It did cost me. But I'm putting my faith in the Phillies' organization now. I believe if I show them I can play healthy and productive they'll take care of me next year."

Someone pointed out that this was what he thought of the Tigers, too, before his contract ran out.

"Hey," he said, his voice angry, "if it doesn't work, it doesn't work. I'll end up paying for it. Nobody else."

But that is not true. Everybody pays. The Tigers have not only lost their catcher and cleanup hitter, they have lost a gentleman — and gained a critic. Listen to Lance Parrish now:

"I see what the Tigers are doing to the other guys on the team. Where's the loyalty? Everybody talks about loyalty! Arbitration? Yeah. You can win an arbitration, but you have to sit in there and listen to them bad-mouth you the whole time. To me that's not how a grateful employer treats his employes.

"Kirk Gibson had to go through that kind of thing. Jack Morris had to go through it. They cut Larry Herndon down to nothing practically this year. And Darrell Evans? They cut his pay — when he's been the most productive guy on the team the last two years!

"If that's what I've got to look forward to, why should I pursue anything with that club?"

When he said it, his eyes were cross and his expression sour. This was an angry man, and anger was never an emotion you saw much in Lance Parrish — whose strong, grinning, everything-will-work-out style was a fixture in the Tigers' clubhouse for years.

Everybody pays. There are loose ends in this deal that will never be mended. How bad was Parrish's back injury? Each side has a different story. What offers were made in 1985 and 1986? Each side has a different story.

And what difference does it make? He's someone else's hero now. Some other town. Some other park. "Baseball," said the Phillies' new catcher, "has elevated itself — or I should say plunged itself — to the point

180

where all anyone is concerned with is trying to get the upper hand on someone, and cheat them out of everything they can. That's what it's become."

Hear that? That's the bottom line of the Lance Parrish saga. Another player jaded on the game. He is not faultless; he was asking an enormous amount. His agent is not faultless — he played it to the hilt. The Tigers are not faultless, the owners are not faultless. Everybody is to blame. Everybody pays. "This whole thing has been ridiculous," said Parrish. "Everything I didn't want to happen, happened. Like I said, I was naive. I thought I would be different. That's what I learned from all this, that I'm not different. I'm just another employe." If there's a player left in baseball who doesn't feel that way these days, he's either very young or very stupid.

What has been lost in all this? Well. There's an old story about Buzzie Bavasi back when he was handling contracts for the Brooklyn Dodgers in the 1950s — back before athletes used agents. One day Gil Hodges came in all hot about his demands for the next season. Bavasi was ready to pay him $25,000.

Of course, Hodges didn't know this. He demanded $24,000, and not a penny less. "That's a lot of money," Bavasi said. He suggested a game. He would put five pieces of paper into a hat, each piece with a figure between $22,000 and $26,000. "This way," Bavasi said, "you have two chances to exceed your figure, and I have two chances to get you lower." Hodges said OK. Bavasi wrote out the slips. Hodges fished around. He pulled one out of the hat. It read $26,000. "Yahoo!" he yelled. Bavasi shrugged. Fair was fair. Hodges got his money. He never knew that his general manager had written $26,000 on every slip of paper. And Bavasi never told him.

That's what has been lost.

So there goes Lance Parrish. One more heart turned stone cold. This is what all the money is doing. And who on the field Friday even noticed? The equipment manager collected the baseballs, the kid in the Phillies helmet was working on another autograph. Nobody plays taps for spirit. Nobody ever has.

"Well," said a Detroit reporter, offering Parrish a final handshake, "we're going to miss you."

"You'll get over it," he said, and he walked away.

181

MONROE'S DAD KNOWS, AND HE MUST BE PROUD

March 29

NEW ORLEANS — It doesn't matter, all the money and the music and the new clothes and the computers. College is still about kids making their parents proud. It always has been.

The last time Greg Monroe's father came to see him play basketball, Greg was a freshman in high school. It was the first game he would get to start, and Greg recalls his father's only advice: "Do what you gotta do."

That was it. One game. In the games that followed, in the years that followed, through the high school championships and county all-stars and freshman and sophomore and junior years at Syracuse University, all those nights, all those tournaments, Greg Monroe never played before his father again, never saw him waiting in the tunnel after the gym had emptied.

Instead, he "did what he had to do." When the games were over, he visited the hospital, where Walter Monroe would spend the better part of seven years. A stroke put him there. Another stroke robbed him of his speech. Then cancer struck, brain cancer, and yet he somehow survived, he lived for years in that bed, and his son grew up and brought him newspaper clippings and videotapes of his blossoming basketball career.

"We communicated a lot through eye contact," Greg Monroe said. "Every now and then he'd try to mumble a few words. Usually he just smiled, and I guess the smile was telling me, 'Don't worry about it, keep your head up, don't let this situation bother you.'

"That's the kind of guy he was. Very strong."

And then, last summer, Walter Monroe died.

On Saturday afternoon, Greg Monroe was introduced to a thunderous roar inside the sold-out Superdome. The Syracuse Orangemen were in the semifinals of the NCAA tournament, one game from the championship finale. Monroe, a stocky player with sleepy eyes, is their starting guard and co-captain.

The game began and Monroe got the Orangemen's first shot. He went up from the right of the key and buried a three-pointer. And in the stands behind the Syracuse bench, his mother, Mary Monroe, quietly applauded. To almost everyone else watching, he was another college ball player on another magic carpet ride to glory. "Lucky kid," they would mumble, eyeing the screaming fans and the national attention.

Mary Monroe knew better. She knew of the daily hospital visits, of the agonizing silence, of the slow ooze of life that those things bring about. Her son had dedicated this season to her and her late husband. And so well had he played, that his teammates dubbed him "Money" — as in "Money in the bank."

And Saturday, Money delivered. He hit several key three-point baskets; he shut down Providence's Billy Donovan, the man deemed most dangerous in this contest; and then, with less than 12 minutes remaining and Syracuse mired in a sudden slump, Money stole the ball from Delray Brooks, ducked his head and drove the length of the court, dishing off for a basket and getting fouled in the process. The play was worth three points and that, more than any single occurrence, turned the tide back in Syracuse's favor.

The Orangemen would win, 77-63. They are going to the NCAA final, the top of the mountain. And as the last seconds ticked away, it was Monroe dribbling past defenders, his shirt dangling out of his shorts. Do what you gotta do. He had scored 17 points. The TV announcers named him player of the game.

The buzzer sounded and as his teammates leaped up and down, he walked off the court quietly. One more to go for his team. One more for his personal quest.

When the game was over, there was no father to congratulate Greg Monroe, but his mother was there, and she kissed him. And when this is all over, whatever happens Monday night, Monroe plans to go to the Rochester, N.Y., cemetery where his dad is buried. He'll go alone. No crowds, no cameras.

"I'll just have a quiet moment there with him," he said. "It'll be the end of my college career and I'm sure he'd be very pleased to know that I graduated on time, that we had a chance to go to the Final Four, that me and my Mom are coping as best we can."

So it really doesn't matter, all the hype and the attention and even the final score. College is still college. It is largely about one thing. "I just hope my father's proud of me," Greg Monroe said before leaving, and somewhere, no doubt, he is.

INDIANA'S SMART RISES ABOVE THE CROWD

March 31

NEW ORLEANS — A huge electronic TV screen hovered over the Superdome floor Monday night, like God's eyes, and the players below in this NCAA championship flashed across in glorious motion. This was basketball of the '80s, instant-instant replay. Look up and see yourself dribbling. And as the final minutes evaporated before nearly 65,000 crazed spectators, there was only one question in the house: Who would be the star? Who would be the final face on that massive screen, looking down at us all?

No one knew. For this was, after all, a great game, a hell of a game, and everybody on both Indiana and Syracuse seemed to have done something by the end, some basket, some rebound, some steal. So when hysteria set in, the final minute and a half, it was a crapshoot, because the score was tied, 70-70, and anybody could grab the hero's halo. Who would it be? Who would be that face?

First it was Syracuse's Howard Triche, a senior forward who had played a terrible first half, but he leaned in and sank a basket to make it 72-70, and then, on the next possession, he was fouled and he went to the line to ice it with a one-and-one. Only 38 seconds left. Here came Triche's giant face, high above the highest seats, looking down at himself. His first foul shot went in. But his second clanked away — and so did his glory.

And Indiana came back with a short jumper.

So now it's 73-72, and a pass goes to Derrick Coleman, the lanky Syracuse forward, and he's fouled. Just 28 seconds left. Up he walks. Up comes his face on the electronic screen, larger than life. Will it be Coleman? All game long he had played with a swagger beyond his years, a freshman showing no more nerves than if someone had phoned him and said, "Come on down, we got a game going at the schoolyard."

Dribble, dribble. Stop. Shoot. The ball clanked off the side of the rim. Glory would have to wait until Coleman grew older. Indiana grabbed the rebound, and now it trailed by a point, and the clock was down below 10 seconds. Who would be the star? Steve Alford, the IU scoring machine, the best shooter on the team? It would be Alford, right?

It would not be. The ball worked around, and Keith Smart, a junior college transfer and the shortest man on the floor, took the ball to the corner, leaped into the air, and bucket! 74-73! Five seconds left, four, three, two, one. Time out! And Syracuse, with one second left, tried a desperation pass, and who should intercept it but Smart, who squeezed the ball, leaped into the air, and hurled the thing into the stands as the buzzer sounded. Look in the sky! The eye in the sky! It was Smart. It was very Smart.

"What were you thinking? What were you thinking?" reporters screamed at Smart as the mob rushed the floor in celebration. "What was in your mind on the final shot?"

"It just came to me," he screamed, "it just came to me and I hit it!"

Oh, did he hit it! Smart had been the catalyst in this, yet another Indiana comeback — its tightest championship game ever. Bobby Knight's first two championships (1976 and 1981) had been over long before the final seconds. Not this one. For a while it looked as if this would be his first defeat, for Syracuse looked strong, played a great inside game. But when the Orangemen needed their free throws at the finish, they didn't get them. They had been missing them all year. And with everybody looking for Alford, it was Smart who stole the thunder.

"He's been doing it all year!" screamed Alford, his arm around the 6-1 guard. "Whenever they have me covered, Keith's the guy who gets it."

Smart grinned. He had been overlooked somewhat in the hoopla of this contest, the scribes focusing on Alford and Knight, and Rony Seikaly, Coleman and coach Jim Boeheim for Syracuse. Smart had actually been benched midway through the game by Knight. But when it became apparent that this would be an athletic contest, speed and quickness and leaping ability, Knight turned to his best athlete. Smart. Very smart.

"I can't describe how I feel right now!" Smart said. "This is the dream. I can't describe it."

Perhaps Knight can. He should describe it this way: Thank God for junior college. Knight, who had always combed the high schools for his talent, changed his pattern with Smart and Dean Garrett, his center. And the move paid off.

"This is nothing for me," said Knight. "I'm the coach. It's these guys, these players, this is so great for them."

Great for them. Great for the spectators. As the Indiana players stepped up to the hoop to cut the net, the throngs of IU fans went wild.

"Hoooosiers!" They chanted. "Hoooosiers!"

And in the middle was Keith Smart, voted the star of this Final Four. Why not? He had 21 points, he had the crucial points. He had it all.

So here was the finale of a college season that was otherwise dunked in mud, a barrel of recruiting violations, a cover story of a drug scandal, tarnished reputations and tarnished programs and tarnished players. But in the end it came down to a glorious 16-foot jumper by the little guy, who could look up and see himself grinning like a baby on the heavenly scoreboard above. Smart was the face. Very, very Smart.

IS THE SPARK STILL THERE? WHERE ELSE WOULD HE BE?

April 6

Sparky Anderson used to play baseball with Buckwheat. That's right. The Buckwheat. From "The Little Rascals." In a Los Angeles playground, when they were kids. I'm not making this up.

"He'd come in a limo, right from the studio," Anderson says. "He brought all the equipment and the balls. That's the only reason we let him play with us. He was terrible."

Can you picture the two of them, Sparky and Buckwheat, charging from the outfield for the same fly ball?

"Outta my way!"

"O-tay, Sparky."

"I got it! I got it!"

"Ooo-tay!"

Now, I ask you. Can a manager who had this kind of start be thrown by something as ordinary as another baseball season? Can a 53-year-old smoothie, the son of a house painter, the grandson of a Norwegian house painter, a guy who flunked the fifth grade, who once worked as a Rambler salesman, who was a terribly average shortstop, whose hair turned white before his first manager's job, who, in his rookie season as manager, guided the Reds to the World Series, who snared four pennants and five division championships in nine years — then got fired — got a new job, and became the first manager to win championships in both leagues, who says things like "I ain't never had no good education" and "If you don't upchuck now and then, it's time to quit" and who could finish under .500 for the next dozen years and would still rank third on baseball's all-time managers' win list — come on. Can a guy like that be thrown by anything anymore?

"Is The Spark Still There?" the title here reads. As if to say the last two middle-of-the-pack finishes for his Tigers might have siphoned the gas from his tank. As if this is some sort of crucial year for Mr. Sparky.

Perhaps you think so. Here is what I think: I think about the night I watched Anderson pose for a photo — one with fireworks going off behind him. It was cold and windy and they couldn't get the fireworks all lit at once. So they had to shoot it six different times. Six sets of explosions. And Anderson wasn't allowed to move or he'd mess up the picture.

So there he was, on one knee, posing in the middle of a dark empty ballfield, while three prop guys tried to ignite the fireworks behind him. Only the things kept going off in their faces so they were screaming and rushing around and it was like guerrilla warfare because the fireworks make this loud hissing noise and they burn and the prop guys were yelling,

186

"LOOK OUT!" and "RUN FOR IT!" And right in the middle of this, Anderson, whose biggest worry was keeping a smile on his tired cheeks, started singing his laughter, you know, like, "ha-ha-ha-HA-HA-HA-ha-ha-ha," oblivious to all the chaos, all the smoke and the fire and the screams behind him. He was singing to keep his smile. And they got the shot.

And when it was over, he got up, turned around, looked at the burnt-out explosives, and the prop guys who were sprawled in the grass, and he shrugged and trotted back to the clubhouse.

I decided, that night, that very little fazes Sparky Anderson anymore.

Why Sparky doesn't worry, in his own words, reason No. 1: "Gene Mauch don't worry, Whitey Herzog don't worry, Chuck Tanner don't worry, Tommy Lasorda don't worry. . . ."

Let me tell you how Sparky Anderson views this "critical" season. We were sitting in his clubhouse office in Lakeland a few weeks ago, and he was leaning back behind his desk, pipe in hand, and suddenly, he sprang forward and grabbed a piece of paper and a pen.

"Do you know where the experts are picking us this season?" he asked, and he wrote "5th" on the paper and slid it in front of me.

"And do you know what the Las Vegas odds are against us?" he asked, and he grabbed the paper back and wrote "18-1" on it then slid it in front of me again.

"Now," he said, taking the paper back, "what if I finish here?"

He wrote "4th" on the sheet. And again he slid it in front of me. Then he folded his arms behind his head and smiled.

"Hell," he said, "I'm up for manager of the year."

That is how Sparky views this season.

Which is not to say he doesn't care. You could never say that if you knew him. It is to say that after 23 years of managing teams in Rock Hill and Modesto and St. Petersburg and Asheville and Cincinnati and Detroit, Anderson has come to some conclusions: "If we're a fifth-place club, we'll finish fifth. If we're a first-place club, we'll finish first. I ain't gonna do nothing about it. I ain't gonna change us from a fifth-place club to a first-place club.

"Players win and players lose it. Bleep. I was the same guy in '85 as I was in '84. Whitey Herzog's the same guy in '86 as he was in '85. What happened? The players didn't win it. That's what happened.

"It's very simple. If you've got a last-place club, you can send 25 managers in there and it'll still finish last. You can go through history and prove that. Take Casey Stengel. He couldn't win with Brooklyn. He couldn't win with the Braves. Then he got the Yankees, and he could've gone to the Bahamas after spring training. Everybody knows that."

The Bahamas?

Why Sparky Anderson doesn't worry, in his own words, reason No. 2: "I used to call John Wooden, the UCLA basketball coach, and say, 'Hey, John. You got Pepperdine on your schedule? Let's give the Pepperdine coach the night off. You coach Pepperdine, and I'll coach your team. I ain't never coached a basketball team in my life. And you can have the point spread. Whatever it is. Who are we kidding? How you gonna beat me? I got the best horses. The best horses win.' It's that simple."

Now, OK. I hear you. If Sparky Anderson can't turn a fifth-place club into a first-place club, if it's all up to the players, just what is it, you ask, that he does for a living? What difference does the manager make? It is a legitimate question.

In his autobiography, Bear Bryant, the famed Alabama football coach, described his first meeting with a thousand Texas Aggies this way:

"I took off my coat and stomped on it.

"Then I took off my tie and stomped on it.

"Then, as I was walking up to the mike, I rolled up my sleeves."

Now that kind of technique you can understand. That approach works in football. It does not work in baseball. For one thing, you can't just rip off your uniform and stomp on it. The damn things are too tight.

So what is it that Sparky does if his team finishes fifth? "Well, you can be fifth one way and fifth another way," he explains. "Take a look at our clubhouse. It's a professional atmosphere. When the young players come in here, they know immediately what it's going to be. If you're fifth place, but you remain professionals, remain businesslike, eventually you're going to turn things around. Two or three young guys replace the older guys, then two or three more, and then suddenly, you got a hell of a ball club.

"That's what happened here. We had (Lance) Parrish and (Lou) Whitaker and (Alan) Trammell and (Kirk) Gibson. All young kids. And they grew with the system and all of a sudden — wham! — all four were ready, along with Jack Morris and Dan Petry, and it all just fell together. It just clicked.

"The players, like I say, are gonna win it or lose it. What the manager does is create the right mood. Create the system where the right players can succeed. That simple. Hell, my best season of managing, pure managing, was 1978. I got fired."

You can buy this theory, or you can leave it. The problem, critics will point out, is that the Tigers aren't sending in many of those good young kids Sparky refers to. It's mostly the same old kids, with a little less hair. This season, Lance Parrish is gone. Kirk Gibson is hurt. And Detroit just completed the worst spring training record of any team in baseball. Yet Anderson recently proclaimed this "the best spring we've ever had."

But then, he is always doing that. Words don't give him much pause.

Remember, this is the guy who predicted a championship when he arrived in Detroit (which came true), and superstar status for Chris Pittaro (which did not) and who always predicts the sun will come out tomorrow (which it does, though he really can't take credit for that).

Because he juggles his lineup, because he says one thing, then contradicts it the next day, because he always seems to find a silver lining on even the dimmest of hopes, there are many who believe George Lee (Sparky) Anderson is full of it. Here is what I believe. I believe he speaks from the heart, he speaks spontaneously and optimistically and with passion and with a genuine love for the game and the people who play it. And sometimes, he is full of it.

But then, who isn't?

Why Sparky doesn't worry, in his own words, reason No. 3: "You think I'm gonna worry about if the Detroit Tigers are gonna fire me? God Almighty! Let 'em fire me. You know what happened the last time I got fired? I got twice as much from the next club."

There is a point in baseball where it's up to them, and a point where it is up to you. Sparky Anderson — now the 12th-winningest manager in baseball history — says he has reached the latter stage. And he is probably right.

"I'd have to be a bleeping maniac to worry about losing my job," he says, his voice tinged with anger. "I know my stature. I'm not gonna pretend I don't know what I've accomplished.

"Put it this way. We go to the winter meetings. I put all the major league managers in a crowded room, scatter them around. How many of them are you gonna recognize? Who'll be the most recognizable? Who do you think's got the biggest crowd around him?

"You think if I was fired the phone wouldn't be ringing? Let me ask you this. Who won more games than anybody in the 1970s? The Cincinnati Reds. Who won more games than anybody in the 1980s? The Yankees — but you know who's second? The Detroit Tigers. What more can I do for you? You're talking lunacy here when you suggest I should be worried about a job. If I'm worried about a job, there's 24 other guys out there who might as well commit hari-kari."

Which doesn't mean he can't be fired. On the contrary, he expects it sooner or later. (We should note that he did not expect it the one time it happened before — in 1978 with Cincinnati. The Reds had sent him on a winter tour of Japan, used him for promotional purposes, then let him go when he got back. A guy who had won more games than any other manager that decade. He remembers coming home and finding only his youngest son, Albert, in the house. "Your daddy just got fired," he told him. He has never forgotten that.)

These days, Sparky, sufficiently realistic, employs what you might call the Anderson Theory of Animosity: The longer you are anywhere, the more animosity builds up. Eventually the animosity spreads within the organization. Eventually it reaches the top. And eventually you are gone. "Has to happen," he says. "But I never worry about it. Never. That's the truth."

Which, again, does not imply that Sparky doesn't care. On the contrary, he cares plenty — but only about each game. "His intensity is the same now as it was when he was a player," says George Scherger, who was Sparky's first manager back in the early '50s and who, like Billy Consolo and other old-time friends, Sparky always manages to take care of. "He hated to lose, even then. He was crazy about it."

It is true, Anderson's hands still shake when he comes in after the ninth inning. He still vomits a half-dozen nights during the season from anxiety ("My wife laughs. She says, 'I see you were at it again last night'"). But that is warfare. A mandatory element of baseball. Sparky says he will quit if he ever loses those jitters. But they are not the same as worrying about a job.

"If I was fired from the Tigers," he says, "you know what would happen? Jim Campbell would tell me, 'Go on home to Thousand Oaks. I'll see you next week on the golf course.' That's what would happen. Then I'd go home and wait for the phone to ring."

Why Sparky doesn't worry, in his own words, reason No. 4: "You think Pete Rose honestly ever cared who was managing him — me or Dave Bristol or Freddie Hutchinson or any of those guys? For one minute you think he cared? Not for one minute. Not for one second."

So, is the Spark still there? That is really some question. It's true that Anderson has turned more of the club over to his coaches in recent springs. ("I'll be the bad guy soon enough," he says. "Spring's the only chance I have to be the good guy.") But once Opening Day arrives, Sparky is back on center stage. He remains the team leader. Him. Not a player.

Anderson wants to keep managing until he's 65 — half for financial reasons, half because, as he puts it, "Jeez, what else would I do?" Yet winning the big one can no longer mean the same thing now, not because he has done it in both leagues, but because he has seen how quickly its glow evaporates. After his first World Series victory, in 1975, Anderson expected to be the toast of Cincinnati for the winter. Instead, he woke up on Monday and football season was in full swing. He was back-page news. Then no news.

In those days, he used to race around the off-season dinner circuit. He has given up that chase. He rarely makes winter appearances anymore, preferring to stay at home in California. When he does have to give a speech, it takes him a week, he says, to think of an opening line. "In the summertime I can rattle those things off the top of my head.

"In the summer there are so many people around, so many accolades, you start to believe, hey, wait a minute, your opinion really means something. In the winter, I'll be honest, I feel very inadequate. I feel incompetent. I realize without being a baseball manager, nobody would ever pay any attention to me. It's a lack of education. No sense lying about it. You take me out of this uniform, the lack of education is apparent. At least I understand it."

"Understand what?" he was asked.

"That without baseball, I don't have nothing. It don't need me, I need it."

Why Sparky doesn't worry, in his own words, reason No. 5: "I got 24 players. Every one of them has a fan club. Tommy Brookens has a fan club. Kirk Gibson has a fan club. So every time I bench one of them, I lose some fans over here. Every time I take one out of the lineup, I lose some fans over here. The longer I stay around the more I lose. That's the way it works."

So here comes another baseball season. The Tigers are projected to be average at best, and Anderson, who once sold cars on Olympic Boulevard in Los Angeles — "I was excellent until it came to closing a sale" — will put on his full-scale salesman's smile and take charge. And let us not forget a few things before we paste him. He now has the longest tenure of any American League manager working. He is the only guy besides Leo Durocher to win more than 600 games with two different teams. Only once has a major league squad of his finished below .500. There is a reason for this stuff.

People in Detroit may be growing, well, used to him. Maybe tired of him. Yet the delight in this guy is that something new can surface any time. He is the verbal equivalent of water above a sunken ship. We were talking once about nothing special, and suddenly, out of the blue, he admitted that he has never liked people with money, and he has a hard time remembering rich people are not necessarily bad people.

"It's a terrible fault I have," he said softly, "but I feel so inferior around them."

And then someone walked in and his voice jumped three octaves and he was chattering about curveballs as though the previous conversation never took place.

I don't know whether Sparky Anderson is the best manager going. I will tell you this. You don't find his players bad-mouthing him. You don't hear whispers behind his back. You don't hear rumblings. Some would say that's because anyone who rumbles will be gone. There is some truth to that.

191

"A ball player who blames the manager for his problems is an ass," says Anderson. "Why would I want to spend seven months around an ass?"

That makes sense to me.

So take him or leave him. Complain that he yanks pitchers too fast. That he tinkers with the lineup. Is the Spark still there? Sure. Where else would he go? Anderson has reached that rare stage where the dugout is his privilege, not his prison. He can sit there, pipe in hand, talking baseball and dishing out the philosophy like an army chef dishes out mashed potatoes. First place? Fifth place? What, him worry? This is a guy who played with Buckwheat.

"You know," he muses, "I asked Vin Scully once, 'What does success mean?' He said, 'For the moment.' That's all it means. No more. Some guys seem to think one success should last them a lifetime. Shoot. Those guys don't last.

"What does success mean? For the moment. That's the greatest piece of philosophy I ever heard. Yes, sir. That's what I believe. That, and one other thing. 'Don't tell me, show me.' I love that philosophy, too. I believe it with all my heart. 'Don't tell me, show me.' Oh yes."

"Who said that?" he is asked. "Herzog? Stengel? Connie Mack?"

"I seen it on a bumper sticker," he says.

LEONARD VS. HAGLER: GREAT FIGHT, GREAT CON

April 8

L AS VEGAS, Nev. — Sugar Ray Leonard was hanging on the shoulders of his trainers, his legs stringy, his expression dazed, and Marvin Hagler was doing a boogaloo shuffle in the middle of the ring. This was the paradox of what they're calling "the greatest return in boxing history," because in seconds, Leonard would be crowned the winner by split decision, the new middleweight champion, the comeback kid of all time, and Hagler, the guy doing the dance, would be thrown to the wolves.

"Oh, Jesus. . . ." Hagler would cry when the decision was announced, his seven-year middleweight reign over. "Oh, come on. . . . I won this fight! . . . They stole it. . . . Come on! . . ." He was babbling, walking in circles, he still looked strong, his muscles taut, his face wore no blood after 12 rounds, nor did Leonard's, but Leonard was exhausted over in the other corner, and his mother was kissing him, then his wife was kissing him. The cameras worked their way through the crowd and suddenly, almost imperceptibly, he seemed to straighten, and then he winked, and you knew he'd had this thing all along.

Leonard wins! And in the aftermath of this mini-war, Hagler and his camp would blame the 12-round limit — to which they had agreed at Leonard's insistence, although championship fights are usually 15 — and they would say Marvin was the aggressor, and they would point to Sugar Ray's exhausted collapse after the final bell as evidence their man was better. "He was dead on his feet!" Hagler would moan. "He couldn't have gone another round."

He didn't need to. Know this. Leonard won this fight. He was exhausted because he executed his plan perfectly, he used the last drop of gas in the tank while Hagler was left with a boxer's most useless possession, a surplus of strength. He had plenty left. He could have knocked out five men. But he had lost the fight, without a cut, without a knockdown and without a single punch that even registered a stun.

How could Leonard, inactive for nearly three years, come to this desert, move up a weight class, and steal the belt right off Hagler's waist? Easy. He came as Hagler's nightmare. He came as himself.

And this fight was all but over before it started.

S ugar Ray Leonard had haunted Marvin Hagler's sleep for years. Like a wallflower watching a prom queen, Leonard seemed to Hagler all he could never be: glib, witty, younger, a sweetly heroic persona with a face for TV and an Olympic gold medal to get him there.

And what was Marvin? A wolf. He scared people. He was brooding, silent, bald-headed with a goatee. Women and children never approached him the way they would Sugar Ray. Hagler had no medal, he was right off the streets, the Newark ghettos, and when he started fighting in Pat and Goody Petronelli's gym in Brockton, Mass., it was strictly small-time, earn your way up. He got 50 bucks for his first pro fight.

In another life, Hagler, 32, and Leonard, 30, might never have met. But in boxing, they reached a peak like two men climbing different sides of the same mountain. Hagler fought twice as often and made half as much, and every time he saw Sugar Ray, sweet Sugar Ray, dancing Sugar Ray, popular Sugar Ray, he was just waiting for the chance to face this little squirt in the only place they might be equal.

Both men became champions. And then Leonard retired in 1982, a rich man with eye problems. Hagler ached. He came to Leonard's retirement press conference. "It'll never happen," Leonard said to him then of their bout. "It's over." Hagler's chance was gone.

He fought other men, beat them, made money, but it was like dancing with every girl except the one you really want. So when the talk started last year that Leonard — after several years as a TV commentator — wanted a fight, one fight, only with Hagler, well, forget the delay and Hagler's retirement plans. Those who really knew the champion knew it was a yes.

Deep down, Leonard knew it, too. "Hagler has this thing about me. He is obsessed," Leonard said. The challenger used that knowledge to hold out for 1) the gloves he wanted, 2) the ring he wanted, 3) the 12 rounds he wanted. Hagler gave in on all three.

Obsession. Muhammad Ali, in his prime, had opponents beaten simply by being who he was. They could never get past that. In the five years from Leonard's first retirement, Hagler — bitten by such a bug — had been chasing his ghost, looking for the kind of adulation Sugar Ray once commanded. And he never got it. Oh, the men Hagler beat! Duran. Hearns. Mugabi. Beat them decisively. Took every challenge. Yet, he looked in the mirror and he was still Hagler. "You guys," he would lecture the press, "you never give me the credit a champion deserves. Everybody talks about Sugar Ray, Sugar Ray. . . ."

In Hagler's mind, Leonard was now more than an opponent. He was a demon, a nightmare. And slowly, Hagler began to sense, in the dungeons of his heart, that he somehow did not deserve to take over Leonard's pedestal. Sugar Ray was now larger than life. And Hagler was his to beat.

When the fight began Monday night in that ring in the middle of Caesars Palace parking lot, Hagler didn't throw a punch for 30 seconds. Leonard taunted him from the beginning, first refusing to look at him during the handshake, then refusing to look away. Leonard scored with the first combination. He flitted about like a bug.

For that round and the next and the next, Leonard was pure motion, he drew Hagler in, herky-jerky, as if attached by a loose string. He played peek-a-boo, he stuck his chin out. In the fourth, he suckered Hagler with a bolo punch to the right kidney. The crowd roared. Hagler was off-balance, switching between righty and southpaw, missing badly, and never once landing a truly painful punch.

Understand the psychology at work here. Leonard was acting out all the things Hagler hated him for — the showboating, the quickness, the fluid grace. The more he did this, the more angry Hagler became. And the more anger, the more fuel for Sugar Ray. "Hagler doesn't get tired, he gets frustrated," Leonard said last week. "If he goes back to his corner shaking his head, I've got him."

He had him. That early. The judges awarded the first four rounds to Leonard — so right there, if this was going the distance, Sugar Ray had money in the bank. Hagler continued to stalk him relentlessly, throwing wild punches for Leonard's head, not his body. Body shots would have been smarter, they would have slowed Leonard down, but Hagler wanted a definitive statement. He wanted to kill the devil, once and for all.

In the fifth, Hagler landed blows, he shortened the ring, and he won the round; but in the sixth, he got Leonard in a corner and still couldn't score. The emotion of the long wait, the years, the buildup, seemed to hit Hagler like a sudden injection, and while Leonard could not hurt him, he could not unleash any bombs himself. So for much of the round, much of the fight really, they were at a dance, chasing and flicking and tap-tap-tap, get in, get out, circle, flurry, take one, give one. This was Sugar Ray's type of fight and Hagler knew it.

Now, frustration began its drum roll. At one point in the seventh round, Hagler stuck his tongue out at Leonard. He was trying to beat Leonard at his own game — showmanship — and that was fatal. Leonard danced and feinted, and lay against the ropes, a la Ali, and then moved away.

And then came the ninth, and Hagler's sky caved in. Four times, Leonard engaged him in toe-to-toe exchanges, and four times Leonard danced away with little damage. Leonard lost that round on two of three cards, but he found his second wind.

Now in Hagler's corner, they were worried. They had been this route before, against Vito Antuofermo in 1979, Hagler's first title shot, and that one went the distance and Hagler should have won but it was called a draw and Antuofermo kept his crown. All week long, Hagler had boasted how he would let his fists, "K" and "O," be the judges, because leaving it to judges in Las Vegas was like suicide. "We need these two! Don't let up!" Goody Petronelli urged him in the 11th.

So the fight for Hagler had reached desperation. Where was Sugar Ray? He could whup him if he could find him. But Leonard was in his element now, sensing victory, moving and dancing. He ducked under a bad miss by Hagler and taunted him with a windmill fake. Had there been four more rounds, Hagler might have taken his time, worn Leonard down, clubbed him with a killer punch. But that is why Leonard wanted 12. And before that final round, he raised his hands in apparent victory and taunted Hagler to come to the center of the ring, he wanted to shake his hand.

Hagler was outfoxed. Three minutes later — in the din of the crowds chanting "SUG-AR RAY! SUG-AR RAY!" — it was over. Hagler claims Leonard told him, "You beat me, man," prompting his boogaloo dance. But when the decision was read, it was two judges for Leonard, one for Hagler, and one of the judges, somebody named Jo Jo Guerra, actually scored it 118-110 for Sugar Ray, giving Hagler just two rounds. "That guy ought to be in jail," Pat Petronelli would say. "We were jobbed."

When Leonard came out from his post-fight dressing room, he was wearing a yachting cap and a T-shirt. His face was pretty. "I got something to say," he began, pulling out a list of fight "experts" who had predicted a Hagler win. "Let's see here. . . ."

No one groaned. He was entitled. This was a remarkable feat no matter what, springing from retirement to a title. It was something Jim Jeffries couldn't do in 1910 and Joe Louis couldn't do in 1950 and Ali couldn't do in 1980. Leonard had done it against a beast, a man whom he had seen looking at him, envying him. Obsession. Sugar Ray Leonard had Marvin Hagler's number and Leonard knew it all along. "I didn't want the belt," Leonard said of the WBC middleweight title, "I just wanted to beat him."

A half-hour later, Hagler, too, would emerge, looking weary, not beat up. "I've never seen a split decision go against a champion. . . ." he would say. "I feel as if I'm still the champion. . . ."

But, all right. These are merely words, and the words of a fighter are no more reliable than the fists of a politician. Fighters speak with their bodies, and in the final rounds Monday night, Hagler's said defeat, he had been stumped, stymied, tripped up by light punches and fast footwork and a psych job that he knew was coming. And that must have been the worst part. Like a man who can stay awake no longer, Hagler closed his eyes and found his old nightmare — right in front of him. "I knew this would happen," he mumbled at one point.

Hagler lost everything on this fight — his title, his streaks, his "unbeatable" reputation — and in weeks to come, second-guessers may wonder why on earth he ever took it. It is a useless question. Obsession does not die with the bell. Marvin Hagler never had a choice.

YOU MUST PLAY HARDBALL TO WIN AT SOFTBALL

April 15

L et us deal today with a timely sports question. How do you choose a company softball team?

I can answer this. The answer is, there are lots of ways. My favorite way is in a bar, late at night, with a hat, 50 pieces of paper, and a group of people who like to sing in Swedish, even though they don't speak Swedish. And plenty of ice. But that is just my way. And I don't hit very well.

Others take the process more seriously. In fact, to certain types — investment bankers, account executives, anyone from New York — softball leagues have become roughly the equivalent of, oh, say, holy war.

So how do you compete? First of all, because it is already April, it is too late to even ask such a question. In today's competitive business world, the winning softball teams make up their rosters back in November. They conduct spring training in Florida. Several players actually are under contract. They will never admit this. But if you know a burly salesman who hasn't met a quota in years, chances are he's somebody's first baseman.

Still, there is hope for your group. Their bus could crash. Or corporate headquarters might phase out their entire division. And if that kind of luck should strike, you better be ready.

Here then, as a public service, and I don't do this for everybody, are my 26 tried and tested methods for picking a winning softball team. And I emphasize the word winning, which is not the same as wearing a sweatshirt and waking up with a hangover. Ready?

1. Never pick the boss.
2. Never pick the boss' secretary.
3. Pick Vinny from the shipping department. If there is no Vinny, pick Frank. No doubt Frank will know a Vinny, probably from some other shipping department, and Vinny will know another Vinny. Or Eddie. So you end up with three guys, either Vinny, Vinny and Vinny, or Frank, Vinny and Vinny, or Frank, Vinny and Eddie. This is your starting outfield.
4. Never pick a Seth.
5. If you hold open tryouts, and a player shows up with a large radio on his shoulder, grab him.
6. Unless the radio is playing Barry Manilow.
7. Are we dealing with co-ed teams? We are?
8. In that case, anyone named Brenda gets on automatically.
9. Take anyone with his own ice chest. (If you do not understand this, you should join the company racquetball league, where they drink Perrier.)

10. No vice-presidents.

11. Never take a guy wearing a batting glove. Batting gloves do nothing. Batting gloves are an excuse for people to spend $10, so the owner of the sporting goods store can take his wife to France.

12. Anyone with a tattoo starts.

13. Two tattoos bats cleanup.

14. IMPORTANT TIP: LOOK AT THE GLOVE. If it is ratty and frayed and has masking tape all over it, you want the guy. If it is shiny and orange and is signed by Rusty Staub, you better pass.

15. If he owns spikes, he's in.

16. Never take the boss. I know we covered this already. I don't want you to forget.

17. ANOTHER IMPORTANT TIP: LOOK AT THE CAR. As a general rule, people who drive Volkswagen beetles make good softball players. I don't know why this is. But then, I don't know why Vinny from shipping is so good, year after year. I do know I have never seen a decent softball player pull up in a Chrysler New Yorker. Ever.

18. No more than four players with glasses.

19. Only a player named "Pepper" or "Spike" or "Scooter" can be your shortstop. But only if that is his real name. Have him bring a birth certificate. I mean, anyone can call himself "Scooter," right? You want the guy whose parents thought it up.

20. Pick someone with spare bats.

21. Get at least one person from sales. Even if he or she can't play, at least you'll find out what all those other sneaky salespeople are planning.

22. Choose a loud and obnoxious catcher. One who will say to a batter, "Hey. If you had a brain, you'd be outside playing with it." Don't worry about angering the opponents. You have Frank, Vinny and Eddie, remember?

23. NEVER PICK THE BOSS! Just a reminder.

24. No Dr Pepper drinkers. I don't trust them.

25. If Rita, the redheaded receptionist, is at all interested, sign her up. The hell with her average.

26. (In the case of an all-female team, the above words "Rita, the redheaded receptionist," should be replaced by, "Sven, the tall, blond shipping clerk." And to hell with his average.)

So there you have it. Of course, these rules apply only if your goal is to win the softball trophy and go to the awards dinner. Once you do that, everyone else in the company will wish you a slow death, and you will, naturally, have no future outside of the shipping department.

But for you, it may be worth it. On the other hand, if your goal is to get ahead in business, I advise only two things:

Pick your boss. And let him play shortstop.

A SHOT, A BLOODSTAIN, AND LIFE GOES ON

April 19

The blood is still there, on the asphalt, in sad little stains. When the sun is hot, the stains seem to take color, to wet, and the kids from the neighborhood ride their bikes past and say, "That's where he got it, man. Right here. Damn! Chester!" And then they ride on, past the rusted green trash dumpster to the basketball courts. No guards at this burial ground. This is a public high school. When a student gets shot in the middle of lunch, in the middle of the parking lot, for nothing, and now he's dead, there is a ripple of pause and then everything goes on.

Kids and bullets.

On the day after the murder, Robert Jackson, a ninth-grader who weighs maybe a hundred pounds, was sitting in a hot dog joint on West Warren Avenue across from the school, Murray-Wright High School. A newspaper was folded on the table in front of him. The headline read "STUDENT SHOT DEAD, 2 INJURED." He stared at it.

"Did you know Chester?" someone asked.

"Yup," he said softly. "I knew him."

"Was he a friend of yours?"

"Yup."

"Did you see what happened?"

"I was in the cafeteria."

"Do you know who shot him?"

"He was a tall kid."

"A tall kid?"

"Yeah. Light-skinned. But I don't know him."

"But he had the gun?"

"Yup."

"What kind of gun?"

"A .357."

"Where'd he get a gun like that?"

"From the street maybe."

"He bought it?"

"Probably so."

"What's a gun like that cost on the street?"

"Maybe a hundred dollars."

"Was this kid in your grade?"

"Yup."

He fidgeted in his chair.

"How old are you?"

"Fourteen."

Kids and bullets.
The day before, Chester Jackson Jr., 17, a star running back for Murray-Wright, had been shot in the head by this tall ninth-grader. And now Jackson is dead. And another student, Damon Mathews, 18, a senior on the basketball team, is in the hospital with a bullet wound in the face. And the suspect, who reportedly tried to look tough as the police drove him away, is in a youth home awaiting a hearing.

It is the second shooting in a Detroit public school in less than three months. No one is sure why this trigger was pulled. What kind of reason do you think? The "assailant" was 14 years old. There is one story about a food fight. There is one story about a chase. There is one in which the last words Chester Jackson said to the kid before being snuffed out were, "Why are you shooting at me?"

There are stories.

Robert got up to buy some cookies. He slid his money under the bulletproof glass over the counter. Then he sat back down.

"What do you remember?" he was asked.

"We were sitting in the lunchroom, and we heard the gunshot and everybody started running. I went outside and I saw Chester lying on the ground where the kid shot him."

"Was he still alive?"

"Yup."

"How do you know?"

"I saw his hands moved, and his eyes were open. The janitor was saying, 'Don't move. Don't move.' "

"The janitor?"

"Uh-huh."

"Then what?"

"They told us to go back into school."

"And?"

"And we went back into school."

"And? . . . "

"And the janitor put a coat over Chester's head."

The kid spoke softly, but without horror. He is 14. He has seen guns before. He has even fired one. Children, you might feel, should never be exposed to such things. But this is the inner city, the veins of Detroit, a place that most of us forgot about in between headlines. Today politicians are making statements and parents are screaming for changes. But it's the kids, the Murray-Wright students, who must endure security guards and police officers and ID checks, and none of it was enough on

Thursday. A few days earlier, Robert said, a man walked into the school, into a classroom, beat up a female teacher — "she was his girlfriend" — then walked out. Untouched.

"They told everyone it was a student who did it," he said. But he and his friends claim otherwise. Until Thursday, however, even Robert had never seen someone killed. Now he has. In cold blood. He is a member of the richest potential resource of our city: He is a student in our public schools. This is his education.

"Our security ain't s—," he said.

A friend came into the food store, Armondo Neal, broad-shouldered with short hair and a little goatee. Armondo was wearing a sweatshirt and a blue cap. He said he was 16. And a friend of Chester's.

"Gimme some," he said to Robert, grabbing a piece of his cookie.

"Not so much, man!" Robert protested.

The two walked outside and leaned against a fence, watching the cars. School was out. Easter break. The shooting had taken place just a few hours before vacation.

Robert looked sad. He grabbed the links of the fence and pulled himself back and forth. Armondo started talking about Chester, about the Public School League final a few years ago, and the football game in which Chester ran for 109 yards. "Chester was dominating," Armondo said.

"Where did the kid get the gun that killed him?" he was asked.

"He can get a gun anywhere around here."

"Anywhere?"

"You just find somebody on the street. You see the guy, you say, 'Hey man, I need a piece.' Easy as that. He says, 'How much money you got?' You say, 'I got 50 dollars.' He says, '50 dollars will buy you a .38.' You say, 'Awright, that'll do.' He says, 'I'll be right back.' He comes back with a bag, you give him the 50, he gives you the gun. Just like that."

"Even a 14-year-old?"

"Don't matter how old you are if you've got the money."

A car passed and the driver waved. Armondo waved back. Robert was still quiet, hanging on the fence.

"What would you do to that kid if he were here now?" they were asked.

"I'd tie him to a pole and break his ribs and his arms and his legs," Armondo said quickly, his voice rising. "I wouldn't kill him, but I'd make him wish like he was dead."

"Wouldn't that be just as bad as what he did to Chester?"

"Yeah, but there'd be a point. I'd be thinking, 'I'm doing this for Chester.' I wouldn't mind going to jail for beating that boy. They'd ask me why I did it? I'd say, 'Because he killed Chester.' They'd say, 'Who were you to Chester?' I'd say, 'He was my friend.'

201

"You know, when I heard the news, I cried, man! A guy crying for another guy? But we were in the same grade together. I owed the blood five dollars man, to this day! I felt for him! I didn't want it to be him. Out of all people, it's like, damn! Chester! Why Chester? Why Chester? Why Chester?"

Armondo paused. He cocked his head, as if listening to his words float away.

"What would you do to the kid?" the question was repeated to Robert, who was staring at his shoes.

"I'd beat him down," he said softly.

n the street "blood" is a word for friend, brother, a fellow black. At about 3 p.m., Robert and Armondo crossed Warren Avenue to look at the blood of their blood, near the trash dumpster in the Murray-Wright parking lot. Every now and then a car would pull up, and people would get out and whisper and point, and then they'd shake their heads and get back in the car and drive away.

Robert and Armondo, who have already seen too much for their years, stared without words at the blood stains. Then they wandered over to a nearby concrete wall and lifted themselves up. Another friend, a small kid with a big head whom they called "Peanut," came by and sat with them.

"Chester, man," said Armondo. "He was gonna be a pro football player. Born to play football! You'd see him run into a pile of guys, it seemed like they got him and all of a sudden you'd see the blood with his head up, going down the field, sprinting."

"He was the best," said Peanut.

"He was the best Murray-Wright ever had!" said Armondo, gesturing with his hands. "He'd come out fired up for every game. He'd be banging on his helmet. He'd say, 'Ain't nobody stopping me, I'm Herschel Walker!' "

"He's Herschel Walker!" laughed Peanut.

"Damn!" said Armondo. "He was gonna go to a big college somewhere, like, um, he might've gone to, what's that, UCLA?"

"Yeah!" said Peanut.

"UCLA," said Robert.

"And I can say I knew Chester a long time."

"He's my boy."

"He was in the fifth grade with me," said Armondo. "We went on a school trip to Boblo Island and I ran out of money and he give me five dollars. And he ain't never pressed me for it."

"No."

"Nuh-uh. He'd see me at Murray-Wright and he'd say, 'You got my five dollars, Mondo?' and I'd say, 'Aw, Chester, man, you caught me broke again.' And he'd say, 'Ain't no thing. You want a hamburger?' And I'd say, 'Yeah.' And he'd buy me a hamburger.

"Damn! I wanted to see him go to college so I could brag about him. You know, like we'd be somewhere, when we're grown up, watching the football game and I'd say, 'Yo man. I know Chester Jackson.' And they'd say, 'Bull, you don't know Chester Jackson.' And I'd pull out a picture and say, 'Man, you wanna see a picture of me and him?' "

"Yeah!" laughed Peanut.

"Put your money where your mouth is," said Robert.

"HE'S A PRO FROM THE GHET-TO!" yelled Armondo.

"And he'd never dog you, man," said Peanut. "He didn't care if you were small or a freshman, he'd treat you the same way. We were wrestling with him the other day, me and Robert, right, Robert?"

"That's right."

"He didn't hurt us, though."

"Blood was straight," said Armondo. "He never used drugs, he never drank. He just had football and his girlfriends. That was his thing. He earned everything he got. He wouldn't start a fight. If somebody called him a name he'd say, 'I ain't got time for you.'

"And he never failed a grade either. I don't think he ever failed. He was smart. I failed a couple times, and when I got here to Murray-Wright you know what he said? He said, 'Damn, Mondo! It's about time you got here.' "

They stopped and caught their breath, the three of them, sitting on a concrete wall, paying homage. In certain religions, it is a custom to remember the dead in a wake. This was the schoolyard wake. Chester Jackson, a good kid who should still be here today, but is not.

"He made you want to come to school," said Armondo. "Even if it was just to play with him. You'd say, 'Today I'm gonna chase around Chester.' It made you want to come."

Can there be a sweeter tribute?

As the afternoon wore on, more and more kids from the neighborhood came by. They brought basketballs. They rode bicycles. They were 14 and 15 and 16 years old, from the row houses off Vermont Street and Putnam Street and Rosa Parks Boulevard. They wore Adidas sneakers without shoelaces, and caps turned backward. Most of them stopped at the blood stains for a moment, still dribbling the balls, then continued on.

Mourners.

"Are you scared now?" the kids were asked.

"I ain't scared," said Armondo. "That kid is in jail today. I'll bet he's saying, 'Damn! I shouldna done no s— like that. It was wrong.' "

"The security in our school is so bad," said Peanut. "They don't ever check for guns."

"In some ways I'm scared, and some ways, I ain't," said Robert.

"Which ways?"

"The way I'm scared is, if I mess with the wrong person now, he might pop me."

"Pop you?"

"Shoot me."

"You worry about that now?"

"Uh-huh."

"In what way aren't you scared?"

"Well, if I do get away from the guy, I just live down the street, so I have protection."

"You mean because you live a few blocks away, you think someone couldn't catch you if he had a gun?"

He looked off for a moment. "Not if I had speed like Chester."

"Chester had the utmost speed!" said Armondo.

"The utmost speed!" Robert echoed.

No one corrected them. What's the point? Chester is gone. Athlete or no athlete. Star or no star. We can forget sometimes that our football heroes are human, too, in high school they are just kids, and kids should never know from bullets, but this has happened, it is horrible, tragic, and it is not new.

Today and tomorrow they will be arguing about random gun searches at the Detroit high schools. Parents will demand hand-held metal detectors, the type they use at airports. Tighter security. Constant checking. More police. More guards. Gun sweeps. Locked doors. High school. Why Chester? Why Chester? Why Chester? Here is what we have become. Kids and bullets.

"Will you go to the cemetery for a funeral?" the kids were asked.

"That's one place I won't go," said Robert Jackson, shaking his head. "I won't go to no graveyard."

"Why not?"

"I don't like 'em. All the tombstones and stuff."

He pushed himself off the concrete wall and unzipped his jacket. He walked within inches of the blood stains of Chester Jackson, the blood of their blood, which glistened now in the heat. And he continued on. He was going to play basketball.

"Graveyards give me the creeps," he said.

ISIAH HAS FACE OF A CHILD
AND BURDENS OF A LEADER

April 26

I t's over! It's all over! The Pistons win the NBA championship, the seventh game of the final series, and the sellout crowd at the Pontiac Silverdome is screaming, delirious, dancing in the aisles. And here comes Isiah Thomas, the hero of the game, bursting into the locker room. And there he goes. Out the back door.

The back door?

Within seconds he is in the parking lot. He jumps into his car, still in uniform, the sweat still moist on his skin, and hits the gas. Off he drives, fast as a blink, one mile, two miles, five miles, off, until he reaches a park, any park, quiet and empty and very far from the celebration he just started.

"And then?" someone asked. "What do you do in the park?"

"I sit there," he said, shrugging, "and be happy."

T his is Isiah Thomas' championship fantasy. And OK. 'Tis the season for dreaming. But what do you think? Leave the building and go to a park? What would Freud call it? The Id and the He-go? Oedipus Zeke?

Call it classic Isiah. For Thomas, who has led the Pistons since he was 20, is at 25 still a mix of innocence and grizzle. He can be seriously silent. He can laugh as if hearing God's first joke. He creates basketball brilliance, and studies its implications, like a kid who invents dynamite in his basement, then hides in the attic to peek at his family's reaction.

For all his wellspring of talent — and you felt a splash of it Friday night in his 34-point performance against Washington — for all his years in Chicago's mean streets, the time under Bobby Knight at Indiana, the wins, the losses, the travel, the coaching changes, the new teammates, there is still wonder inside Isiah Thomas. There is still a wide-eyed fascination.

And here is what he sees today: Happy days. For this, he says, is the best team he has ever been on.

"There's no comparison. We're better in every aspect of the game. In years past, we used to really have to gear up to play in playoff-type basketball. With the team we have now, all we have to do is be ready."

"Do you think you'll surprise people in the playoffs?" he was asked.

"The only people we'll surprise are people outside the game," he said quickly. "Everybody inside basketball already knows how good we are."

O n Friday night, Thomas himself looked awfully good, a one-man force in the Pistons' 106-92 opening-round win over the Bullets. Tonight he will go at it again. By now Detroit has come to recognize his game:

205

a happy-faced whippoorwill weaving through sequoia trees, in, out, in, out, driving to the basket, dishing off, arching soft high lay-ups, almost cooing as he goes, drawing your attention like a magnet draws steel.

That is his style. It has been for a while. So those who just tuned in to this season Friday night may have said to themselves, "Yep. Same as usual. Still the Isiah Thomas Show in Detroit."

They are mistaken.

Friday night aside, this has not been the easiest of seasons for Thomas. Change is never easy. And with the addition of Adrian Dantley, Sidney Green, Dennis Rodman, John Salley and Kurt Nimphius, he has had to change. His game has been resculptured. At times he has heard it criticized ("He tries to do too much," goes a gripe among certain media members). Meanwhile, he has had to tiptoe around his mouth, making sure he said nothing that could be interpreted as trouble between him and Dantley, "because if I did, it would be headlines the next day." And on top of everything, he has had to endure a persistently sore left knee that kept him from practicing Saturday and may require surgery after the season.

Yet the team has jelled. That is largely to his credit. The personality clash with Dantley never materialized. Once the Pistons got used to each other, they got used to winning, tying the best record in club history with 52 victories. And while he is no longer the leading scorer (Dantley averaged 21.5 points a game, Thomas 20.6), playoff time will reveal that Thomas is still the leader. Even Dantley will tell you: "This is Isiah's team. He is the man."

"Are you comfortable with that phrase, 'Isiah's team'?" Thomas was asked. "It doesn't bother me," he said.

"Do you like it?"

"I never thought about it to like it or not. You gotta understand, ever since I was 20, when I first came here, it was my team. I was the leader."

"You were, or you were expected to be?"

"I was," he said.

D id you know that Isiah Thomas often drives to Detroit area parks by himself and watches kids play basketball? He never gets too close, he says, and he never interferes. "I just like to watch. See if the ball goes in. Since I was a kid I always went to the park. I even swing on the swings."

"Still?" he was asked.

"Yep," he says.

He swings on the swings. You hear that, you look at him, that kindergarten grin, and it's hard to remember he is a six-year veteran in this league. That he has waited a fair time to be on a championship team. That he has played more than 400 grueling professional games, his knees and ankles and wrists taking the nightly pounding.

He has been with the Pistons longer than any player on their roster, and the changes he has seen — and brought about — in the franchise are significant. Years ago, this was a mediocre team that had to be dragged into the win column. "Now," Thomas said, "there's not a player in this league who wouldn't want to play in Detroit.

"You talk about Detroit now, you're talking about a great place to play basketball. We sell out every night, we lead the league in attendance.

"In this league, a guy gets traded to Boston, he's happy. A guy gets traded to LA, he's happy. A guy gets traded to Detroit now, he's happy. Ask Sidney Green, who came from Chicago. That's the change."

He sighed.

"It happens with winning."

Thomas takes a lot of pride in the winning. Pride runs deep in him. And this is the other side of Isiah; older, wiser, stubborn enough to play hurt. Despite his gentle public persona, he is protective of his turf, of his role, of his leadership. He is giving it away to no one.

"You know, even if I never won a championship," he said, "but the team won one after I left, I could take a lot of gratification in that."

"How's that?" he was asked.

"Because I started it. I more or less planted the seed for this franchise to be good for a very long time."

"How does one person do that?" he was asked.

"By winning a lot of games."

Now, he said, it is time to win more. The Pistons have been a team in recent years that makes the playoffs, then exits early. Thomas has had enough of that. So have the fans. "I think this is the basketball team the Detroit fans have been waiting for," he said. "The fans here are not like the fans in, say, Boston. In Boston, they expect their team to make the finals. Here the fans are ecstatic if the team has a legitimate chance."

"Does this team fit that description?" he was asked.

"Oh yes," he said.

So it's fantasy time, the playoffs, you dream about winning it all. And Thomas, the veteran youngster, can still fantasize about that moment, that getaway drive in his sweaty uniform, with the echo of championship holler still in his ears. Drive to the park? That is really what he'd do if the Pistons won it all?

"Well," he said, "that's mostly what I fantasize. But there are times I think it would be nice to celebrate, too. You know, hang in the locker room, pour the champagne on each other, go crazy and everything."

"Wait a minute," someone interrupted. "Those are pretty different fantasies."

"I've had a lot of time to think about it," he said.

A TOOT OF THE HORN
FOR JACQUES DEMERS

May 3

Sometime this afternoon, I will drive to Jacques Demers' house and honk the horn. And that should make two bikers in this city very happy. I am talking about the two guys in leather jackets and leather pants and spiked hair and boots who stopped me outside Joe Louis Arena before the first game of this Toronto-Detroit playoff series. This was all they wanted to know: "Did you drive Jacques to the game tonight?"

And I said no, not this time.

"Damn!" they said, groaning. "You gotta drive him, man! You gotta! You're the good luck charm! Damn! Now what? Now we're gonna lose!"

And I shrugged.

And I went inside.

And the Red Wings lost.

So relax guys. I will honk. He will get in. I am not sure when my car and the fortunes of the Red Wings actually became intertwined. I do know Jacques Demers and I have now driven to five playoff games together and Detroit has won all five, and now even Demers, who is not superstitious, is asking me what time we're leaving. And it has been great fun, and a little spooky. And it will end today. No matter what.

I will be honest; it is not without some regret. What began as a simple interview on the way to Demers' first Detroit playoff game — and the column that got the bikers so worked up — has turned into a sort of regular appointment with this quixotic hockey coach, the way two buddies might meet for breakfast on Saturday morning, or carpool in from the suburbs. Bowling night. Bridge night. The ride to the game.

"You ready to go?" I say.

"I'm ready," he says.

And six hours later they win.

Not bad, huh?

But there is more. In the last two weeks, I have done "the drive" with Demers in Detroit, Chicago and Toronto. I have heard him talk hockey, weather, his wife, the Kentucky Derby, airplanes, music, French, Greg Stefan and truck driving. I have seen him joke with toll collectors. I have seen a Canadian customs officer ask for his autograph. I have even parked in his Joe Louis Arena parking spot. Once. Just to see what it was like. (The answer is: It is near the door.)

And I will tell you this: The guy is a great car-pool partner. He doesn't play with the windows, he doesn't tune to country music stations. He is also very tough to figure out. You get the feeling you are carting around two men; one a general who is in complete control, the other a baby leprechaun, absorbing the human race with wide-eyed wonder.

Take, for example, the first ride in from Windsor — Game 1 against the Blackhawks — where we drove along the river and he suddenly said: "You know, I love water. It makes me calm. I like to stand by the hotel window and just look out on it and see the Detroit skyline, and say, 'Tonight, over there, there's gonna be a big hockey game.'"

Or the time in Chicago, when we drove through a rundown section of the west side, dirt-poor, and Demers couldn't take his eyes off of it: "Look at that. To live like that. . . . We have no right to complain. Jeez. Look at that."

Before Friday night's Game 6 in Toronto, certainly the biggest game of the season so far, Demers told me to take a sudden right turn en route to Maple Leaf Gardens: "Let's drive up Yonge Street. You'll see how beautiful it is. . . . Look at all these shops. Wow."

And yet, there was also the ride after he benched Stefan, the team's No. 1 goalie. He'd told the media Stefan "would not see the Leafs again" and he asked what I thought, and, trying to be nice, I said he probably wished he hadn't made that statement. And he said firmly: "No. I meant it. I still do. We're all big boys here. I'm the coach."

So who's chipping in for the tolls here? Who's the real Jacques Demers? The genteel French-Canadian who was unloading trucks before his first coaching job? Or the hard-line leader who said, "We'll be back for a Game 7" even when the Wings trailed Toronto, three games to one?

The answer is both. That is his magic, the secret of his success. Demers can work with characters without losing his own. He is never far from humble, yet he will not permit his players the comfort of feeling second best. "No excuses," he told them during Friday night's 4-2 victory. "We have played 90 games this season. If you want to play 91, you better win this."

He is at once charming and determined, blue-collar and sacre-bleu! I cannot recall the last time a coach turned on a city this much. Yet there is no denying Demers is as big a Detroit star as anyone wearing skates and a helmet. (This, by the way, has been another car subject: "I'm afraid people are getting sick of me," he says. "All these interviews. How much can I say? Won't the people get sick of me? What do you think?")

But remember this. Demers, 42, has transformed a hockey team that left its fans ashamed last season. He has instilled pride and guts. And now it is on the verge of the NHL playoff semifinals — a round Demers reached last year with St. Louis, considered far superior to these Wings in pure talent. One year? He did that in one year?

How is it that Demers gets his men to play so well for him so quickly? Some say it is because if you don't, you are gone. A peek at the Wings' opening and closing day rosters will bear that out. So will Stefan's benching, and that of Petr Klima Friday night. "These are the times you gotta produce," Demers said fervently during a recent ride. "The playoffs, there can be no excuses. No, sir. Not now."

Then he fished into his pockets.

"Need change for the tunnel?" he asked.

On Friday, before what could have been the season's final game, I asked Demers if he could even remember the season opener anymore.

"Loss to Quebec, 6-1," he said quickly. "I told the guys right then, 'This won't do. We can't have this.' "

"Did you have any idea then you'd go as far as you have?"

"Oh, yes," he said. "Even then I believed we would make the playoffs."

Well, why not? Here is a man who was about to take a job as a computer operator when a hockey coaching spot opened up. The son of a butcher who wanted only enough to eat and who now lives quite well in the suburbs as a Motown celebrity. An Inspector Clouseau look-alike who figured his sport would have to be his mistress, until he met his future wife (his second) behind the desk at a hockey team office. Hey. Why shouldn't he be optimistic? "So many good things have happened to me," he will say.

He says it, on average, about once a day.

"What happens when this ends?" I asked before Game 5. "What will it feel like?"

"It's hard," he said. "The day after your last game, you feel very sad. You wake up lonely. It's like a dream that you don't ever want to end. But you know it has to."

He paused, and looked out the window. He asked me about my travel schedule. I rattled off a string of meaningless flights to places like Atlanta and Louisville.

"Boy, you got a great job, eh?" he said.

I have a theory about Demers' occasional language bloopers: French works differently than English. In French, you put the object between the subject and the verb. So "I see you" would be "je vous vois." Which in English would be "I you see." I think. Unless I'm wrong. I was never good at French.

Anyhow, maybe this is why Demers, a native of Montreal, has the occasional spot of trouble with English, which has led to dozens of impersonations, and a few good laughs.

It is true, he can create some beautiful phrases. He once explained himself to a Sports Illustrated reporter: "Everyone said when he gets to Detroit he'll take a landslide, but I think I've done a commandable job. . . . "

Huh?

He also once said: "They can recuperate a lot of pucks out there." And a personal favorite, after a congratulatory note from Sparky Anderson: "Isn't that nice? He doesn't know me from Adams."

But OK. The malapropisms are merely part of his charisma. So is the smile. So is the camaraderie with his players, the way they all say, "Oh, Jacques, you know, he's. . . ."

And tonight, in a fever pitch, Oh, Jacques, you know, the charismatic coach, will take his spot behind the bench for a game no one imagined when this season began. Game 7. Leafs vs. Wings. "We want to win for the fans, we want to win for ourselves. I personally, you know, would like to win, too," he said.

And perhaps they will. But whatever the result, there is a sense that no season will be as sugar-coated for Demers as this one has been. There will eventually be negative press. Eventually, criticism. History proves that people get used to anything, even manna from heaven. So surely the Detroit fans will expect big results next season, and will find fault if they do not arise.

But tonight will be madness. Tonight will be pandemonium. Horns, crowds, buzzers, millions of hopes and dreams. So for now, a simple appreciation: for the coach, and for the team he has put together. It is not easy to restore lost pride. It is not easy to spin "straw" defeat into "we can do it" gold. Where were the Red Wings one year ago? Do you remember? When they drop the puck tonight for Game 7, it would not hurt to marvel at that distance.

So listen up, bikers, wherever you are. This is it. We're square. The last lucky car pool. If the Wings can advance to play Edmonton, they certainly don't need me or my wheels. But for now, I will throw some gas in, and pick out a decent radio station. And we'll see, we'll see. Playoffs mean different things to different people. Victory. Heroism. But in a funny way, these, at least for me, have meant something I didn't count on: a mirror to a good man's thoughts. Can I butcher some French here? It's only fair. Je vous salute, Mr. Demers.

And don't make me honk twice, OK?

WINGS' DREAM LIVES; EDMONTON IS NEXT

May 4

The fans were going insane, the players were slapping each other in celebration and even coach Jacques Demers, dressed in his lucky wedding suit, walked out across the ice, raised a fist, and suddenly leaped toward the heavens. Why not? That's where these magic words seemed to be coming from:

The Red Wings are going to the semifinals.

Amazing.

The Red Wings? Hockey's little train that could? The semifinals? This was the worst team in the league last season? This was the joke, the embarrassment, the reason fans around here considered putting bags over their heads, or moving?

This is the team. And this is not the team. These players carry the logo, they carry the uniforms — they do not carry the memories, or the fate, or the weight of failure.

"How far are you now from your lowest point last year?" someone asked fourth-year center Steve Yzerman, who was drenched in champagne after the Wings' 3-0 seventh-game win over Toronto.

"It seems like centuries apart," he said, beaming. "I've never won a Stanley Cup, but if the feeling is any better than this, I can't wait!"

Stanley Cup? Dare they talk about that? Well, why not? They have a fresh taste now, these Detroit players, a clean plate. They have a coach who keeps booking charter flights for the next step and an intensity that will not be crushed by odds. They've been pushed now to a Game 7 and they've come out winners.

This morning they have eight playoff victories.

And eight'll get you a shot at 12.

The Red Wings are going to the semifinals. Amazing.

Have you ever heard a cheer that loud?" someone asked right wing Joe Kocur about the final-buzzer explosion from the Joe Louis crowd when the victory was finally official. "Anywhere? At a rock concert? At another game? Anywhere?"

"Never," he said, his young eyes bulging. "It was heaven out there."

Heaven? Well, hockey-wise, perhaps. What happened at this arena Sunday night was not merely a win, it was a refusal to lose. This was a whale of a series, a series the Wings had trailed, 3-1, a long time ago. But they threw the thing on their backs and lugged it back and forth across the Canadian border, and here, in the biggest of the big games, Game 7, they

212

simply refused to put it down. Not for a moment.

What a night! What noise! What power! What colors! The red and white smeared the blue all over.

Here was Adam Oates, circling behind the net and spinning and shooting and getting his rebound and, score!

1-0.

Here was Yzerman, goal-less in this series, breaking away, drawing closer, and . . . score!

2-0.

Here was Darren Veitch taking a beautiful cross-ice pass from Oates and winding up, winding up, then slapping that puck as if all the frustrations of hockey in this city were unloosed in his one mighty swipe.

Let it fly . . . in the net . . . score!

3-0.

And, through it all, here was goalie Glen Hanlon, called upon as a mid-series replacement, whacking and smacking and flicking away everything that came close to his net, finishing a masterful series in which he would not allow a single goal to be scored by the Leafs in this country. Not a single goal? Two Detroit shutouts?

Say good night, Toronto.

The Red Wings are going to the semifinals.

Amazing.

I am so proud of these players," Demers said afterward, a cigar in his hand, his eyes watering from both a cold and the emotion. "They had plenty of chances to quit. People would have said, 'Hey, you swept Chicago (in the first round). That was good enough.' But they wouldn't accept that."

Halfway through the evening, it became clear they would accept nothing less than total, unquestionable victory. No last-second flukes here. By the second period, this was no longer a game, it was a shooting gallery, every Red Wing gets a swipe, and history and defeatism and bad news were suddenly gone as if sucked up by the Zamboni machine.

So dominating was this finale that it almost seemed pre-determined, carved in the ice. Didn't it? Everyone thought the patient named Toronto was merely asleep, it would awaken in Game 7, but the patient was dead. Where was the Leafs' offense? Where was their pressure?

Meanwhile, the Red Wings were loading up the emotional scales. Even the Ostrom sisters — those curly-haired little girls who have sung the national anthems throughout this series — brought their mother out with them this time. Their mother? And Demers wore his wedding suit — "only the second time I've ever worn it." His wedding suit? Their mother? Come on. You can't fight that kind of karma, can you?

No way.

The Red Wings are going to the semifinals.

All right. Some perspective. True, this was not like beating the Flyers, the Canadiens, the Oilers (Detroit's foe in the next best-of-seven series, Gretzky and all, starting Tuesday). No doubt outsiders will look at Detroit this morning, leaping and laughing and whooping it up, and say, "Boy, are those people desperate for a party."

But remember the failure that has been hockey around here in recent years, the red faces, the "Dead Wings" jokes, the revolving door of coaches and players. It was as if a filmy residue had dried on this franchise, so even when these Wings finished with a better regular-season record than Toronto, there was still doubt.

Forget that now. With Sunday's final buzzer, these players have brought a cleansing rinse that leaves them fresh and new and ready to establish their own tradition in this town, Demers and Hanlon and Yzerman and Oates and Gallant and Ashton and Burr, et al. However far they go now, it is their doing, not a shadow from the past.

So they may not win a game against the great Oilers. Or they may push the Oilers to places they never dreamed of. Does it really make a difference at this moment?

Nah.

"Tell us about that leap!" someone yelled at Demers. "What was going through your mind?"

"I was . . . I . . . I'm so happy," he said, choking up. "I was . . . you know. . . ."

Ah, forget the words, Jacques. Go ahead and leap, leap all the way to the freaking sky. Stay up there for a moment with the echoes of words not heard in this hockey town for too, too long. . . .

The Red Wings are going to the semifinals. Amazing.

'GREAT TEAMS COME TRUE' FITS THE HEROIC RED WINGS

May 15

The game was lost, the season was over, the plane was taking the Red Wings home. It was after midnight. I glanced around. Here was Gilbert Delorme, the defenseman, sitting behind me, saying nothing. Here was Shawn Burr, the center, sitting in front of me, his eyes red from weeping. Here were Dave Lewis, Glen Hanlon, Mike O'Connell and Adam Oates, dealing cards in a silent game.

For a moment, I wondered whether this loss to Edmonton in the Campbell Conference final, the last nail in an incredible Detroit hockey season, would hang over the team like a damp rag. It had come so far, played so long. Would depression set in? Would it last the whole flight, maybe longer? No smiles until next season? No forgiving? No forgetting?

"NO BEER?" yelled a player suddenly.

No beer?

"YEAH, STEWARDESS. HOW 'BOUT ONE?"

"Me, too!"

"Over here."

"Gimme six!"

"SIX?"

"Yeah."

"SIX?"

"We're sharing."

"YO! . . ."

Well, I said "a moment."

Can I confess something right now?

I am really going to miss these guys.

What was the highlight of this year?" I asked Steve Yzerman, the 22-year-old captain who had scored a goal Wednesday night in the Wings' 6-3 final defeat. "This year has been so crazy, it's seen so many changes. What was the single best moment of all?"

"For me, the best part was the final minute of Game 7 against Toronto," he said. "The crowd at Joe Louis was going crazy. It was so loud!

"It was so great to be on the ice for that. That one minute alone made the whole season worthwhile."

It was a beautiful moment in a season of moments. Is there anyone out there who didn't start collecting memories somewhere along this magic carpet ride? The Red Wings? The doormats of the NHL last year? Did you ever think this team would dance with first place? This team would sweep

215

Chicago in Round 1 of the playoffs? This team would come back from a 3-1 deficit to beat Toronto in the Norris Division final?

Did you ever think this team would take the first game against Edmonton, mighty Edmonton, and would play rock-hard the rest of the way, would scare the Oilers every time, would come within a crossbar here, a freak shot there, of winning this whole thing, not just hanging on, but winning? Advancing to the Stanley Cup final?

"We really felt we could do it," Yzerman said. "We weren't pretending." So how heartbreaking was Wednesday night, when it all ended, when the Wings came out on fire and still could not burn enough distance between them and the omnipotent Oilers? The game was like a tightly edited nightmare: the bizarre Edmonton goal pushed in by the skate of Detroit's Greg Stefan; the wicked slap shot by Gerard Gallant that rose toward Edmonton goalie Grant Fuhr, struck him, lifted him in the air, knocked his stick from his hands — yet he stopped the shot; he always seemed to stop the shot.

And that final, crazy clearing pass by Kent Nilsson with the score 4-3 Oilers, and the clock down to seconds. Did you see that? Could you watch that? It was not meant as a shot, not really, but the puck hit the boards, and slid toward Detroit's open net, and the whole Red Wings team stared helplessly as Delorme gave chase, man against rubber — "I needed five more feet," he said later. "I would have dove, anything, but just five more feet" — and instead it skittered in, gave the win to Edmonton for certain. Delorme buried his head in his hands and slumped over the net.

Back on the Wings' bench, coach Jacques Demers looked at his players, and they looked back, and then away.

The goodby look.

"What were you thinking as you watched that puck slide?" I asked Demers on the plane.

"Hit the post," he said. "I just wanted it to hit the post. Please hit the post."

In the locker room following the game, Demers had sat on the trainer's table, holding a beer, his eyes watery, his legs dangling like a child's. He carried the wear and tear of the season, in his eyes, in his scratchy throat. But mostly in his stomach. By playoff time, Demers' suit jackets no longer buttoned. He had taken to patting his waist and saying, "When the season is over, boy. . . ." And yet you could look at Demers' growing profile and see the team's accomplishments therein. Somehow it seems fitting that he should grow, well, larger from all he has done.

This is the coach of the year in hockey, a shoo-in, no question, a Svengali of ice play who knows talent and alchemy, how to mix skills and personalities. So you have a Mel Bridgman, 32, and a Burr, 20, as playoff roommates. You have goalie Hanlon, as stable as a board, and Bob Probert, a tinderbox both on the ice and off. You have guys who only want to stay out late and guys who will make sure they don't. And somehow it all works. You have a team.

Demers is the reason. I cannot remember the last time a coach caused so much commotion in a major city. I do remember driving him to playoff games in Rounds 1 and 2, a tradition that became somewhat overblown when the Wings suddenly won every game we carpooled and lost every one we didn't. By the sixth ride — Game 7 against Toronto — the superstition was getting a bit too much attention, and when I picked up Demers at the Windsor Hilton I suggested this would be the last time, and he said, "Oops. Wait a minute." And he ran back in the hotel lobby and grabbed an apple off a fruit basket when nobody was looking and gave it to me. "Here," he said, "it's all I can get right now. I just want to say thank you for the rides."

An apple?

Yeah. Well. Why not?

I have often written fondly about Demers' butchering of the English language (his native tongue, as most people know, is French). Wednesday night, in speaking about the Oilers, he said: "Great players come true, that's all. Great teams come true."

He meant to say "through." Great teams come "through." But it sounded like true. And I kind of like that better.

Great teams come true, Detroit.

Was that not his season's greeting, all season long?

Here is what I will miss most about this team. They are regular guys. No big shots. No super egos. I think the reason Detroit fell so deeply in love with the Red Wings is that they reflect the workingman's image of the city itself.

But such is ice hockey. It is, as far as I know, the only major sport in this continent where players do interviews between periods. It is also the only major sport in this continent where common courtesy is still the norm rather than the exception.

So it was that Wayne Gretzky, the incomparable Oilers center, was standing near the exit of the Northlands Coliseum, by himself, shaking the hands of Detroit players as they left.

And so it was that Joe Diroff got his plane ticket paid for. Diroff is a fanatic booster, a 64-year-old retired schoolteacher who waits at the airports when the Wings come in, and who cuts out construction-paper signs and leads cheers. He is odd-looking, with a large forehead and prominent eyebrows that have earned him the nickname "The Brow."

On other teams he might be ignored, shunted aside as an embarrassment. But Diroff paid to fly to Edmonton for Game 5, to support his team, and when the Wings found out they invited him on the charter home. And a few hours into the flight, when the players were finally relaxing, having some farewell fun, right in the middle of that, Hanlon came around collecting $10 per player.

"Let's chip in and pay for Brow's ticket up here," was all he said. And instantly the players stopped their games and boozy laughter and dug into their pockets. Dave Barr pulled down his garment bag and began fishing around for his wallet. Jeff Sharples, called up to the team only a few days ago, came back to his seat for his jacket.

They got the money in a matter of minutes, somewhere around $300, and gave it to Diroff. And then, to really make his night, one of them said, "Brow! Let's do the Strawberry Shortcake cheer!" And right there, at 30,000 feet, this unlikely group of hockey players broke into one of the dumbest cheers you have ever heard:

Strawberry shortcake
Gooseberry pie,
V-I-C-T-O-R-Y

Amazing. Here were these bruising, scarred, often toothless men, on the night of their season-ending loss, singing a high school cheer. Simply because it made the old guy happy.

Many people will remember goals and saves and slap shots from this season. I hope I never forget that cheer. I think it says something.

So there goes the hockey season. With the sound of a horn in Edmonton we are let off the hook of this roller-coaster ride, thrilled and tired and curious about the next run. Is a Stanley Cup possible? Does it ever get better than this?

"Later," Demers said as he exited the plane. "Right now I'm going to just take time with my wife."

"I'm going to Mexico," Burr said.

"LA," Bridgman said.

"Hey, tomorrow night, 7:30!" Yzerman yelled. "Team dinner. Wives and girlfriends. Don't forget."

The Red Wings nodded.

And that was that. This season is history.

I caught a ride home with Yzerman and Brent Ashton. It was about 6 a.m. We drove over the Windsor bridge and along the nearly deserted highways. Neither player was talking much, and I figured maybe the pain of the loss was finally hitting, so I kept quiet, too. We rolled along in the morning light of Detroit. The radio played softly. And suddenly Ashton turned to Yzerman and looked him squarely in the eye.

"You know," he said, "Edmonton ain't so hot."

Uh-oh.

MEET BILL LAIMBEER, PISTONS' MR. PERSONALITY

May 22

H*ey, if I were somebody else, looking at me? I'd think I was an a------, too."*
— **Bill Laimbeer**

BOSTON — Wait. Don't tell me. You hate his guts. He's a stiff, a boor, a spoiled brat, an actor, a loudmouth; he can't jump, he can't block shots, he runs like a pregnant deer, his nose is pointy, and, when he high-fives, it looks like party time at nerd training camp.

"Who cares?" says Bill Laimbeer, sitting across the breakfast table. He reaches over with one of those long arms. "I'm gonna have some of your grapes. Thanks."

Yeah. Who cares? Have a grape. Just 12 hours earlier, during a playoff game in Boston Garden, Laimbeer, the Pistons' center, had been roundly booed, cursed, despised; the hate rained down — as it would in the Pistons' Game 2 defeat Thursday night. Who cares? During the Atlanta-Detroit playoff series, a sold-out Omni crowd chanted, "LAIMBEER S - - - -!" And, after the Hawks lost, someone threw a glass of beer in his face. Who cares? Knock, knock. Hey! It's Mr. Popularity.

"I do what I have to do. That's my style of play. I bump people. I'm not fluid. I'm herky-jerky. I try to get other players out of their games any way I can. That's why people don't like me."

He smirks. "These grapes are lousy."

W*illiam Laimbeer Jr. To paraphrase Kojak: Who bugs you, baby? Anyone more than this guy? Unless, of course, you are a Pistons fan, and you love the way he snares all those rebounds, and bumps and grinds his opponent and never gives up. But even then. . . .*

Did you hear the roar whenever he fouled a Celtic or missed a shot? He had a poor game offensively (1-for-6, two points) and they wouldn't let up. What is it about him that gets under people's skin? What doesn't?

Here is an NBA star who never set foot on a ghetto playground, a rich kid who had a car by his 16th birthday, who flunked out of Notre Dame as a freshman, who quit his only summer job after two weeks; a guy who is sarcastic, caustic, who moans, who complains, who would rather be playing golf, and who, by his own admission, takes off his dirty clothes and lets them drop wherever, figuring his wife will pick them up.

Are you ready to smack him yet?

And look. He's laughing. You rattle his faults in front of him and he laughs like a baby in a crib. Is that what makes you shake your head, grinning, every time you go to insult him? Is it that curious Laimbeer ego that, instead of proclaiming greatness, seems to send him loping downcourt, pounding his chest and screaming: "I AM . . . MEDIOCRE!"?

Who bugs you, baby? Laimbeer is vilified by everyone from opposing centers to radio announcers. And yet, he has made the All-Star team four times, the Detroit fans love him, and even Isiah Thomas, everybody's favorite NBA cherub, calls Laimbeer a best friend.

Obviously, what we have in this 6-foot-11, 260-pound jigsaw of a body is either a gifted and misunderstood man or the world's largest dork.

O r something in between. It is true, if not caring is a sin, Laimbeer is guilty right down the line. ("Damn, man!" laughed teammate John Salley, upon hearing someone call Laimbeer an atheist. "Do you believe in anything?") He does seem to lope through life with a private safety net, as if no matter how awkward, inconsiderate or annoying he gets, he still wins. Like a child in the house of mirrors, he sees all of his unkind reflections. And they only crack him up.

"Look, I'll never be able to fly through the air like so many guys in this league," says the center who has still managed to win an NBA rebounding title (1985-86), average 15.4 points and 11.6 rebounds this season and shoot 18-footers like a silky guard — and who is a crucial player if the Pistons hope to win this Eastern Conference final against Boston. "I realized early I was not going to be an all-time great player.

"So I do what I have to do to survive. I jostle people. Like when a guy is going to his favorite spot, I step in his way; I bump him; I don't let him get there; I bump, bump, bump.

"I laugh at my reputation as a tough guy, though. I never fight. I walk away from it. I may have some altercations, but they're never real fights. People don't like that style? So what? As long as people in Detroit appreciate me, what do I care about Boston or Atlanta or Milwaukee?"

OK. Laimbeer has, of course, given those opposing crowds more than an occasional bump to remember him by. Last time the Pistons met the Celtics in the playoffs (1985), Laimbeer was knocked to the floor by Robert Parish and came up swinging (he missed). And after an insinuation by Larry Bird that Boston would sweep that series, Laimbeer found the star forward during the Pistons' second win and yelled, "Where's your bleeping broom now, bleep bleep?"

So he's not getting any free passes to Boston Garden. His license plate should read: "Born to Irritate." He pushes. He bad-mouths. When he is introduced, he often runs out and points at his teammates (no hand-slapping) with this tight-jaw expression that is supposed to be his tough look, but actually suggests that he needs to use the bathroom.

"If you were somebody else playing against Bill Laimbeer, wouldn't you want to take a swing at yourself?"

"Yeah," he says. "I guess I would."

Case closed.

And yet there is surprise to Bill Laimbeer, an itchy feeling that — no matter how often you speak with him — always leaves you wondering if you weren't this close to discovering a whole different guy.

"You know, I don't really even like to play basketball," he says suddenly, grabbing a glass of orange juice. "It's not fun to just go out and play. The competition in a real game is fun. But just to play pickup? That's stupid. . . . I stink at that. I need referees."

Yeah, say his critics. He needs referees like Don Rickles needs the front tables. There's no act without them. This, after all, is the man Sports Illustrated once dubbed "master of the theatrical fall."

But what Laimbeer is saying is, he needs rules. So that he can bend them. Like him or not, here is a player of limited ability who has figured out just how much he can get away with, an ugly duckling set loose in a makeup factory. "As long as I don't break the rules," he says.

So what is it with him? You can list 100 things to hate about him. He'll list them for you. Why do some still find him, well, intriguing?

Maybe it's the notion that the most hateful crime is pretending you are something you're not. Of that, Bill Laimbeer is completely innocent.

Unlike most of us, he wears his faults on the outside. His good qualities, like long johns, remain underneath. "He makes a terrible first impression," says Steve Glassman, 34, a Cleveland restaurateur and a close friend. "I introduce him to people and they walk away saying, 'Where does that guy get off being like that?' But they don't know him. And he doesn't care, or at least he says he doesn't."

Laimbeer "doesn't even try" to fit in the slick black subculture of his NBA peers. He does not downplay his privileged upbringing. He is not interested in having loads of friends.

"Do you have a conscience?" I ask him.

He pauses. "Uh . . . well . . . with regards to what?"

"Well," I say, "do you have a conscience during basketball?"

"No."

"How about off the court?"

"Well . . . yeah. . . . I suppose."

Nothing like putting your best foot forward.

And yet here is something you probably didn't know about Bill Laimbeer. Four years ago, he and his wife, Chris, lost their first child. A baby boy. It was born prematurely, lived two days, and died. "We buried him and said our goodbys," Laimbeer says. He does not use the statement to launch into a speech about being misunderstood. Few people even know the story, because Laimbeer thought it was nobody else's concern. He admits he cried. But he shrugs off any sympathy.

"He felt that loss more than he lets show," says Glassman, who was with Laimbeer at the hospital that day. "The whole time he was worried about Chris, about us, about everybody else. I think about that time and I hear people say he's the biggest agitator in the league, and, I don't know; I can't put those two things together."

And this is the paradox of the man people love to hate. Just as you are convinced he is a selfish cynic from his sneakers on up, somebody tells you a story. His charity golf tournament. A surprise gift he paid for. Some little thing. And you look at him, smirking, that "I-know-something-you-don't-know" look, and you say, "Wellll . . . "

"I don't let people get too close to me," he admits. "I always want a buffer zone."

"Is that because you're afraid you might not be worthy of their attention?"

And instead of laughing at the pseudo-psychology of the question, he says quietly: "Yes. Possibly."

So there is more than just the lonesome, scowling boy behind uniform No. 40. There is also this: Laimbeer is crucial to the Pistons' success. Check the box scores. When Laimbeer has a bad night, they almost never win. "The record bears that out," says Pistons coach Chuck Daly.

So what are you going to do with the big lug? You may hate him and say he is lazy and cynical and a crybaby and a stat-keeper and annoying, aggravating, infuriating and a jerk. But you don't know everything. And that gnawing sense he may be smarter than all this keeps you from walking away from Bill Laimbeer convinced you really understand him.

And that is the way he wants it. Give him your boos, your heckles. Your grapes. "I'm never gonna be small and cuddly," he says. "So I figure I might as well play the part that's already here for me. People aren't going to change their minds about me. I could come to Boston Garden for six years and give up 60 points every time and they'd still think I was a bleep. So forget it."

And there goes Mr. Popularity, to another playoff game. Who bugs you, baby? Everyone expects him to push, grope, complain, rebound, score, and, in seasons to come, probably make a few more All-Star teams. Do you know what I expect? I expect one day to accidentally bump into Bill Laimbeer somewhere, in a grocery store, or a nursery school, or just a quiet corner of the Silverdome, and catch him in an act of niceness.

And I will do him a favor. I will not tell anybody.

CELTICS' MAN OF STEAL MAKES IMPOSSIBLE REAL

May 27

BOSTON — "BIRD STOLE THE BALL! BIRD STOLE THE BALL! BIRD STOLE THE ..."

The words echoed across the New England airwaves, across cable television stations, they splashed onto morning headlines and morning talk shows and they pierced the hearts of every Detroit Pistons fan alive.

Bird stole the ball! What happened in those final five maddening seconds of this Eastern Conference playoff game? How could it happen? Even here, in the Boston Garden, where they ask for your next of kin when you step on the court, where the Pistons haven't won in five years, where something always happens — even here, this was unbelievable.

"I was open at halfcourt, waving my hands," said Dennis Rodman, who made the play we should have been writing about this morning — a brilliant block on a driving Bird, giving the Pistons possession with five clicks left and a 107-106 lead. "Then I saw Isiah throw the ball in and I saw Bird steal it and DJ make the basket and the whole time I was just frozen, man. It was like a dream. I just stood there. I couldn't move."

Who could move? Who could breathe? All the air had been sucked out of this humid arena by that point. "The world should have ended after this," a Boston writer remarked in the pandemonium that followed. He was right. There were bodies bent, and bodies fouled out, voices gone, fans hanging from the rafters, there were tears and cheers and hearts and dreams all over the place. Life and death. Blood and glory. All that remained was a giant earthquake to swallow us all.

How had it come to such a finish? How had the Celtics grabbed a 3-2 lead in this best-of-seven conference final? The Pistons had played their gutsiest game of the season, looking for that lead themselves, desperate to avoid a return here for Game 7. They weathered every Boston eruption, every flurry, every six- and eight-point bulge.

It was like dodging hand grenades. Bill Laimbeer, the house villain, took a fist to the face from Robert Parish that drew blood in the second quarter and no foul was called. Nothing. Every Boston basket brought a deluge of noise, incredible, painful noise, and yet the Pistons fought back with everybody, the rookies, the veterans.

And with 17 seconds left in the game, Isiah Thomas, the star, did what he was always meant to do, dribbled and spun and hurled a top-of-the-key swish over Jerry Sichting, giving Detroit the lead. Shouldn't it have ended then?

Instead, Isiah grabbed that ball (Rodman's block that went out of bounds) and lofted that oh, too soft inbounds pass to Laimbeer, even as Chuck Daly raced downcourt screaming for time out as if trying to forestall Armageddon.

"Was it a great steal or a bad pass?" Thomas was asked afterward.

"A bad pass," he said, his lips tight.

Miracle to manacle. Hero to less-than-hero. The ball floated up, and Bird, who raced toward Laimbeer with the intent of fouling him, found, instead, his destiny hanging about nine feet in the air. "I guess Isiah just didn't throw it hard enough," Bird said later. "I was lucky. The whole play was lucky."

Ha. It is never luck here. It is something else that lives inside these rickety walls. Bird came down with the ball, found himself falling out of bounds, and he dished to a streaking Dennis Johnson, who laid it up — did you even think for a moment he would miss it? — and hearts all across Michigan dropped to the floor, even as those in New England, which still remember when John Havlicek stole that pass to end the Eastern final 22 years ago, were learning a new lyric:

"BIRD STOLE THE BALL! . . ."

And here, in the post-game locker rooms, was all of sports, every moment, glory and mud, crystallized and polarized and held at their blissful extremes. Here was Thomas, grim, sad, the pain of this hadn't even hit him yet, answering the same questions over and over. "You can second-guess a lot of things," he whispered. "Why didn't I call time out? Why didn't I throw it to someone else? Why didn't Bill step up? The end result is still that we lost the game."

Around him sat his teammates, shell-shocked, deluged by reporters, talking bravely about Game 6 in Detroit. And down the hall, in the crazy Celtics quarters, sat Bird, calm, dressed, answering questions as if it were just another play. Say what you will about this guy. He is simply brilliant on the court. Most players would have been so angry at being blocked on their team's last shot, they never would have kept their eyes so glued to the ball. Even when he stole it, he was counting seconds in his head. Destiny three, destiny two, destiny one.

"If Johnson wasn't there, would you have taken the shot, even falling down?" he was asked.

"I would have," he said, "but it probably would have hit the side of the board." On this night? In this house? Under these dark green skies?

Nuh-uh. It would have swished.

FOR ONCE, LET CHUCK DALY WIN IT

May 28

Has this ever happened to you? You are screaming until your lungs explode for something you want desperately, passionately, but you are drowned out by 14,000 hysterical, towel-waving, beer-drinking fans?

Well. No. I guess not. But that is where we left Chuck Daly Tuesday night, rushing down the Boston Garden courtside, waving his arms, shrieking, trying madly to get Isiah Thomas to call for time-out with five seconds left — and instead, his voice lost in the deafening crowd, he watched Thomas throw the ball inbounds, a lazy pass. . . .

You know the rest. Larry Bird stole it, Dennis Johnson scored it, and, gal-oooomp. Daly swallowed a pound and a half of anguish, along with the assurance that, once again, he would not sleep five minutes all night.

Listen. I'm going to do something shameful here. OK? I'm going to take sides. I'm going to say the Celtics — who lead this Eastern Conference final, three games to two — are great, marvelous, truly impressive, and if there is any justice in this world, the Pistons will kick them right off the sports page. Not for the players, not for the fans, but for all of life's runners-up, for anyone who has ever come in second, anyone who has one digit from the jackpot, or best man at his secret love's wedding.

Take a look at your coach, B-team. The guy on the Detroit bench with the slick coiffure and the neatly pressed suit.

Chuck D's in love. With basketball.

And she may break his heart again.

"High school?" I ask.

"My team went to the state semifinals once," he says. "The year after I graduated, they won the state championship."

"The year after you graduated?"

"Yeah."

"How about college?"

"I got a scholarship to St. Bonaventure. But a lot of guys were coming back from the war, so . . . I ended up transferring."

"Coaching?"

"As a college assistant, I made the Final Four."

"As an assistant?"

"Yeah."

"And the pros?"

"Made it to the NBA finals. With Philly. I was an assistant there, too."

"Assistant. Semifinals. You know. . . ." I say, looking over the notepad.

"There is a pattern here."

"I know," Chuck Daly says, "second banana."

Second banana. Runner-up. The guy is three years from his 60th birthday, he has put in his time, he has taken no shortcuts, 32 years of coaching, including Duke, Boston College, Penn, Cleveland, Philly, Detroit, he has won a lot and yet he has never won it all, at any level. A year ago, he had "pretty much accepted the idea" that he would probably never see an NBA championship. And suddenly, a few trades, the system clicked, the Pistons are now further than ever before, within breathing distance of the final — and Bird has the audacity to steal that pass?

Forgive me, Boston. You have, in K.C. Jones, a terrific coach, a hell of a coach. A coach who also has, on his hand, or in his sock drawer, or wherever he keeps them, two NBA championship rings as Celtics skipper and Lord knows how many as a player.

Chuck Daly has his wedding band.

N ow I don't know about you. But this affects my sense of, well, distribution. A lot of would-be NBA coaches want to jump from the court to the bench in a single bound. No sympathy here for them. But Daly has played fair. He has touched every square in the hopscotch board. Seven years in high schools. Seven years as a college assistant. Four years as an NBA assistant.

Not many people consider reaching Punxsutawney, Pa., a milestone in their careers. Daly does. "Hey, I was a Depression kid," he says. "My father was a traveling salesman. I used to go riding with him on his runs. I'd sit in the front seat of the car while he called on customers.

"To me, getting to Punxsutawney (his first high school job) was great. I mean, I was coaching." Which is only a big deal when you consider the alternatives. Prior to Punxsutawney (and I keep repeating it here because I am amazed every time I spell it correctly), Daly had worked as a furniture loader, a dishwasher, a night watchman, a construction worker and, while in the Army, a bouncer in a Tokyo nightclub. "One summer in college I had a job in a leather factory. They'd bring in these hides from South America with blood on them, and we'd throw them in the lime pits so the hair would come off. And then I'd have to go down and clean the lime pits.

"Those kind of jobs really helped me decide what I wanted to do with the rest of my life."

"Like get out of the lime pits?" I ask.

"Right," he says.

T oday, it is true, Daly is out of the pits. And into the glitz. In fact, at their pin-striped, silk-tie best, Daly and assistant coaches Ron Rothstein and Dick Versace could be pictured running some Las

Vegas casino; Rothstein at the blackjack tables, Versace — white hair and all — crooning into the lounge microphone, Daly sort of walking around with his jaw set, the man in charge, the kind of guy they whisper to and he waves a couple of fingers and an hour later, somebody gets shot.

"Chuck was always slick, from the day I met him," Rothstein said. But he means slick in dress. Earthy in character. Remember, this is a guy who worked for Ted Stepien in Cleveland. His first head-coaching job. He lasted 93 days. He lived in a Richfield hotel room. The entire time. When he was fired he just checked out. You gotta like that.

The fact is, it is tough to find anyone around who doesn't like the guy. (Except maybe Stepien.) Even some of the Boston writers privately concede they'd like to see him get one before he quits, even if it means beating the Celtics. Why not? Here is a guy who is, well, relatable: He likes golf, Mel Torme, New Jersey. He will bury you in optimism, then turn and say, "But hey, they may fire me tomorrow, so what do I know?" He can talk clothes with rookie John Salley, he can talk best-sellers with a bookstore owner. He is the type to come to lunch in Sergio-this and Georgio-that, and still slurp his soup.

I have seen him, at various times, racing through a shopping mall in Atlanta, leaning over a piano in a Boston bar, pacing the halls in the Houston Summit. I have heard him deny contract rumors, admit he was about to be fired, choke up at the prospect of leaving, and laugh at the Pistons' playoff success. I have seen him yell at players, yell at reporters, and remark that "practice today will be just long enough to throw up." And this is my impression: Daly, 57 in July, is like a salesman who has grown tired of the sandwiches and the long drives and the feeling in the pit of his stomach when the customer says no. But he still can't resist the prospect of the one big one, the consummate deal, and so he trudges on.

He deals with egos that are insatiable, players who all want "48 minutes and 48 points a night." He takes the barbs of a Bill Laimbeer and the silence of an Adrian Dantley and the explosive leadership of an Isiah Thomas. He kills the road boredom with shopping malls and books. And he fields all of it, like a shortstop, even though it is a flat-out pain in the butt, even though he is the second-oldest coach in the NBA (behind Jack Ramsay). One time, you would figure, for all this, he would get the brass ring.

And it keeps eluding him.

When do you feel oldest in this job?" I ask.

"Mid-January around 5:45 a.m." he says. "I get that wake-up call, another bus, another airport, and I say, 'Oh my God.' I couldn't sleep all night because we blew a 10-point lead and lost a game. I was up every hour. I must be insane. A normal guy is going home at 5 o'clock today. And he's got a future!"

The last word is always on his mind. No coach in this league should feel particularly secure. But Daly — perhaps because of the ugly, almost-switch to Philadelphia after last season, and the season he had to spend doing TV commentary after the Cleveland collapse — seems particularly job-sensitive. "I tell the guys even now, hey, with all we've done this year, 10 days into next season, I could be gone," he says.

"Doesn't that bother you, never knowing if you'll hold onto your job?"

"Yeah," he says. "That's partly why I'm interested in GM jobs. I had a good chance at one last year, before I signed the new contract here (he would not say which team)."

"Why didn't you take it? Why didn't you get out?"

He shrugged. Then he laughed. Above all else, Chuck Daly has a hell of a laugh.

"I'm in love," he said, sing-song. "I'm in love. I still want to coach. What can I say?"

I should add here that the guy is not a saint. I mean, I have witnessed Daly blow his top. Firsthand. Last season during the playoffs, I wrote a story about Isiah Thomas' bladder ailment — which threatened his play. Daly, naturally, didn't want it in the papers. When I told him it was in there, he went "ARRGH!" His eyes bulged, I thought instinctively about ducking, and then he wheeled on me, yelled, "FINE! FINE! THAT'S ALL!" and marched away.

Isiah got better. The Pistons got eliminated. I didn't speak with Daly the rest of that season.

So this is not a fan letter. Just an appreciation of a guy who has put in his time. Chuck D's in love, but she keeps teasing him, inviting him in, onto the couch, dimming the lights — then taking a phone call in the kitchen. Enough. Let the guy have his moment.

The Pistons had only one big, closed-door team meeting this year. The highlight, Daly said, was this unexpected dedication by Thomas:

"I read where you said you don't think you're gonna be named coach of the year," Isiah said.

"That's right," Daly answered.

"Well, I'm not gonna win the MVP award. And Laimbeer's not gonna win the rebounding title. And Adrian's not gonna win the scoring title. So why don't we dedicate ourselves to winning the whole thing instead? Kind of all the second-bests? Let's just go for it all, for all of us."

I like that. So maybe tonight, for all the second-bests, all the also-rans, all the guys back in the lime pits, things will turn out OK. And who knows? Maybe the Pistons and Daly will go back to Boston and take it all there in a stunning finale, and then go on to beat LA for the title?

In which case, Chuck, forget I said any of this.

CELTICS PUT GREMLINS TO WORK ON PISTONS

May 31

BOSTON — Danny Ainge threw up a shot, the Pistons scrambled madly for the rebound, and it flew over their heads, back into the Celtics' hands. And another shot went up, this time by Larry Bird, and the Pistons scrambled, and again it caromed over their heads and back to the Celtics. Surely some devil was at work now. And it happened again, Kevin McHale missed, rebound Boston, and again, Robert Parish missed, rebound Boston, and again, another shot, another rebound, and by now the sold-out Boston Garden was laughing, taunting, and the basketball was becoming the very spirit of the Celtics, unexplainable, unreasonable, undeniable. And finally it was swung into the hands of Ainge again, standing out in never-never land, three-point soil, and with just over three minutes left in somebody's season, up it went and down it came, straight through the hoop. They should have checked that ball afterward. There was blood all over it.

Life goes on. The Pistons do not. There is no way they deserved to lose this thing, this 117-114 decision in the seventh game of the Eastern Conference final. No way except from a scoreboard point of view. And that is all that counts. So when the final buzzer sounded it was the Celtics leaping and laughing and celebrating in each other's arms. And the Pistons were staring at the parquet floor that had been their burial ground.

"That's it?" they seemed to say.

That's it.

What was going through your mind every time they got the ball back?" someone later asked Dennis Rodman of that painful sequence, which turned a 99-99 deadlock into 102-99, Celtics, a lead for good, and which seemed to suck the destiny out of the most courageous game these Pistons have ever played.

"It was like, we got it — no, we don't," he answered, looking at his feet. "We got it — no, they got it. Finally it felt like, 'God, what do we have to do to win here?' "

Here was guts in every human form. Here was Isiah Thomas, with four fouls early in the second half, begging coach Chuck Daly, "Lemme stay, Chuck! . . . I won't get another! . . . Please! . . ." Here was John Salley, half-blinded by an elbow in the eye, going to the hoop for a slam and drawing a foul. Here were Vinnie Johnson and Adrian Dantley diving for a loose ball and banging heads, and Dantley, the team's most reliable solo threat, being wheeled out on a stretcher, semiconscious, his eyes closed, spending the rest of this game in an ambulance and a hospital bed.

D id you ever want a game more than this?" the Pistons were asked, one by one, in their cramped locker room afterward.

"Never," said Thomas softly.

"Never," said Bill Laimbeer.

"I've never played in anything like this," sighed Joe Dumars, the quietest Piston, who seemed the most dejected of all. He had played brilliantly, scored 35 points, kept his team in this war with Isiah on the bench. He was symbolic of a group that had found strength from unusual places all series. Now he sat, hands on his knees, his lips pursed tightly.

"Tired . . . dejected . . . hurt," he said when asked what he was feeling. "It just hurts so much to lose like this. I really felt we played well enough to win."

And they did. Which may be what hurts the most. It was difficult for anyone with compassion to watch the final three minutes — the Pistons staying close, playing foul-and-pray, rebound-and-pray — and not feel something. How sad for Daly, who turns 57 this summer, and must wonder whether he'll ever get this close again. How sad for Thomas, who has been in Detroit for so long, and for Laimbeer, who endured more Boston hatred than one man should ever have to, and for Johnson, who had his game knocked out of him because he dived for a ball, and for Dantley, who never even knew what happened in the biggest afternoon of his career. When he awoke in his hospital bed, when they told him the score, what could his reaction have been?

That's it? That's it.

N o fair, it seems, that now and forever the picture of Bird stealing that pass in Game 5 will haunt the memory of this series, it will always be there, like a dull ache, like a scar. And however bad the fan feels, the players involved — Thomas, Laimbeer, Dumars — feel worse. They may say nothing. They may shrug it off. You never shrug it off.

And this hurts more: If you flipped this series around, if the Pistons had won Saturday, the Celtics would have little to complain about. They had already been soundly beaten three times, virtually beaten in Game 5, and held close in Games 1 and 2. The Pistons' victories, conversely, were sure, unarguable. Yet they will be the ones cursed to wonder how such talent and desire did not translate into four wins.

"Did the best team win this series?" Thomas was asked.

"No, because I felt we were the best team."

"Did the best team win this series?" Laimbeer was asked.

"I'd say the team with the home-court advantage won," he grumbled. From other teams, one might consider this sour grapes. And yet, well, don't you feel that way, too? With their backs to the wall, the Pistons had the intensity of a surgeon holding a human heart. They could take every punch the Celtics threw. They just couldn't take all of them.

This place. This place. Playing the Celtics here is a choke-lock. You can wiggle, but you rarely get free. Bird was brilliant (37 points) and McHale was gutsy and Ainge did so much damage at the worst moments. With 25 seconds left, there was still a Detroit prayer, still a razor of hope, and Ainge once again uncorked and — up, down. Over. The Garden crowd went wild, thumping, jeering, going hoarse with exultation.

Seconds later, they had done it again, this green team that never dies. And the Pistons dragged themselves to their tiny visitors' quarters, and took their uniforms off for good.

That's it? That's it.

The summer goes on. The Pistons do not. This hurts terribly in Detroit, because the city desperately fell in love with basketball during these last two weeks, or rather, fell in love again, a rekindled affair. Isiah's pops, Dantley's spins, Laimbeer's flicked-wrist jumpers — they had all become part of the household recently, like knick-knacks collected and put on the shelf. And suddenly you wake up this morning, and they are behind glass.

That's it.

Hadn't the Pistons become the sentimental favorites of basketball fans across the country? With each passing game, each slice of clamped-jaw determination, the Detroit bandwagon was more and more full. In Portland and Milwaukee and Boise and Squaw Valley and Charlotte and New Orleans and Brooklyn? Weren't they rooting for blue?

But such desire reaches only the out-of-bounds line. On the floor, it's the players, and, on this day, the Celtics were just too much the Celtics. Complain not about Dantley, for Boston had more than its share of injuries and absent players, too. What can you do? Salute the Celtics' pride, their obstinacy, even their arrogance, for if you admire victory, then you will understand these are all qualities that ensure it. They just belong, in the Pistons' fans case, to the wrong people.

It seems too cruel to say the Pistons "lost" this series. It sounds better to say they finished second, in a photo at the tape, and depending on the angle, you could maybe, possibly, say that. . . .

Never mind. It ends here, in a steamy Boston Garden on a muggy Saturday afternoon. You look at the court, where everything came crashing down, now empty and quiet, and the finality of it comes to you like the end of summer, like the last guest leaving a party, like a rebound flying helplessly over your head and into the hands of your laughing opponent.

That's it? That's it.

OUR INTREPID COLUMNIST HAS A BERRY GOOD TIME

June 30

WIMBLEDON, England — Don't tell ME about strawberries and cream. I loaded the things. On a truck. At 4 in the morning. That's right. Wimbledon strawberries. And I ripped open a box and munched a few juicy ones, too, right there, on the dock, with the sun coming up, and. . . .

But wait. I'm getting ahead of myself. To understand this little tale, which I call "How I Saved Wimbledon" (a slight exaggeration), we must go to the beginning. To the bar. Late at night. Where I got this idea: Everyone talks about the strawberries and cream here, right? Why not trace those strawberries from the field to the paper cup?

OK. So it's a bit stupid. I said I was at a bar. Besides, how often can you write about Mats Wilander? I don't even like Mats Wilander.

"STRAWBERRIES!" I yelled at the bartender, moments before I fell off the stool. . . .

Let us skip ahead here to Sunday, at midnight, at the New Covent Garden Fruit and Vegetable Market, which is somewhere in London, and, at midnight anyhow, is very dark and very quiet and full of trucks and smells like my garbage disposal.

Why do fruit people work at midnight? Well. Let's see. How the hell should I know? But this was where I stood, at the fruit vendor's gate, with my friend Jimmy S., whom I persuaded to join me for the thrill and because he owes me money.

And here came a man on a forklift.

"Sir?" I began. "We'd like to do a story on the strawberries. . . ."

When he stopped laughing, 20 minutes later, he was fine. Yes, his firm handles the famous strawberries. They are grown in Kent and Hampshire and he sells them to a distributor, who takes them to Wimbledon, and who'd be picking them up in a few hours, if we cared to wait.

Hey. Sure. Why not? We're not busy.

Can I explain again why we did this? Because people have been eating strawberries and cream at Wimbledon since it began, 101 years ago. This is a fact. I think. And in America, most folks figure the things just dance off the trees right into the paper cup, with a little sugar on top.

But I'm a journalist. I get to the bottom.

Besides, strawberries don't grow on trees.

We waited. And we waited. Three hours. "You the Wimbledon delivery guy?" I asked a bearded man who finally arrived at 3 a.m. He nodded.

"We'd like to do a story on strawberries. . . ."

When he stopped laughing, 20 minutes later, he was fine. His name was John, a bill collector for British Gas, but for these two weeks he delivers the Wimbledon fruit, as he has the last eight years, because he loves it, and because his brother-in-law owns the company.

"Well, mate," he said, jumping inside the truck, "if you want a chat, you can 'elp me load 'em up, and we can chat."

Did I mention my bad back?

And suddenly, there I was, loading crate after crate, 3,000 pounds of Wimbledon-bound strawberries. What a thrill! What tradition in my hands!

"Good batch this year?" I asked John.

"Dunno." He ripped off the plastic wrap and popped a fistful into his mouth. "Quite tasty, actually," he said.

What the heck? We ate a few. We ate a few more. And finally, at 4 a.m., we finished loading, which was good, because by that point we needed a bathroom desperately. And besides, a few more crates and I'd have had to join the union.

Oh. Here was good news: John would let us help deliver the strawberries to Wimbledon. John knew cheap labor when he saw it.

Here was bad news: He didn't leave until 6 a.m.

So Jimmy and I found a tiny cafeteria near the loading docks. And we waited. And waited. I can barely describe the fun of sitting at a Formica table, for two hours, next to a British truck driver named Cheech.

Aw heck. I won't even try.

A t 5 a.m., I had my fifth cup of coffee. At 5:15, my seventh. I shut my eyes for a blissful moment, taking in the sounds and smells of the market. . . .

"Wake up, you're snoring," said Jimmy.

OK. Back on the truck with John. Off we went. Already there were people waiting for tickets, sleeping on blankets along Church Road.

"Yup," said John, "seen my share of underwear on this street."

What more can I tell you? We unloaded the fruits of our labor outside the main stadium, said goodby, and stumbled back to our hotel room as the rest of London went to work.

So on Monday, I can proudly say we helped bring fruity joy to hundreds of Wimbledon patrons. I can also say when we finally made it back to the grounds, we swore we would never bother with an investigation like this again. And we sealed that pledge with a cup of you-know-what.

I looked at the strawberries, and wondered if they were the batch we had dipped into. Then I wondered if John had washed his hands. Ah, forget it. Our journey is over. Right? Jimmy put the spoon to his lips. . . .

"I wonder where the cream comes from," I said.

MARTINA, CHRIS: FRIENDLY RIVALS EXIT, LAUGHING

July 3

WIMBLEDON, England — What you noticed most was the laughter. How often do you hear that during a Wimbledon semifinal? Chris Evert would hit a great shot, and Martina Navratilova would shake her head and chuckle. Then Martina would scoop a volley out of the grass and Chris would drop her racket. And smile. It was not loud. It was not even often. But it was there. Quiet, gentle, familiar.

Laughter.

"Wasn't that a little strange?" someone asked Evert afterward. "For such an intense match? To smile and even laugh at certain moments?"

"Yeah," she answered. "I usually don't give anything away when I play my opponents. But when I see Martina ... well, we've played so many matches that by now, if there are light moments, it sort of relieves the tension."

Laughter. Why not? They have been playing each other forever, haven't they? Chris and Martina: a never-ending dialogue between two rackets and a little yellow ball. For years, even the dullest tournaments had hope if these two met. Even the weakest fields could be excused if a Martina-Chris showdown was possible.

How many matches? Seventy-three, counting Thursday's. They have had major ones and historic ones and good ones and not-so-good ones but in this one — Navratilova's 6-2, 5-7, 6-4 victory — they were simply great, as excellent as they can be. And the prize was sufficiently worthy: a Wimbledon final. How many more will either player get?

So their baseline exchanges were crafty and quick. Their net play was like a video gun stuck on "fire." Pow-pow! Chris lobs a bull's-eye. Pow-pow! Martina dives for a drop shot. Unforced errors? Hardly any. First serves? Almost always in. "That may be the best tennis we've ever played," Navratilova said afterward.

And yet they found time for this: Chris came to the net and poked a winner, then, surprised, she pointed at Martina and yelled: "You were supposed to go there!"

Laughter.

A serve was called out by the center linesman, only his voice cracked when he yelled "OUT!" and Martina rolled her eyes and Chris' lips began to spread.

Laughter.

This is what you noticed. The laughter, the grins, the warm feeling between two supposedly bitter rivals. But this you might have missed: sympathy. "I had tears in my eyes," Martina said. "And it wasn't for me winning, it was for Chris losing. I really wished that she could win this tournament one more time. . . .

"At 5-4 in the final set, I started thinking about our friendship. Then I thought, 'God, you're crazy to be thinking about that now. . . .' It actually overwhelmed me, because I didn't expect to feel so much. I would be as happy if she won this tournament as if I do. . . . But she lost. I feel sad about that."

Sad? About winning? Martina? Well. This is how far they have come. They are longer than vaudeville, the best rivalry in sports, now, then, maybe forever. Chris and Martina. Another suitcase, another show. But Martina is 30, and Chris is 32, and Chris is asked about retirement now a hundred times a day.

For years they were Nos. 1 and 2 in the world, jockeying like the last two players in musical chairs. At first Chris was better. Then they were even. Then Martina was unbelievable. Then Chris came back.

Fourteen years of intense rivalry. Now everything is changing. Evert has fallen to No. 3, behind Steffi Graf, the 18-year-old bomber who will play Martina Saturday for the Wimbledon championship. Graf is a blip on the screen that grows brighter every second. Who knows if Evert and Navratilova will ever hold the wishbone again?

"What would it be like if you started showing up at tournaments and Chris wasn't in the draw?" Navratilova was asked.

"Pretty strange," she said softly. "I would miss her a lot."

The Centre Court crowd Thursday at Wimbledon obviously shared the emotion. Here was Navratilova, fighting for a record try at an eighth title, and yet Evert was the one cheered as if history rested on her racket. Surprised? Well. Doesn't emotion always rule over numbers?

So when Evert, down a set, took Navratilova to 5-5 in the second, beat her in the sixth game, broke her in the seventh, won it with a strong net volley — well, the crowd was a cloudburst, applause raining down.

And when Evert pulled ahead in that final game, and all she needed was one point to tie the set, 5-all, and send them playing on and on — win by two; it could have gone till nightfall! — the crowd was ready to leap. Instead, Martina muscled a killer serve, won the point, and soon, the match. The fans applauded politely the victory.

But they were thinking about the defeat.

"She plays one of the best matches of her life and she loses?" Navratilova said. "Of course you're sad. It takes a lot away from me winning because I had to beat Chris.

"When we shook hands at the net, do you know what she said? 'I hope I didn't take too much out of you for the final.' What a thing to say. I put my arm around her when she said that."

A nd that was how they walked off — side by side, dipping in sync toward the Royal Box, then disappearing into the tunnel. Seventy-three matches together. Who knows if they'll ever do that here again?

"What if you came to the major tournaments and Martina wasn't here?" someone asked Evert, a switch on the earlier question.

"I wouldn't have anybody to talk to in the locker room," she said, laughing. "No. . . . I'm just kidding. But it's almost like she's family now. We've been together so long. We've seen other players come and go, but we've been the constants. . . ."

Longer than most? Longer than any of them. Any sport. Longer than Magic and Bird, than Tunney and Dempsey, than Snead and Hogan. How long have they been out there? All the Wimbledons and French Opens and U.S. Opens and Australian Opens and Tokyos and Romes and Clevelands and Atlantas and Team Tennis and exhibitions and clay and cement and indoor carpet. How long? When they played their first match, in 1973, Chris was single, and Martina was a brunet Czech. And today Chris is single again and Martina is blond and American. How long have they been out there? Two hair colors, one husband and a country. That long.

"You know, over the last years we've gotten to know each other better," said Evert, smiling despite her defeat. "Before it was always a lot of respect on the court, but 'see you later.' Now it's more socializing. We say, 'Do you wanna go out to eat?' It's more of a family thing now. . . .

"Friendship," she said.

"Friendship," Martina said.

There is no more enduring rivalry in sports. There is no more enduring quality in life. Finally, it seems the two have come together: prodigies, challengers, enemies, friends. That is what we can say now, after saying all the other stuff about Chris and Martina. Friends. They are friends.

So this latest Wimbledon semifinal, this magnificent display of tennis, was a loss for Evert, but not a defeat. A victory for Navratilova, but not a celebration. Consider it a great production number in the closing act of a great play, an occasion to marvel and applaud and yes, even laugh. You were allowed to laugh. They laughed.

"I really wished we could have stopped this thing at 30-all in the last game," said Navratilova, sighing. "When people talk about the greats of all time, they'd have to talk about both of us. . . ."

Not to worry: They will anyhow. Here's laughing with you, kids. This was splendor in the grass.

PAT CASH CANCELS WIMBLEDON'S CZECH

July 6

WIMBLEDON, England — He had just won Wimbledon, no worries, mate, and now he jumped into the stands and started running up the steps. Never mind that the Duke and Duchess of Kent were waiting at midcourt, that all the pomp and circumstance of this tournament was waiting, that the guy he had beaten, Ivan Lendl, was alone at the net, fuming. Does he care? Naw. Hold your water, yabbos. He's gotta hug somebody.

Pat Cash wins Wimbledon. Pat Cash runs up steps. Pat Cash steps on man's head, jumps into the box, hugs dad, hugs coach, kisses girlfriend, removes headband, waves — then searches for a way back to the court. Australia waited 16 years for this. Let the Duke hold the trophy for a minute.

"To be honest, the whole time I was posing with it for photographers I just wanted to get off the court," said Cash, 22, after squishing Lendl in straight sets, 7-6, 6-2, 7-5, to win the first Grand Slam title of his career. "I just wanted to be with the people who meant the most to me, that's all."

Good day for G'day. Cash In. The latest thunder from Down Under is a precision server with a Mel Gibson face who boasts an earring, a bandana and a post-tennis ambition to "go to the pub with the boys and be a real yabbo" — which is sort of Australia's answer to Billy Carter.

"Were the yabbos back home watching at the pub?" he was asked.

"I bloody hope so," he said.

Well, this is what they saw this hot afternoon: Cash all over. He was magnificent against Lendl, like Zorro minus the cape. Cash slamming from overhead. Hah! Cash diving for a backhand. Hah! Cash stretched like gum near the net, returning the ball with a glorious boink. Hah! Hah-Hah! Die, you dog!

Which brings us to Lendl, once nicknamed "The Choking Dog." Oooh. This has to hurt. Even the staid British TV commentators suggested the No. 1-ranked player in the world swallowed it out there. That is hard to back up — although he did lead, 5-2, in the third set. But he has never won Wimbledon. He has never won anything on grass. The bet here is he returns to his Connecticut mansion and puts in a rock lawn.

Besides, even Mercury might have had trouble with Pat Cash on Sunday. His serve was a laser, and if you can't return a serve you can't win too many games, unless the other guy dies or something.

Consider this: The first game Sunday, which Cash served, took two minutes. The next game, which Lendl served, took 12. The third game, which Cash served, took two.

Get the idea?

"He places it so well," said Lendl afterward, shaking his head at the man who won 20 straight points on his serve. "And he mixes it up. I hardly knew where it was going to go. . . .

"I said to myself before the match, 'No matter what happens, just keep fighting. You can come back from anything.' "

Nice thought. Dead wrong. Only in that third set, after slashing Lendl to cold cuts for two solid hours, did Cash finally lower his gloves. He played a few sloppy games, and Lendl was suddenly serving for the set at 5-3. If there was ever a moment for him to take control, that was it.

Instead, Lendl lost by double-faulting. He never won another game. He barely won another point.

Next thing he knew he was shaking hands with yet another Wimbledon champion (he lost last year's final to Boris Becker) and watching as this one jumped the rail and did a Crocodile Dundee impression — stepping on people's heads into the arms of his loved ones.

Cash Out.

What did he say to you?" someone asked Ian Barclay, Cash's coach of 11 years, whom Cash hugged tightly in the impromptu guest box celebration.

"I can't say," Barclay answered, smiling.

"Can you hint?"

"Well, all right. I'll leave out the expletive. He said, 'We — showed them.' Get the drift?"

Of course. We're not all yabbos, you know.

Besides, leaving out expletives is standard practice when dealing with Pat Cash. He was at his charming best Sunday — would you be in a bad mood after winning Wimbledon? — but the record shows Cash has been an Aussie terror for years. He was recently fined $8,000 in Dusseldorf, West Germany, for obscenities, both visual and audible. Three years ago, after losing to Lendl at the U.S. Open semifinals, he threw his racket into the stands and hit a guy in the head.

Even the Australian journalists are cautious about interviewing him, because his tone can quickly go arrogant or aloof. "He won't deny he has a temper," Barclay admitted, "but that's part of his competitiveness. That's what enables him to win."

That's no excuse. But face it. How long can you knock a guy who tells the British to stuff their ceremony while he hugs his dad?

"Was this the greatest moment of your life?" he was asked.

"No way. The greatest moment in my life is when my son was born."

So will the real Pat Cash please stand up? Sure. Now that his back is OK. Remember that Cash missed most of the 1985 season with back injuries, then needed an emergency appendectomy before Wimbledon last year, just five days after his son was born — are you keeping up with this? — and yet he played, and made the quarterfinals, despite a world ranking of No. 413.

We should have suspected something then. He obviously had the flair — he threw headbands and wristbands to the screaming girls in the crowd — and he clearly had the strokes. This is a gifted athlete: fast, fluid, instinctive. Compared to Cash, Lendl moved like a man dodging spears.

"I've had a few ups and downs in my career," Cash said, sipping a glass of champagne during his post-match interviews, "and the downs were pretty steep. A lot of people haven't really helped me in my career, so I have always said my fans are the most important people to me. That's why I've started the fan club in Australia and London."

No one asked him why he started the fan clubs. Isn't that usually someone else's job?

Whatever. Here is a new joke: How much does it cost to join the Pat Cash fan club?

I don't know. But they take Czechs.

Hah!

So Wimbledon ends, with Pat Cash finishing for Australia what Peter Doohan began when he upset Becker, the defending champion, in the second round. The Aussies have waited since John Newcombe in 1971 to hear that familiar accent in this winner's circle. The yabbos must have done a lot of Foster's pounding Sunday night. Or this morning. Or whatever time it is down there.

So be it. Here was a Wimbledon that began with rain and ended in sun, that featured a Jimmy Connors comeback and a Steffi Graf arrival. It saw Chris Evert and Martina Navratilova give us one for the ages, and Stefan Edberg, 21, Gabriela Sabatini, 17, and Natalie Zvereva, 16, warn us that the ages may have nothing to do with it.

And it all ended with this: a final precision serve by Cash, a volley, and Lendl sending his fondest wish into the net yet again, losing Wimbledon, while the newest heartthrob champion took off for the seats.

"Well done, Pat," a BBC-TV man said in the closing interview, "and now, go have a drink (he needs to tell him that?), enjoy yourself, celebrate, but before you go, sum up in one word how you feel right at this moment!"

Cash looked straight ahead, champagne in hand, the title in his pocket, the country at his feet, and smiled.

"Stuffed," he said.

LOVE OF GOLF TAKES SCOTS FROM CRADLE TO GREEN

July 16

MUIRFIELD, Scotland — "Maybe you can help me with directions," I said, unfolding a map as I stepped to the counter. "I'm trying to get to the British Open, and I can't seem to. . . ."

I looked up.

I was talking to a 12-year-old.

"You . . . don't drive, I take it?"

"Afreeed noot," he said.

I have this problem whenever I go to Scotland. Actually, I have three problems whenever I go to Scotland. I keep getting in the wrong side of the car. I keep driving on the wrong side of the road. And I can't understand a thing they say.

And here I was again, en route to the Open in Muirfield, lost, confused, hitting curbs. I had rented a car at the Edinburgh airport. I had asked for directions, and the lady had said "goo to the fuurst rooondaboot" and look for the signs.

So I went to the first "rooondaboot." I went rooond and aboot. And I was back in the airport.

I did this three times. Each time I wound up back in the airport. It was on my fourth attempt that I noticed the only slab of business in this otherwise deserted little loop: A driving range.

Yes. The Port Royal Golf Range. I am not making this up. Right there. Maybe 1,000 yards from the airport. I knew golf was big here. But I figured they could wait until they got home.

Anyhow, I pulled in for directions. Which is how I wound up with this Scottish Little Archie; red hair, freckles, thin and that accent. He said his name was Grant.

"Do you golf?" I asked.

"Aye."

"You have your own clubs?"

"Aye."

"When did you get them?"

"Two years agoo," he said.

"Two years ago? How old were you? Ten?"

"Aye."

Now, forgive me. Where I come from, you don't have your own golf clubs when you are 10. You don't even touch a golf club when you are 10, because the only golf clubs around are your father's, and if you

240

touch those you hang in the closet by your ankles for a year.

"What's your handicap?" I asked, joking.

"Sixteen," he said, serious.

"And you play, like, all 18 holes?" I just couldn't see this little kid teeing off, choosing a driver, studying a putt.

Just then the door opened. In walked two more kids. One of them was chubby with apple cheeks, the other thin, wearing a Los Angeles Raiders sweatshirt. Ah, I thought. Normalcy.

"Where's dee Putulssomby golf?" the chubby kid asked. Or something like that. It was then that I noticed the second kid was lugging a bag of clubs, with little red fuzzy things on the club heads.

"Go dune de rood," Grant instructed, "go rayt den leeft den rayt. . . ." Out they went, presumably with a tee time.

"More golfers?" I asked, once they'd gone.

"Aye," he said.

I felt as if I'd walked into Saturday morning television. I could see these kids walking to school, books under one arm, 5-iron under the other.

"You wooont to hit a few?" Grant said.

What the heck? I wasn't getting any closer to Muirfield. We walked outside. The sky was gray, the grass thick and wet. Plane engines roared overhead. I stood at the tee and stared at the yard markers, 100, 150, 200. Above them, you saw "EDINBURGH AIRPORT" on the side of a hangar.

"Goo aheeed," said Grant.

Just then I remembered how I play golf. You know how there are bad golfers, horrible golfers and the absolutely laughable golfers?

Yeah. Well. The last group? I carry its clubs.

But now I had a 12-year-old watching me. He scratched his chin. I drew back the driver like a sword and brought it down.

The ball dribbled off and died.

"Well, I gotta get going. . . ." I said.

And so I did. I got in that car — on my second try — and banged against curbs on the wrong side of the road until I found my way here. And when I arrived, everyone was talking about the Open, which begins today, about its tradition, its history, and Scotland's love for golf.

What more need be said? You want to learn about the heartbeat of a sport? Start with the children. Check the schoolyard. Check the sandlots. Check the airport.

As I drove off from the Port Royal Golf Range, I noticed Grant had taken over my tee. I watched him in my rearview mirror. His swing was true. The club head whammed across. The ball rose like a tiny jet, high and strong into the friendly skies.

TIGERS' JIM WALEWANDER: THEY'RE PLAYING HIS SONG

July 27

L et us pause here for a day in the life of the Tigers' latest hero: Jim Walewander.

Uh, that's W-a-l-e-w-a-n-d-e-r.

Right. OK. He is a rookie. He has played in 23 big-league games. Here is how he learned he was starting Sunday: Lou Whitaker, the Tigers' second baseman, came in at noon and said he couldn't play. Bad back. The game was 90 minutes away. A call went out from Sparky Anderson's office, a call to arms, a call to destiny. . . .

"GET ME . . . WALEWANDER!"

Now. This had already been a special day for Jim Walewander. Earlier in the morning, he had met his favorite punk rock group. Perhaps you've heard of it. The Dead Milkmen? Yeah. Well. Maybe not. Anyhow, on Saturday night the Dead Milkmen played a gig in Hamtramck. If it's called a "gig" in Hamtramck. I'm not sure about this.

Anyhow, Walewander had gone to see his idols. He had gone alone. Why? I'll let you figure that out. And now, during batting practice, they were returning the favor.

Here they stood, on the Tiger Stadium field, dressed in their Sunday-best combat boots. They posed for photos. It was great fun, and Walewander was having the time of his life, especially when they signed a poster. One member wrote: "To Jim — Satan Is My Master, (signed) Rodney." You can imagine how special that must have felt.

And then the Dead Milkmen got to meet Sparky Anderson. I missed that. I can only imagine:

PR MAN: Sparky, meet the Dead Milkmen.

SPARKY: Well, hello, boys.

MILKMEN: DEATH TO CAPITALISTS!

SPARKY: Well, gotta go, boys.

(Actually, Sparky related this story after the game: "One of them had on combat boots, a camouflage army shirt and an earring. I told him, 'Son, don't take no prisoners.' ")

You gotta love a manager like that.

F or most of us, meeting the Dead Milkmen would be enough for one day. Or maybe a week. But there was more in store for Walewander.

He came to bat in the sixth inning with Chet Lemon on first and the Tigers clinging to a 2-1 lead. This was an important game. If the Tigers won and the Yankees lost, Detroit would move into first place for the first time all year.

And what did Walewander do? He cracked a fastball high into right-center field, up, up — it slammed off the upper deck! The crowd went crazy! His first major league homer! Goodness. As we reporters watched him circle the bases, we thought about this and the Dead Milkmen in one day, and, well, we got all choked up. Mostly when we thought about the Dead Milkmen, though.

And of course, as you now know, the Tigers went on to win the game, 6-2, and stay right on the Yankees' tails. And in the clubhouse after the game, Walewander, the hero, was given his home run ball, and the privilege of choosing the music to dress by. He chose one of the Dead Milkmen's more mellow numbers, something just right for the moment. "Bomb The Sewage Plant," I think it was called.

"What will you do with the ball?" someone yelled, trying to be heard over the bass guitar.

"Put it in my glove compartment," he yelled back, "along with my first major league hit."

"How many balls do you have in there?"

"Just these two for now," he said. "When I fill it up, I'll be able to buy myself a new car."

He grinned like a high schooler, which is about how old he looks. His T-shirt featured a smiling cartoon cow. A cow? Yes. A gift from. . . . Oops! The music changed! A new number.

"What's this one called?" he was asked.

" 'Take Me To The Specialist,' " he said.

Gotcha.

So the day was a real thrill, as any music lover can imagine. And baseball fans enjoyed it, too. After all, one telltale sign of a pennant contender is winning games with your No. 9 hitter blasting a home run, while your starting pitcher (in this case, the inimitable Walt Terrell) goes all the way.

Good stuff. Promising stuff. This is simply the hottest team in the major leagues right now. There is no telling who today's hero will be, where he will come from, what size combat boots he will wear. But no matter. The fact is, the Tigers are getting something out of just about everybody.

And Sunday, it was a perfectly timed debut homer by Walewander, who figured his biggest thrill had already come before the starting call.

"Did the Dead Milkmen stay for the game?"

"Nah," he said. "They had a gig somewhere."

Livonia, perhaps?

JIM EISENREICH REVISITED STILL HARD STORY TO TELL

August 5

I first encountered Jim Eisenreich three years ago in a Florida parking lot. He was walking out after a spring training game, and I was sitting in my car, waiting. I had driven 200 miles. I wanted to interview him. But as he passed, I just sat there. After a minute, I watched him drive away.

You're always a little nervous when you first interview somebody. But in Eisenreich's case, it wasn't my nerves I was worried about. For years, he had been suffering from a disorder that made him twitch and gasp for breath uncontrollably. It happened during ball games. Sometimes he ran off the field, scared, choking. No one was sure what it was, although certain doctors called it "stage fright syndrome" because it tended to happen in the outfield and among large crowds.

Whatever it was, it had clipped his baseball career each time he reached the major leagues — and Eisenreich belonged in the major leagues. He has tremendous talent. Great power hitter. Good arm. But people had been cruel, fans had heckled and laughed and doctors had made him feel like a freak. He was trying a "final" comeback with Minnesota that spring of '84 — after failing in two previous seasons — and, in that frozen moment in the parking lot, I sensed my questions would only make things worse.

So I said nothing. Later that season, Eisenreich's problem acted up again, and in June 1984, he voluntarily retired from the Twins and, ostensibly, major league baseball.

I had often wondered what he was doing. And this past winter I read of his planned comeback with the Kansas City Royals. I made a few phone calls. Finally, in January, I went to visit him at his home in St. Cloud, Minn.

We talked there for several hours. He said he had finally learned what the problem was: Tourette Syndrome, a neurological disorder that causes certain uncontrollable responses, such as twitching and barking sounds. He was taking medication to keep it in check. He denied ever having "stage fright syndrome" and expressed anger at the Twins' doctors who diagnosed him that way.

He seemed a little uncomfortable with all my questions, but he answered them. At times he even joked about it. By the end, we had a nice rapport, and I left there thinking I had met a man of remarkable courage.

Journalists are people, too. They prefer to be liked. But if they follow the rules of their job, that's not always easy. I would have liked to have written Eisenreich's story without calling anyone else. I would have

244

liked to have written that in person he seemed like every other big league player I've ever interviewed.

Neither would be accurate.

So I called the Twins' doctor, Leonard Michienzi, who maintained that Eisenreich does not suffer from Tourette, but is just using that theory to cope with his problem. And I included his opinion in the story. I also included the fact that only one doctor (whose name Eisenreich couldn't remember) had diagnosed him as having the syndrome. I included impressions of his behavior; his foot tapping; his voice, which was, at times, unsteady. And, of course, I included a great deal of what Eisenreich himself had told me. This is part of painting the whole picture. It is what they teach you when you get into this business.

The article was very long. It concluded with the thought that Eisenreich deserved a happy ending, but a happy ending was not for sure. When it appeared, in February, the reaction was considerable. Many readers were moved; they wrote asking to get in touch with Eisenreich, and hoped he made the Royals' roster.

And since then, he has. He was called up in June as a designated hitter. He is doing OK (.219, three HRs), and while he does not yet play the outfield, where his problems often occurred, that may come in time. He has had no troubles in two months.

Which is great. I don't know for sure whether Jim Eisenreich has Tourette. I doubt anybody really does, including Eisenreich himself. But he is in the big leagues for now. He has won a few games with his bat. Take that for the wonderful news that it is.

S o I called Eisenreich Tuesday morning at his hotel. The Royals are in town to play the Tigers, and this was the first time our paths had crossed since January. I wanted to congratulate him.

"Yeah, it's you," he said over the phone. He did not sound friendly.

He said he hadn't liked the article, that it had upset his family. This was not the first time an athlete has told me that. Journalism is not public relations. But this was the last person I ever wanted to be unhappy.

"What about it upset you?" I asked.

He didn't have specifics. He remembered one part where I described him. "You made me sound like a bum," he said.

(I checked the article. I wrote: "His face is unshaven, his eyes sleepy-looking, his mouth a crooked line." That is precisely how he looked that afternoon. Maybe I should have called him cheerful and apple-cheeked. But that was not the way he appeared.)

"That's really what bothered you?" I asked.

He said I wrote he appeared "nervous." He did appear nervous. He was fuzzy on other criticisms, but I imagine some of his objections lay in the claims by the Twins' doctor, and my impressions that he was not a sure bet, no matter how much I wanted him to be. What could I say? Perhaps he thought, because we had gotten along, that I would simply write things the way he saw them. But that is not my job.

"All you guys just write what you want," he said. What we want? What I really wanted was for him to hit .400 and win the MVP. I have never felt more for an athlete in my life. This was a guy who from age five had been teased, hospitalized, insulted, and yet he rose to the top. Good for him.

My initial reaction was to tell him this, argue it out. I started to. Then I thought about all he had already endured, and I felt as I did in that car three years ago — as if I never should have asked anything.

I apologized. Not for the words in the article. But for the reaction they brought him.

"I really just called to say I'm glad you're in the majors, and I hope you stay long enough to make everybody forget the other stuff," I told him.

"I'll never do that," he said quietly.

We hung up. I have re-read that article five times. There is nothing in it that is false. Nothing that I did not see or hear. But they are still my words, my thoughts. About somebody else. Eisenreich is going to read them one way. You another. Me another. It is the nature of this business. And I cannot describe, as I sit here and write this, how lousy I feel. A bum? My God. In many ways, he is the biggest hero I've ever written about.

I don't know how to get that across to you, Jim. All I know is this: You want to tell the truth and you want to be somebody's friend. And sometimes there's no way you can do both.

DARNELL COLES:
SO HIGH, SO LOW

August 8

The phone call came in the morning, and by noon he had emptied his locker at Tiger Stadium and was headed for the parking lot. Nobody was around. That was fine. That was better.

"Throw some stuff in the car, hit the road, and I'm outta here," said Darnell Coles, making a herky-jerky motion with his arm. "Goodby to this place."

Goodby to this guy. The young man who was once labeled "the future" at third base for the Tigers has been sent to Pittsburgh, in exchange for a 34-year-old infielder named Jim Morrison. Gone? Just like that? A year ago Coles was a starter, a crowd favorite. The writers voted him second to Jack Morris as Tiger of the Year. Yet on Thursday night, in what would be his last game as a member of this team, he sat quietly on the bench while every non-pitcher got a chance to bat. Except him.

Goodby to this guy.

"FROM FAME TO S—!" he bellowed now, with a mock laugh that echoed off the concrete walls, "that's what it's been like for me!"

Then his voice lowered. He looked at his feet.

"Actually, it's . . . it's been really tough. . . ."

Part of the game. That's the expression players use when a teammate is traded. Part of the game, happens all the time. But this was a story that went unusually sour, unusually fast. Try out, make out, psych out, fade out. Darnell Coles didn't just see "part" of the game in his 16 months here.

He saw most all of it.

How far had he fallen? As far as he had risen. He came into spring training last year all bubble gum and cartoons; you could hardly shut him up once he got talking. "I got a different Mickey Mouse for every day," he once told a reporter, pointing to seven T-shirts with the famous Disney character. "When I get to Detroit, I'm gonna get some more. You can never have too many Mickeys."

He was named the starting third baseman — at age 23 — and once he hit Detroit, he didn't have time to shop for shirts. On a team that was only good, and a tad too familiar, he was the new face, the promise of promise. Darnell Coles finished 1986 with 20 home runs, a .273 batting average and the gratitude of nearly every Tigers fan in the state. "At last! A third baseman!" they seemed to say.

He did commercials. The radio and TV people sought him. He was easy to like, when things went well. He was one of the Tigers chosen this year for the pre-spring tour around Michigan, shaking hands and eating banquet meals and drumming up fan interest. "He's so cute!" they would comment. "He's so young! He's so funny! Just think of how good he'll be this year!"

"I love it up here," he said then.

"Thank the Lord I am out of here," he said on Friday.

What happened in between was a remarkable testament to the power of the brain turned in the wrong direction. Coles got off slowly in the spring, he tried too much too fast, and when it didn't come, he tried even harder. His hitting suffered. His fielding suffered. His hands developed blisters. So did his confidence. When the regular season began, he was making mistake after mistake.

"It was ridiculous," he said Friday. "No way I should have been playing that bad." But the negative thoughts had slipped into his system like a coin in a washing machine, round and round, and he couldn't shake them. He made three errors in one game. He made three errors in another. He would look to the dugout whenever he made a mistake, and the reaction he saw there, the shaking heads, the disgust, just made him more nervous. And he'd make another error. "It got to the point where a batter got up and I was praying, 'Don't hit it to me! Don't hit it to me!' " he said a few weeks ago.

Who knows how these things start? Who knows how to end them? Coles claims he was ostracized by Sparky Anderson (Anderson denies this) and many of his teammates once his playing slacked. He claims that made things worse. There was a clubhouse skirmish following a game in Texas — Coles and a few teammates had to be separated — and since then, he had talked to a select few.

"Hi and bye," he said of his relationship with many of the Tigers. When asked Friday about his relationship with Anderson, he rolled his eyes.

"What relationship?" he said.

Give Coles this much credit. If you bothered to ask him, he would admit that all of it — the 17 errors, the .181 batting average, the eventual trip to the minors, the loss of his job to Tom Brookens — was his fault. "I blame no one else," he said Friday. He is not the easiest guy to be around when things are sour. He is moody and sensitive on a team where do-your-job-and-don't-complain is the preferred style.

So obviously, Coles needed a change of scenery. The Tigers had no intention of using him at third if they could help it. And a brooding non-player is not the kind of influence a pennant-contending team wants around.

He had gone to Bill Lajoie, the Tigers' GM, a few weeks ago demanding to be traded. Lajoie had pacified him. "He told me, 'You're our future,' " Coles said after that meeting, " 'and we're not gonna just trade away our future.' " Not, at least, unless they can get something they wanted in return.

Friday, they apparently got what they wanted. A 34-year-old veteran is not a 25-year-old second-year man. But youth is a relative factor. In truth, Coles had no future here. He had been given "his chances" by this organization.

The trade was made. Lajoie couldn't reach Coles — Coles' phone was off the hook — so he called Dwight Lowry, who lives near Coles, and Lowry's wife walked over to the house and told Darnell to call the office. Coles turned to his wife. "I'm gone somewhere," he said.

And he was. To Pittsburgh.

Try out, make out, psych out, fade out.

Move out.

H ey, this is great. I'm happy," said Coles, his hands dug in his pockets. "I'm going to a team where most people are 24, 25, 26. Not to say this is an old team, but just more veterans. Maybe I didn't fit in, for whatever reason."

He paused. "Maybe when you make errors, you don't fit in."

He said he would miss Detroit. The fans. Several of the players, most notably Larry Herndon, who, he said, "really helped me through a lot of these bad times."

"But hey. Whatever. As far as I'm concerned, my season starts today when I set foot in, what is it? Three Rivers Stadium? Is that what it's called?"

Yes, he was told.

"My season starts when I get there," he said.

Goodby to this guy. It's hard to say if the Tigers gave up too soon on Coles. You would think so, by his age. But perhaps what was broken they saw as unmendable. Or perhaps the chemistry was simply bad. Baseball is not always about right and wrong. More often, it's about fitting in.

"Do you have anything to say to your old teammates before you go?" he was asked.

He thought about it.

"I hope they win it all," he said.

And he walked to his car. That's it? That's it. Part of the game. Darnell Coles is not as sunshine-young as when he first joined the Tigers. But he took his better and his worse and he climbed into the front seat, closed the door, and drove out of the stadium lot, past a small group of fans waiting in line for tickets.

DOBRONSKI'S FRIENDS CHERISH FINAL MEMORIES

August 23

I t was hot inside the church. The bride and groom stepped to the altar. This was last weekend, Joe Maiorana's wedding, and his college pals were serving as ushers. Bill Ryan. Dave Maine. And, of course, Kurt Dobronski, his ex-roommate, his best friend, who had flown in from Phoenix for the occasion. "It was the first time," Bill remembers, "that all four of us were together in tuxedos."

They had laughed about that because back at Central Michigan it was always jeans and sweats and football gear. Tuxedos? Us guys? True, Bill was now a salesman, Dave worked in a credit union, Kurt had the real estate business in Arizona. But together, somehow, they still felt like kids. "Let's take a picture," their wives and girlfriends had said back at the house. And in their tuxedos, because they couldn't resist, the guys grabbed at one another and stuck their tongues out and mugged for the camera.

Friendship. At the reception afterward, they sat together on a patio and had food and drinks and talked about college days. They had been doing it all week. At the bachelor party. At the rehearsal dinner. At the hotel the night before. Reminiscing. "Like old men, right?" says Bill. "I mean, we're only 28."

That night they danced. They ate cake. They drank champagne. A guy with a video camera came around and gave Kurt the microphone, and he made a little speech for the groom, his closest friend: "Joe, I hope when you're 50," he said, gazing into the lens, "you'll look back at this tape and remember all the good times we had when we were 20."

It was a nice thing to do. But then Kurt was always doing things like that. Joe watched the tape Thursday night — four days after a Northwest Airlines jet crashed horribly upon takeoff at Metro Airport — and then he tried to sleep. The next morning, he met Bill and Dave and they drove quietly to the church to serve as pallbearers at Kurt's funeral.

This is a story about death in an instant, and about friendships that last forever. Kurt Dobronski was not a famous person. But his was a life that touched another life that touched another and another, and in the horribly gray week that followed one of the worst air crashes in U.S. history, those lives were pulled together tighter, like shoelaces, one big tug that they will never forget.

I was watching TV Sunday night when they broke in," recalls Bill Ryan. "They said there was a crash at the Detroit airport and then they said the flight was going to Phoenix, and that's when I got nervous. At the wedding so many people had asked Kurt when he was leaving for home and he said Sunday night.

"I said to my wife, 'Oh, my God, I think Kurt was on that plane. I know he was going on Northwest.' For a while they weren't saying if there were any survivors. We sat there for an hour, not knowing anything. . . .'"

This much Bill Ryan felt he knew: It couldn't be Kurt. Kurt was too, well, too healthy, too much in shape. He was a football player back at CMU — where they had all become friends in the late 1970s and early '80s — a defensive end who would make all-conference twice. On Friday, two nights before the crash, Kurt and Bill had slept in the same hotel room after a big wedding-eve dinner with the families. "We stayed out late, all of us, talking and drinking, and when I woke up Saturday, the first thing I saw was Kurt doing sit-ups. Fifty sit-ups! At like, eight in the morning!"

This was not the kind of guy who dies. This was Kurt, who was always grinning and never complaining and who was doing so well in Arizona. Everybody loved Kurt. "No way it happened to him, I kept saying. He was so together. We had just spent the best weekend of our lives and then . . . well, there's just no way."

He sighs.

"He was too much of a friend to die."

Dave Maine was watching television Sunday night, too. He heard the announcement that Northwest Flight 255, bound for Phoenix and Orange County, Calif., had crashed moments after takeoff, leaving debris and bodies scattered all over. He saw films of the wreckage, of flames licking off I-94.

What do you do in such a moment? Like Bill, Dave immediately focused on the recent mental pictures — the bachelor party, the rehearsal, the wedding — because these were real images, images of life, familiar and right and comforting. Dead? No way. Dave, Kurt and Joe had played on the football team together. They had celebrated two Mid-American Conference championships. At the wedding they had done their celebrated "Victory Dance," in which they slide across the floor, jump in the air, scream "HEY!" and slam into somebody.

Dead? No. Couldn't be. "You only have a few good friends," Dave says. As if that might make them immortal. These good friends had always kept up. Kurt would return to Michigan for the CMU homecoming games, and not too long ago, Dave had visited Kurt in Phoenix, had slept in his house, and had told him the big news: He was going to get married. "I said, 'You wanna put on a tux next June?' And Kurt said, 'Heck, yeah.' He was always happy if you were happy."

So there was a wedding to go to. He couldn't die. He wouldn't. Dave thought about the time Kurt tried out for the Dallas Cowboys, and when

251

that didn't work out, how he tried the Arizona Outlaws of the USFL. "He was writing George Allen all the time, just asking for a look. I told him to quit; he had a nice (real estate) business growing out there. But he wouldn't quit. He wouldn't quit anything."

People like that don't die. Not him. Not him. Wasn't that the thought of so many loved ones when the horror of last Sunday night spread across the nation? Not him. Not her. Not mine. What do you do at such a terrible moment? Dave Maine did what was instinctive. He called Kurt's parents' house.

"Kurt?" he said, hopefully, when a male voice answered.

"No," answered Kurt's brother. "That was Kurt's plane. There were no survivors. I gotta go. . . ."

L ove is only chatter; friends are all that matter." A poet wrote that once. And is there ever a friendship like the one with your college roommate? What a time! Grown-up bodies without the grown-up responsibilities. Parties and late night talks and beer and late night talks and girls and late night talks.

For five years, Kurt Dobronski and Joe Maiorana shared a room, shared a bunk bed, walked around Joe's pile of clothes in the middle of the floor. ("We called it 'The Pile,' " says Bill. "It was so big we used to sleep on it.") They had grown up near one another in Detroit. They had heard of one another through the high school athletic grapevine. After two weeks of freshman football practice at Central Michigan, they decided to room together.

So telling Joe of Kurt's death — which Bill volunteered to do — was going to be the hardest thing. Joe was on his honeymoon. He and his bride had just reached the island of Kauai, in Hawaii. Because of the busy produce business in which Joe works, these two weeks were to be the longest stretch the two of them ever spent together. They had enjoyed one day of island fun when the phone rang at 7 a.m.

It doesn't seem fair — a guy on his honeymoon.

It isn't fair.

"When I heard Bill say he had bad news, I thought somebody had broken into my house or something," says Joe in a soft voice still choked with grief. "Big deal. That wouldn't have mattered.

"Then he said it was a plane crash. My God. What pops into your head? People die in plane crashes."

You need only talk to Joe Maiorana to know what he had with Kurt Dobronski was more than average friendship. This was one of those rare meshes, a sharing of a soul, two guys who could live together for five years and never have a fight. Their best memories were snapshots that included both of them: the first game they started together, Joe at offensive guard,

Kurt at defensive end, the showers after winning, the trip to California, the trip to Florida, the championship rings they received.

"Have you ever had a friend that you just didn't have to say anything to? He just knew? That's how we were. When he got hurt his freshman year and couldn't play, I was there for him. I got hurt the next year and couldn't play. He was there for me. When we got out of school, I remember that first summer, thinking how weird it was not to be going back in September to our room. We had been together so much."

So what do you do when a piece of your soul is suddenly yanked away? Joe hung up the phone, went for a short walk, then began making plans to return as quickly as possible. He and his wife had these honeymoon reservations for eight months. Thousands of dollars would be lost. It never entered his mind. "I was just doing what a decent human being does. When your best friend dies, you go back, no matter what. There was never a question. He came to my wedding. . . ."

He pauses, the words strained. "I just feel like, I wish I hadn't invited him. . . ."

On the plane trip back from Hawaii, Joe and his wife had to stop in Honolulu, Los Angeles, Minneapolis and Detroit — all on Northwest Airlines, which paid the fare and whose last-minute mistake caused the couple to miss their first flight.

The journey home took nearly 24 hours. The takeoffs were the hardest part. "I kept looking out the window as we lifted off," says Joe. "I tried to visualize what Kurt saw. My God. It must have been terrible. He's a smart guy. He had to realize what was going on. He had to face the terror of knowing he was going to die. That's what bothers me the most. That's what I can't accept. It just isn't fair. . . ."

It isn't fair. Kurt Dobronski was a 6-foot-2, curly haired, always grinning young man who, by all accounts, never spent a day pretending he was something he was not. Quiet. Confident. Loving. You can ask people from work, school, the neighborhood. They come up with the same words. During the last week of his life, he visited CMU. He was crazy about his old school. He saw his old coach, Herb Deromedi, and he even worked out with the freshman football players. "He told me he had a lot of equipment and football souvenirs at home but what he really missed was just getting into the simple gray sweats and working out," says Deromedi, "so I gave him a pair."

Before he left, Kurt made sure to take a young player to lunch, a kid who had gone to Edsel Ford, Kurt's old high school, and was now playing for Central. Nobody asked him to do it. He did it anyway. "He loved that place," says Bill. "He never forgot it."

A week later, in the charred wreckage of Flight 255, workers would somehow find Kurt's CMU championship ring and send it back to the family.

Where is the rhyme and reason for this heartbreak? Where is the sensible chord? "I know people say this is part of God's plan," says Deromedi, who recruited Kurt out of high school, "but I don't believe that. God did not plan this. Not this kind of tragedy."

You need only to have seen films of the crash site, of the makeshift morgue that was set up in an airplane hangar, to realize where those words come from.

Isn't it crazy? Without a plane, Kurt Dobronski never would have made it in for the wedding. He never would have been there for the bachelor party, for the time with his family, his brothers, his sister, and his fiancee, Cheryl Kolakowski, whom he'd dated since their freshman year.

He would have missed those homecoming weekends, and the reunions at the bar. Isn't it crazy? Without a plane.

These are the times we live in. "Days of miracle and wonder," goes a popular song. Long distance. Computers. Cellular phones.

Planes.

The last time Kurt, Bill, Dave and Joe were alone together was the limousine ride to the wedding. It may be their fondest memory. They were so happy, so giddy, so mischievous. And they were so late. Joe was nervous. He was tapping his hand without realizing it on Bill's shoulders.

"You can still back out," Kurt teased.

"Yeah," said Dave, "we can take this limo right now and go to the airport."

"We'll go to Vegas."

"Yeah."

"Vegas?"

"Or Phoenix."

"Yeah, Phoenix."

"Right now?"

"Come on."

"To the airport."

"Right now."

"Let's go."

Planes.

It was hot inside the church. The silver casket was adorned with flowers and two photos of Kurt, one a picture of his handsome face, the other a college football shot. The room was packed with relatives, friends, ex-football players and coaches, some of whom had to stand outside and watch through the open doors, because there were no seats left.

The preacher spoke about life and death. The soloist sang "Somewhere," a song that contains the lines: "It helps to know, we both are sleeping, 'neath the same blue sky."

When the service was over, the pallbearers carried the casket outside. There were eight of them, including Bill, Dave and Joe. They looked straight ahead, into the coming rain. They appeared too young for this duty. But nobody was very young anymore.

The real grief of a tragedy like this comes not when the plane crashes to earth, but when reality does. Tonight and tomorrow night and all the tomorrows that follow will contain a dull ache for Kurt Dobronski's family and his loved ones, and for his friends. There will be no church then, full of supporters. No newspaper stories. No one they can see about the sadness. Except perhaps each other.

"We had one of our best weeks ever together that last week," says Dave, who will be married next year. "I keep thinking about that. I want to see that picture we took in our tuxedos. I'd really like to have that. . . ."

"You know, for some reason," says Bill, with his child on his lap, "when we were at the wedding I just grabbed Joe around and told him I loved him. I had never done that with any of them before. You know, to tell a guy you love him. But it was such a neat evening, and Joe was just making the rounds, and I just said it. I'm glad I did, too."

"I was so concerned for Kurt's family," says Joe, who has a honeymoon to finish, some day, some way. "When I went up to them, I couldn't believe they were worried about how I was feeling. I'm so insignificant compared to what they're going through. They said they'd like to see more of me, to make sure I stay in contact. I'm going to."

Where is the rhyme? Where is the reason? Perhaps only in this: the appreciation of what we have today, right now, before something sudden and horrible takes it away. There was a moment when the four of them danced and drank and felt as if they would live forever. But that was last week. And last week was a very long time ago.

LIGHTNING START SETS UP BEN JOHNSON'S RECORD

August 31

ROME — "ON YOUR MARKS! . . ."

Carl Lewis crouched low in the starting blocks, head down. Ben Johnson crouched next to him, a mirror image.

"SET! . . ."

Their backs arched. Lewis still looked down, awaiting the gun, as did six other sprinters. Only Johnson raised his head and looked toward the finish, as if destiny was cooing his name. . . .

This would be the start of something big. For days, this city had buzzed about the "the confrontation" of this world championship 100 meters, the two fastest men on the planet — Lewis, 26, the big name, the Olympic king, the defending world champ, versus Johnson, 25, the shy Canadian, who grew up running barefoot in his native Jamaica, and who had beaten Lewis several times, but never in a competition this big.

The stadium was packed. Every head was turned. Even the vendors and the teenage volunteers came out from the corridors and lined the steps. Here is what they saw: Seven sprinters, heads down. One sprinter, head up.

"POW!"

Johnson exploded out of the blocks as if cannon-shot — "It was either the best reaction time of his life, or the slowest jump I've ever seen (for me)," Lewis would later remark — but it was ruled clean, no false start, and after the first 20 meters it was evident that this whole race was Johnson and Lewis, and likely in that order. Their bodies grooved quickly into their individual styles: Lewis fluid, straight ahead, no wasted motion; Johnson an earthquake of power, feet slamming the track, arms muscle-tight and churning madly. Is he for real? He looks as if he'll blow up before the tape!

He passed 40 meters easily ahead. Fifty. Sixty. Johnson is the better starter anyhow, while Lewis is famous for motoring past people as they slow toward the finish. But Johnson wasn't slowing this time, no way, no how, and the crowd began calling his name, first quietly, then quickly, and with each stride: "JOHN-SON!" Seventy. "JOHN-SON!" Eighty. "JOHN-SON!" Ninety. No coming back from this. Lewis pressed the final 10 meters, but it didn't help, it wasn't close. . . .

"JOHN-SONNNNN!"

Victory! He eased up, and the whole stadium, perhaps the whole world, did a double-take as the scoreboard clock flashed unbelievable digits: 9.83

— a world record by a tenth of a second!

No wind. No altitude. No asterisks. A world record! A tenth of a second? It had taken 15 years for the record to drop two-hundredths of a second! Wow! The stadium exploded, and so did Lewis, chasing Johnson halfway around the track in an effort to congratulate him. "He deserves a handshake," Lewis would say. But the winner, who has taken his fill of Carl Lewis questions and comparisons the last two years, barely acknowledged him. "I didn't see him coming," Johnson would say later. There was more to it than that. This was Johnson's moment. And he wanted it that way.

Lewis slunk back to the tunnel. In the wild applause for the new hero, no one yet realized, not even Lewis himself, that in finishing second, he had run the best time of his life, a 9.93, which would have given him a share of a world record had Johnson not been there.

MEEESTER JOHN-STON!" the Italian reporters screamed in the sticky-hot press room afterward. "MEESTER WORLD RAY-CORD!"

Johnson, a 5-10, 180-pound muscle ball, answered their questions briefly, sedately. Whereas Lewis is the ultimate media creature (he habitually fixes his hair before any TV interview), Johnson would rather be anywhere else. He speaks with a stutter he has had since youth, so talking is not his forte. He shied away from waving a flag after his win. On the victory stand, he wore only dark green sweats. "I don't have any Canadian singlets," he explained.

And yet, what he had done! Shattered a mark that earned him the title "World's Fastest Human." Shattered? Is that the right word? There are ruins in this city with less damage. You don't take a tenth of a second off the 100-meter record. Not in one swoop. Do you?

He did. "And I think I can improve it next year," he said. "It can be done."

Amazing. Even Lewis had to concede that. And yet, in some way, this was a shining moment for Lewis, too. He showed grace in defeat — the first really big one he has suffered in a while — and it may well have won him more fans than any of his victories. "We are not friends," he admitted of his relationship with rival Johnson, "but we are competitors. I respect him."

A world record. A would-have-been world record. When they analyze this race, they will see that the difference was at the gun, Johnson's thunderclap of anticipation. What was he thinking when he stared down that track? Velocity? Destiny? Perhaps only that this would be the start of something big.

Oh, man, was it ever.

ONCE PERFECT, SCOTT HEADED DOWNHILL FAST

September 7

ROME — The runners were charging to the tape in the 1,500-meter final, but I can't tell you who was in front. I was watching the guy in last place, the tall, sandy-haired American whose steps were labored and whose face was strained. He was way behind, maybe 60 yards, but I kept waiting for him to charge, to kick, to win. It was stupid. I can't help it.

His name is Steve Scott. He is the first athlete I ever interviewed.

That shouldn't mean anything. I have interviewed hundreds since: baseball stars, basketball stars, Super Bowl winners, Hall of Famers. But back then, I didn't know all that was coming. Back then, I was a free-lance writer, looking for work, and Scott was a big name in his field — the best American miler in history, and our top hope for an Olympic gold in the 1,500.

A small running magazine had commissioned me to write a feature story. Two hundred bucks. If Scott would agree. I called him on the phone. My voice cracked with nerves. He agreed anyhow.

"You want a Coke?" was the first thing he said, welcoming me into his home. We sat in his living room, he endured my amateur questions for hours. He even showed me around his neighborhood, because I thought it would "strengthen" the piece.

I liked the guy. He was easygoing, he laughed a lot. He seemed crazy about his family — his wife and baby son. I mentioned that the 1984 Olympics would be a money-making opportunity, and that athletes such as Edwin Moses and Mary Decker already had big contracts. "Yeah," he said, shrugging, "I guess I should do something like that."

Because the magazine could not afford to send a photographer, Scott gave me a few pictures from his family photo album before I left. He trusted me to return them.

That, it would turn out, was a mistake.

Time, since then, has been kinder to me than Scott. I was hired by a newspaper, then a bigger newspaper, then a bigger one. I have made some money. Seen much of the world. Things have gotten better and better.

Scott, meanwhile, finished second in the 1,500 at the 1983 world championships — outkicked by Britain's Steve Cram. Then, determined to avoid the same fate, he tried a different tactic in the Olympics. He ran from the front. It was a mistake. He finished 10th.

He was still one of the best in the world, but the two "big" races didn't work out. The endorsement money came and went, showered itself on Moses and Mary Lou Retton and other Olympic success stories. Scott remained fairly anonymous. He was 28, no longer young for track. What could he do? He kept running.

I would see him at least once a year, somewhere, even though his was now a minor sport in my work. We talked at the '84 Olympics, and the national championships in 1985, and last summer at the Goodwill Games in Moscow. He always remembered me, always smiled when he heard how well things were going. And he always asked about the pictures, laughing, and I always promised to return them, laughing.

"First thing when I get back!" I always said.

I know this makes no sense. But somehow, I always figured as long as I was writing sports, Steve Scott would be a topflight runner. We'd sort of parallel each other. After all, in no small way, his kindness had affected my career choice; he made me want to try another sports article, and another, until it suddenly became my job.

I figured his big success was just a matter of time. But time passed. Once, the mile and 1,500 belonged to Scott, Sebastian Coe and Steve Ovett. Now others rule. New faces. Younger legs. Scott is a "seasoned veteran." Which means: slower.

Sunday in this world championship 1,500 he was the slowest. Dead last. Afterward, reporters crowded the tunnel, where you must request an athlete for an interview.

"Scott, No. 1,080," I said to the staffer. He disappeared, then returned minutes later.

"Mr. Scott has left. He said he is very tired and does not feel good. He is sorry."

I understood. He was frustrated. Embarrassed. Last place. But that didn't matter to me. I only wanted to say hello. I ran outside, looked for him by the exits. But he was gone.

And that, I suddenly realized, was that. Unless he makes the Olympic team next year, which is hardly for certain, I may not see him again. "I can't believe it," I half-mumbled to a colleague.

"Scott?" he said. "Hey. The guy's washed up."

There is a sports columnist in Chicago who loves to criticize the local athletes. I once asked whether he worried about facing his targets. "Nah," he said, "I'll be here longer than they will."

I never understood what he meant. Until now. I have a flight home today, to a pennant race, a football season, a year even better than last. And Steve Scott, the athlete who, in many ways, got me started, is 31 and slipping. Growing older, I guess they call this. But it doesn't seem fair.

Gibson's Big Hit Stops the Clock

September 28

TORONTO — Oh, if home runs could talk! What might this one have said — this ninth-inning speedball that exploded off Kirk Gibson's bat and sailed gloriously over the right field wall, tied the game, silenced the crowd, landed in the Blue Jays' parking area and rolled under a car. What might it have said? "Wait a minute. We're not done yet."

Wait a minute. Time out for a great moment, a great game, a reprieve from the warden on a Tigers season too good to end. Yes, Detroit is still in second place in the American League East. Yes, it still trails Toronto by 2½ games with a week left.

But here, Sunday, for four hours and six minutes, was the chase, the season, everything they play for, everything we watch for. One must-win game — against a team that had seemingly forgotten the phrase: "You gotta lose sometime." Stop Toronto. That was all the Tigers wanted. Stop Toronto. No problem. Stop the ocean, while you're at it. And war, and world hunger.

After all, hadn't these Blue Jays been kissed by some devilish destiny, hadn't they already won three games from the Tigers by one run apiece, with enough ninth-inning magic to fill an entire reel of highlight film? Stop Toronto? How did one do that? The Tigers had already tried throwing their ace, taking early leads, scoring nine runs. Nothing had worked.

And here they were, in the final game of this four-game series — "We lose this, that's it," Darrell Evans would later admit — and so they played their trump card: Doyle Alexander, the hottest pitcher in baseball. And he surrendered one run in eight innings, fought off threats in the fifth and sixth, and handcuffed guys like Lloyd Moseby, Ernie Whitt and Jesse Barfield.

And with three outs to go, his team was still losing, 1-0.

What went through your mind when you came to bat in the ninth?" Gibson would be asked when this thing was all over, when the Tigers had finally beaten the Blue Jays, 3-2, and breathed new life into the final week of the season. "What were you thinking?"

"Honestly?" he would say. "I was thinking that last time up I swung like a bleep!"

Well. What do you want? Shakespeare? The fact is that Gibson, like his teammates, was fed up with all that had been happening, these weird losses, weird bounces, bullpen collapses, and he decided to swing freely —

260

"Go for it," a Californian might say — and bam! Over the wall. Suddenly, the score was tied. And more important, a spell had been broken: It wasn't just the Blue Jays who could have magic in the ninth.

"That was as big an at-bat as we've had in a long time," Evans would say. Indeed. It seemed to change everything. Only one inning earlier, Evans, the Tigers' elder statesman, had smacked his own towering fly ball to right-center, only to see it caught against the wall by a leaping Barfield. Evans stood for a long time on first base after that, just staring off, mumbling to himself. What did the Tigers have to do to win here? Sports writers memorized the scene, stored it like a chestnut for when the Tigers went down.

Only they didn't go down. Gibson hit that homer and they went to extra innings and the Tigers scored again, and the Blue Jays tied them, and the Tigers scored in the 13th and. . . .

Well, we'll get to that in a second.

A few words here about Doyle Alexander: Fantastic. Awesome. Totally. What he did Sunday was no less than save the Tigers' season — in a park that loves him as much as Popeye loves Brutus. All day long, the lean, saggy-faced pitcher (who criticized Toronto after the Jays traded him) had endured jeers from the sellout crowd — at one point a plane flew overhead with a tailing message "LET'S FOIL DOYLE!" — and he ignored it all. On top of that, he was working without a net; the Tigers' bullpen was a tinderbox. Everybody knew it. Alexander had to go long. He went long. Alexander had to choke the rallies. He choked the rallies.

He went 10⅔ innings, before giving up a tying run on Barfield's single, and Willie Hernandez relieved him. "He was unbelievable the way he pitched," Dan Petry said afterward. "Doyle left his heart on the mound."

The Tigers weren't about to let it be stepped on.

So, OK. Back to the game. The 13th inning. By now a rain had already started falling, stopped, the clouds disappeared, and the sun returned. How much longer would this go on? Jim Walewander opened it with a walk. Walewander? But of course. The young man who made the rock group The Dead Milkmen famous, was perfect for a game like this. He took second on Lou Whitaker's bunt, and stayed there while Evans received an intentional pass.

And up came Gibson. One more time. Whiskered. Tight jawed. Realistic. He hadn't celebrated when he'd hit that home run in the ninth ("You never celebrate early here") and he knew, despite the indications, that he wasn't swinging well.

"I've been lousy for a while now," he said. "I just followed that old saying, 'Swing in case you hit something.' " And he did. The first pitch. It blooped toward center field and Walewander and Evans froze on the base paths, watching Moseby, the center fielder, come charging, charging — and, no! The ball bounced in front of him and ricocheted over his head. Flash! Walewander took off, charged around third, as shortstop Manny Lee retrieved the ball and threw toward home. It was close, Walewander went in headfirst, dragged his hand and reached the promised land in a cloud of dirt. . . .

Safe!

"People always tell me not to slide headfirst, because you get hurt," Walewander would later remark, "but I say, 'Bleep it.' "

Yeah. Bleep it. The Tigers had the lead. And this one they would not surrender. Not even a hit batsman (George Bell by Mike Henneman) or a close-but-missed double play, or the appearance of Dickie Noles, who had surrendered the winning hit the day before, could stop this one in the bottom of the 13th. Noles took the ball from Sparky Anderson (who had but one request: "Get the guy out") and, ta-da! He retired Barfield on a broken-bat grounder to Alan Trammell. A flip to second. Score it 6-4 in your books. And the Tigers had won! The season was still alive, still breathing.

What a game! What a glorious game! Gone already for hours were Alexander and Toronto starter Jim Clancy (who pitched seven shutout innings). Old already were Gibson's first blast, and Evans' 11th-inning home run that made it 2-1, and Barfield's RBI single that tied it, 2-2. How great was this game? You had to remind yourself of that stuff. Each inning threatened to outshine the one before it. "My heart is still beating," said pitcher Frank Tanana, who was warming up as the next reliever in the 13th should Noles have faltered. "Whew! Whew! Wow!"

Wow, indeed. The Tigers have control of their destiny now. It is no guarantee of anything. It simply means one more week of baseball that matters — secured by a triumphant home run with three outs to go that said: "Wait a minute. We're not done yet." And proceeded to demonstrate why.

As the stadium emptied after Barfield's final out, and the Tigers players met at the mound, shaking hands, slapping high-fives, Evans wandered back to the spot where earlier — an hour? two hours? — he had stood, wondering what the Tigers had to do to win here. And slowly, almost unnoticed, he began to clap. Faster, now. Harder. Clapping and clapping, over and over, for his team, for the win, for the game. The reason they play, the reason we watch. The greatest game of the year. Clap on, Darrell. The Tigers earned this one.

A TOUR OF THE CLUBHOUSE FOR OUT-OF-TOWN SCRIBES

October 2

I would like to welcome each and every out-of-town journalist who has come for this weekend's big Tigers-Blue Jays series. Unfortunately, that would really run up my phone bill. So instead, I offer a gift: a personalized MAP-TO-THE-STARS of the Tigers' clubhouse. After all, we don't want you walking into the showers.

Ready? First, get inside Tiger Stadium. Go past the Italian sausage stands. NO, YOU CAN'T STOP! FOR GOD'S SAKE, YOU HAVE WORK TO DO! Go through the clubhouse door. Take a sharp left. Smell the pipe smoke? This is Sparky Anderson's office. Sit down. Start talking with Sparky. And we'll come back for you on Monday.

No. Ha. Only kidding. Sparky is the first stop, however, because he is known, in the business, as "a good quote." Of course, the quote he gives you may totally contradict the one he gave the guys from Denver five minutes ago. But hey. Those guys aren't going to read your paper, right?

OK. Once done with Sparky, come out, and take a right past the Wispy Machine. The Wispy Machine is a landmark in the Tigers' clubhouse. It is big and metal and dispenses Wispy, which is sort of low-cal cold white stuff, not really, you know, ice cream, although it comes in chocolate, or, well, brown, I think it's chocolate but . . . ah, I'm not sure what it is. It's Wispy. Eat it and shut up.

Now look straight ahead. Ta da! You are on "Pitchers' Row." Frank Tanana, Dan Petry, Walt Terrell. Who's who? Easy. Petry and Tanana are on the ends. Terrell sits in the middle, on his stool, holding a beer and staring into space. Before the game. After the game. Day. Night. Doesn't matter. I think he sits there through the winter.

OK. Around the corner. Here you find the relief pitchers. Jeff Robinson is tall with light-brown hair. Mike Henneman is tall with light-brown hair. Eric King is tall with light-brown hair. Have fun. Also, you'll find the catchers, Mike Heath and Matt Nokes. (HELPFUL HINT: Nokes is the one who could star in "Leave It To Beaver.")

Next, you'll hit Willie Hernandez. Everybody hits Willie Hernandez. That's the problem.

Keep walking. Ah. Doyle Alexander, the hottest pitcher in baseball. A thin man whose facial expression suggests that he is suffering from severe cramps. Never mind. He is 8-0. LEAVE HIM ALONE! CAN'T YOU SEE HE HAS TO PITCH! MOVE! YOU'RE BREATHING HIS AIR!

On we go. Turn past the showers. And presto! — you have reached shortstop Alan Trammell and second baseman Lou Whitaker. Side by side. What a team! These two have been together so long, sometimes they put on each other's clothes, take the wrong car keys, go to the wrong house, and come back the next day without ever noticing.

Stop writing that down. It was a joke.

And here is Darrell Evans. With a mob of reporters around him. Go ahead. Ask Darrell how it feels to be 40 and still playing so well. I bet it's the first time he hears that one.

Keep going. Tom Brookens. . . . Larry Herndon. . . . Johnny Grubb. . . . Now we are hitting the fun corner. Jack Morris and Bill Madlock. This is the corner from which a flying sock is most likely to originate. You will notice a photo of the two men hanging there: over Madlock's face is written "Mad Dog." Over Morris', "Sad Dog." On a slow day this summer, Madlock and Morris tried to sell signed copies to their teammates.

They're such kidders.

You may notice two smallish, fresh-faced young men running around. They are not clubhouse boys. They are rookies. Scott Lusader and Jim Walewander. They are nicknamed "The Rodents." Lusader thought that up. How about that, huh? Walewander has become a fan favorite for his excellent base running and fine taste in music, which includes "Spit Sink" by The Dead Milkmen. You may notice a "Jim Walewander Fan Club" sticker above Sparky's office. Heh-heh. Pretty funny, huh? Sparky doesn't even pay dues.

OK. Back to the tour. Gibson. Kirk. Big. Blond. Whiskered. See his locker? See that sticker? The one that says "I'M ORNERY"?

Slow down. He's not chasing you. All right. We're about done here. You'll find Chet Lemon and Dave Bergman. It was Bergman who came up with the Wispy Machine. Quick! See if you can find your way back to the Wispy Machine!

Very good. Just testing.

Walk past the coaches' corner, and, voila! The tour is complete. You are back to Sparky's office, where you no doubt can pick up the conversation you began 45 minutes ago, without missing a beat.

So there it is. The map to what most people consider the most easygoing clubhouse in the league — and perhaps, soon, that of the American League East champions. I hope it helps. You may need it should the Tigers win this weekend and have a big celebration, with champagne popping everywhere and leaving you soaking wet.

By the way, should the Tigers lose and you still find yourself soaking wet, I have news for you.

You're in the showers.

In a Classic Battle, Good Guys Finally Won

October 4

The crack of the bat sent them all in motion, three Tigers base runners, one ground ball, 12 innings and a Detroit fairy tale hanging in the balance. What a story in those six moving feet! What a magnificent tale, an all-afternoon adventure, a baseball game played like one of those old serial movies, where danger lurks at every turn and all you know is the heroes prevail at the end.

"I cannot tell you, or anyone else, how much I loved what happened today," said pitcher Jack Morris when this affair was finally over, when the Tigers had squeaked out a 12-inning, 3-2 victory over Toronto that leaves them one crazy victory from the American League East title. "This is the kind of game every kid who wants to play baseball dreams about. Just to take part in it, is . . . wow!"

Wow. And Morris did more than take part. He threw the first nine innings, left with the scored tied, 2-2, and watched the final three innings inside the Tigers' clubhouse, huddled with a few teammates in front of a TV set. Four hours and five minutes this game lasted. Every one important. Scoring threats arose, scoring threats were stymied. Big swingers stalked to the plate, big swingers were struck out. Inhale, exhale. Shiver. Quiver. Somebody deliver!

Somebody did. And what did those clubhouse players do at the final magical moment — when Alan Trammell's hard grounder scooted between the legs of Toronto shortstop Manny Lee with the bases loaded, and Jim Walewander scored from third with the winning run? What did they do?

What do you think?

"We whooped and hollered and yelled, and then, I got so excited I ran all the way down the tunnel and into the dugout," said Morris.

And then he froze.

He forgot he was wearing only his underclothes.

Isn't that the perfect reaction? Isn't it? After a game like this, so chock full of brilliant pitching, clutch hitting. One run was scratched out on a sacrifice fly, another on a two-out single, another on a fielding error and a double. And that final one — Trammell's ground ball that had destiny tattooed all over it. "I hit it real solid, right at him," said Trammell to a mob of reporters in the crowded Tigers' clubhouse afterward.

"But Lee should have had it, right?" someone interrupted. "He just messed it up, right?"

265

"You can't say that," Trammell answered, almost pleading, "you don't understand how hard a play that is."

This was beautiful. Sportsmanship in the midst of one-upsmanship. Sure, the ball might have been fielded — possibly for a double play. But the Tigers and Blue Jays have battled six times now in the final two weeks of this crazy season, the Tigers have won three, the Blue Jays have won three, all have been decided by one run, and there is one more scheduled for today. Nobody is insulting anybody. These are two battle-weary squadrons that have just enough energy to salute each other and do this one more time.

What twists! What turns! Last Friday, Lee beat the Tigers with a ninth-inning triple in Exhibition Stadium. "THE MANNY OF THE HOUR," the Toronto headlines read.

And Sunday, after Toronto's sixth straight defeat, Manny Lee sat alone by his locker, wordless, half-dressed, staring into space as reporters stepped gingerly around him.

Such are the highs and lows of heavenly competition. And Saturday was heavenly competition. From the 11 innings pitched by Toronto's Mike Flanagan (two runs, nine strikeouts) — "The guy was great," admitted Tigers catcher Mike Heath — to Mike Henneman's crucial three innings of Tigers relief (no hits, no runs, four strikeouts, and the win) to a beautiful double play by Lou Whitaker and Trammell in the second, to Heath's clutch double that drove in the tying run in the fifth, to ... oh, my. Who can remember it all? "A classic," Morris repeated, shaking his head. "A real classic."

No moment more than that final inning. It was after 6 p.m. The sun was already punching out. The October cold now was under your skin, in your veins, making your nose run. This was football weather, for God's sake. Yet no one dared leave. The 45,026 who had shivered from Morris' first pitch were determined to get their last looks — no matter how long it took.

And it started. Heath began the 12th with a ground-out. Whitaker singled to right. Bill Madlock singled to left. Walewander, the lovably kooky rookie who seems to be a good luck charm for Detroit baseball, came in to run for Whitaker, and the crowd responded by rising to its feet. Kirk Gibson, hitless all day, battled reliever Jeff Musselman for a walk, and, look out! The bases were loaded.

"ARRRRRRRRRRR!!"

Insanity.

In came relief pitcher Mark Eichhorn. Up stepped Trammell, the converted cleanup hitter, who symbolizes the surprising excellence of this Tigers club. The fans tugged on their scarves, the bleachers began to sway, the place was gloriously exhausted, wiped out, drained, and yet, suddenly, a chant began for Trammell, softly at first, then louder, louder.

"M-V-P! M-V-P!"

Whack. A grounder. And the Tigers started running. Trammell toward first, Gibson toward second, Madlock toward third, Walewander heading for home. It was an instant, a split second, and the ball was through Lee's legs and, hallelujah. The celebrating began in mid-stride.

"I thought I was going to be out at home," said Walewander afterward, "and when I looked back, I saw it go through his legs, and I said, 'Oh! Thanks!' "

"What about you?" someone said to Madlock, who passed Lee just as the ball scooted by. "Did you even bother to round third base?"

"Oh, yeah," he said, laughing. "I rounded third base. I mean, I was heading that way anyhow!"

And there it was. Beautiful. Tigers win, they take over first place, and it has come down to three words that every fan in this motor city is repeating like a mantra now: one more victory. One win, and they are AL East champions.

Remarkable, really, when you consider where this team began this season, in the dumper, with grim prospects, a lousy April, an 11-19 record at one point in May. Only the success of the Pistons and Red Wings distracted the city from an early write-off of its favorite baseball team.

And now. One game? It is as if all that has happened was meant to happen. All the falls, the hot and cold streaks, the injuries, the trades, the front office moves, the emergence of Henneman and Matt Nokes, the arrival of Doyle Alexander, Madlock, Jim Morrison, Walewander, Scott Lusader, all this and all that — all of it woven into some orange and blue tapestry hanging in fate's living room. One game for the title? Who would have thought?

And what of Toronto? Who would have thought? The Jays are a great club, but they are struggling, reeling, coming apart, a team trying to stand on a greased log in the middle of the river. Where is their magic? Where is their power? Where are George Bell and Jesse Barfield and Willie Upshaw? Where is what's missing? And if they rediscovered it all today — if they won to force a playoff Monday — would it surprise anyone?

No way. There are no surprises now. "Today was one of those games that was too good to lose," said Morris. "But, hey — they all are. The shame here is that one of these two teams has to go home. I'd like to keep playing these guys forever."

If only, if only! When Trammell's ball went between Lee's legs, it kept going deep into left field. The Toronto outfielders didn't bother to chase after it. It stopped a few feet from the wall, and sat there, innocent in the grass, even as the Tigers celebrated on the pitcher's mound. Why not? The ball, after all, was merely a prop. In a classic like this, the play's the thing.

TIGERS TAKE TITLE BY BEATING JAYS – PERFECTLY

October 5

This said it all: Frank Tanana darting off the mound, scooping up the ball, turning to first baseman Darrell Evans and — with a lollipop smile already on his face — flipping it underhand for the final out.

One, two, three, leap!

Happy ending.

"Whenever I think of this game from now on," Evans said, champagne soaking his face, after the Tigers had beaten Toronto, 1-0, to capture the American League East, "that's the moment I'm going to see. Frank coming towards me, the ball in his hand, his eyes as big as saucers. . . . Oh, man. Oh, man. I'll never forget that."

Forget it? Are you kidding? For years in this city people will be talking about where they were when the Tigers turned that final out, beat the Blue Jays, leaped into each other's arms having done what everybody dreamed and nobody expected — on the final day of the season.

American League East champions.

Happy ending.

"I couldn't move," said Chet Lemon, who watched that last play from center field. "I should have started to run in, but I was, like, frozen in amazement. Then it hit me. We won! We won! . . . And I said, 'I better move before I lose a limb.' "

They won! They won! In an instant the field was filled with leaping Tigers players, police on horses, fans who made it over the wall. Inside the Detroit clubhouse, the staff wheeled out champagne, and pulled down rolls of protective plastic over everything that could be protected.

And in the stands, the sellout crowd was on its feet, giving thunderous applause, basking in a gloriously winning feeling. As their Tigers heroes galloped en masse toward the dugout, Tanana, in the center, looked up, his hair in bangs on his forehead, a wad of pink chewing gum in his mouth, and gave an expression of joy that was captured in 100 camera clicks and a delightful page of history.

"I felt," Tanana said, "like I was six years old again."

Happy ending.

What a moment! What a day! What a finish! Here was the final piece of a jigsaw season, that suddenly, finally, made sense. "If you had told me this would happen back in April, I would have said you're crazy," said pitcher Jack Morris. "We were playing terrible (11-19 in May). That was the truth then. But there's a different truth now. We're playing pretty darn good baseball."

Good? Is that the word for it? Try great, remarkable. "Awesome," suggested Tanana. OK. Awesome. Best record in either league. It was downright chilling to watch these final seven games with the Blue Jays — three this weekend, four last weekend in Toronto — all of them decided by a single run. History will surely remember this as one of the finest title chases in baseball.

"I've never been involved in seven games like this," said shortstop Alan Trammell, his voice a rasp, lost to screams, shouts, a million interviews. "A week ago, we were really down, trailing Toronto by 3½. But we never gave up. And now . . . this. I'm so emotionally drained right now. But it's the greatest feeling. God, it's great."

God, it was. Seven head-to-head games in the last 11 days. And it all had come down to this — the last one on the schedule. Tigers win, it's over. Blue Jays win, there's a one-game playoff. Tanana (who two weeks ago was slumping so badly, he was removed from the rotation) was back and pitching for the Tigers. And Jimmy Key, Toronto's ace, 17-7, was going against him. A duel in the Sunday afternoon shadows. How would this one go?

A better question: What was left? Already in this crazy series, there had been games as raucous as a 10-9 Toronto win up north, and as tense as Saturday's 3-2 Tigers victory in 12 heart-stopping innings.

What was left? What hadn't we seen? How about a 1-0 game — the slimmest possible victory in this sport — on a wobbly home run by Larry Herndon in the second inning?

Perfect. How absurdly perfect. A series full of big hitters and big talkers won on a single swing by the quietest man in a Tigers uniform. "Pretty fitting, huh?" said Evans, winking. Indeed. Herndon even gave a brief interview afterward.

"How do you feel?" he was asked.

"Great," he said.

What more need be said?

Great. Grreeaaat. Couldn't have been better. And Tanana wins it? The homegrown Detroit hero? A shutout? A complete game? A six-hitter? "Did you ever think two weeks ago this might happen?" he was asked.

"No," he said, "I hoped I'd get a chance. But I wasn't even pitching. My job then was to be a cheerleader."

Is that beautiful? A guy is benched, and he becomes a cheerleader. Outsiders might suspect a tad of corniness here. But that is truly characteristic of this Tigers team. Subs root for starters. Slumpers root for the hot hands. Remember, this is not 1984, a Tigers season of power and dominance. Uh-uh. This year has been spit and glue, a leak springs, you take the gum out of your mouth and plug it up.

269

And because of that, this was the year of Sparky Anderson's life — probably the best managing of his storied career, no matter what happens in the playoffs. "That guy," said pitcher Dan Petry of Anderson, "is the key. In May, when we stunk, he came to us and said we could win it. And a lot of us said privately: 'The guy's nuts.' But his spirit catches on. It really does."

And finally, it gave birth to a title. In the spritz-a-second Tigers clubhouse, Anderson, 53, talked to microphone after microphone, dressed only in T-shirt and shorts, his white hair soaked with champagne. "I've had it all now," he croaked. "If I die and go to heaven — and I hope I go to heaven — I can say I've had it all."

"What about that prediction back in May?" he was asked. "How did you know? How did you know?"

He grinned.

"I didn't know," he whispered. "I was just having fun."

So the Tigers win the division. They go on to play Minnesota for the American League pennant. And the city of Detroit wakes up this morning, happier than it expected to be, with scenes from Sunday that linger like sucking candy:

Here was Toronto's Cecil Fielder, 6-feet-3, 220 pounds, trying for second base in a botched hit-and-run attempt — and sliding desperately into the waiting tag of Lou Whitaker. Out. End of threat.

Here was Lemon, standing in center field in the eighth inning, waiting for George Bell's fly ball to drop lazily into his glove. All weekend long, Bell, the Jays' MVP candidate and biggest threat, had been handled this easily. Up, down, out. Did not drive in a run. Maybe the key to the series.

And here, lookie here, was an octopus flying out of the stands in the seventh, going splat in front of the Blue Jays' dugout as nearby fans pointed and chuckled. An octopus? Isn't that what they throw at Red Wings hockey games? Well. Yes. Maybe someone got confused. The Blue Jays players sitting on the dugout steps simply looked up into the stands, mystified, shaking their heads, as if this was the final insult.

An octopus?

O K. A moment here for Toronto, a great team, a team that should be playing more baseball this season. The Blue Jays may not realize the ugly pitch fate will toss them now; but they will soon enough. The despair of one lost afternoon will not compare to the disgust at 100 afternoons of questions next spring, next summer, forever: "How could you guys lose your last seven games? What happened? What happened?"

Who knows? History will record that the Jays finished just two games behind the Tigers, with the second-best record in baseball. But who really reads history? People will remember that they lost the last game of their tilt with Detroit in Toronto — some say the turning point of the season — then lost three straight to Milwaukee, and three straight to the Tigers. Their last seven games? Yes. People will cast the Blue Jays as losers, chokers, and that is unfair, they deserve better.

"This series had gotten to be so good," said Trammell. "I kind of wanted to keep playing them."

No need for that now. The division is won. The Tigers got it.

"Yeah," said Trammell, grinning at the words. "Yeah ... yeah. ... " Yeah.

An hour after it was over, when Tiger Stadium was empty, quiet, the evening sun just about gone, three figures, dressed in underwear, suddenly appeared on the Tigers infield: Jack Morris. Jim Walewander. Scott Lusader. The highest-paid player on the team, and two rookies. They dropped into a stance at first base, and, smiling, on cue, took off in a footrace to second. Lusader took the lead, Walewander second, Morris trailing. They reached the bag — Morris slid — and they cracked up, laughing, waving, yelling. All alone. Is that any way to behave? The American League East champions? Racing in their underwear?

You bet it is.

CAN EVANS, TIGERS RISE FROM THE DIRT?

October 12

He was on his knees, sunk in the dirt, the weight of the Tigers' season seemingly on his shoulders. What had he done? Darrell Evans? The veteran, the leader, the symbol of the Tigers' experience . . . had been picked off at third base, caught in a mistake, gunned down by an alert catcher and a deadly accurate throw?

Out?

Out.

"That doesn't happen," Tigers fans seemed to whisper. "It just doesn't happen."

It happened. Tigers lose. They are one game from elimination in these American League playoffs. Not because of that one play. Not because of Evans' failed belly-flop back to third that left him only dirty, sorry, and out — and deflated a potential rally. Uh-uh. Not because of that one play.

But because of what it symbolized — which is what had been happening all night.

"The Tigers don't do that," whispered the fans.

They did. All the things they're not supposed to do. All the things they hadn't done in building the best record in baseball. They blew scoring chances. Their big hitters were not big at all. Men were left on base like forgotten car keys. The starting pitching did not hold.

And their opponents are playing like the favorites.

Who are these guys anyway? The Minnesota Twins? Or some ghosts from the past in young, fresh-faced bodies? They have outplayed, outhit and outpitched the Tigers in three of four games, and they lead this unexpected series, 3-1.

"Not supposed to happen," the fans repeated, shaking their heads.

It happened.

Shock," said Evans quietly into an army of microphones. The game was over, the game was lost, 5-3, and what happened in that sixth inning was merely one of a number of bad occurrences. Evans had been on third base, Dave Bergman on second, Lou Whitaker at the plate. One out, Tigers trailing by a run. On the first pitch, Evans tried to get aggressive. He leaned just a tad too much. And suddenly here was catcher Tim Laudner up and firing toward third baseman Gary Gaetti — a called play, Gaetti would admit — and Evans, too late, too late, was tagged out.

"Shock is mostly what I felt. You don't figure it's gonna happen. . . . It's a mistake. I wish I could have it back. You just want to dig a hole and bury yourself."

It did not lose the game. But ultimately, the game was lost. And the feeling now is like spotting an "E" on your gas tank with 100 miles of highway to go. Three straight? Is that really the only way the Tigers can stay alive in this once-magical season? Three straight? What happened to all the World Series talk? What happened to the best record in baseball?

This is what happened: Somebody began a new season. And all the old stuff went out the window. Suddenly, the Tigers are no longer chock full of dominant starting pitchers. Suddenly, they have no big bats in the Nos. 3 and 4 spots. "We're just not doing what we normally do," said cleanup hitter Alan Trammell, 3-for-15 in this series. "I don't know why. I wish I did. I'd like to show the country what kind of team we really are."

So far, they have not. And the Twins? Those terrible road-playing Twins? Those we-don't-really-have-pitching Twins? Too young, too inexperienced, not-ready-for-prime-time Twins?

They have shown exactly the opposite.

Here, in Tiger Stadium, was Kirby Puckett cracking a solo home run off Frank Tanana. Here was Greg Gagne, the No. 8 hitter, doing the same. Here was reliever Juan Berenguer, the hate raining down on him from his former fans, shutting down the Tigers for 2⅔ innings. "I don't think there's any doubt they've played better than us," said Kirk Gibson, who struck out in the bottom of the ninth for the final out. "And as for our situation, I think it's pretty bleepin' obvious."

A moment here for Evans. He did not deserve this. He has played so well all year, led the team by example, proved those wrong who said he was too old (40) to do what he used to. How terrible must he feel this morning. How hard was that walk from third base back to the dugout, his uniform covered in dirt from the failed slide, his face the picture of frustration — with himself, with the situation, with everything. "Look at him over there," said Trammell in the clubhouse, motioning to the crowd of reporters around his teammate. "He's sitting there, taking it. I can't say enough about him. He's been our leader all year."

Unfair. He deserves better. But this is a game, not a courtroom. You get what you get.

Yes, there were plenty of other failed moments. The very next inning, Trammell — the Tigers' MVP candidate — grounded into a double play with one on and nobody out. Earlier, in the fifth, Larry Herndon had lined out on a 3-2 pitch with the bases jammed. And back in the first, Evans, once again, had the bases loaded and lined out.

The whole game was like one of those dreams where you are running in slow motion, where you can see your goal, but you just can't reach it.

Before it began, Sparky Anderson had admitted losing this would "be almost impossible" to overcome. Correct. Not only for the difficulty of three straight victories, but because two of them must come at the Metrodome, where, if you wear a foreign uniform, just breathing is hard enough. "What choice do we have now?" asked Trammell. "We have to win three straight. It's been done (1985 by Kansas City, in the playoffs over Toronto)."

And it must happen again, if the Detroit baseball season is to continue. Didn't the Tigers have the best record in baseball? Didn't Minnesota have the worst record of any division winner? Yes. Yes. And what does it matter? This is a seven-game season now, not 162. The stage has changed; and so, apparently, have the players.

Why has it happened?

It has happened because Detroit's starting pitchers, supposedly its forte, have been average or less against Minnesota batters — Doyle Alexander, Jack Morris, Walt Terrell and Tanana, all unable to last a game or earn a victory.

It has happened because every time it looks as if the Tigers should score in bunches, they score in drops. "And when we score," admitted Chet Lemon, "they seem to come right back and score themselves."

It has happened because of bad things at bad times, and because of aggressive, no-fear play by the Twins. And in the end, all that counts is that it has happened. And the Tigers now need a miracle, three times, to get out of it.

How sad a scene Sunday night: Evans, caught, out, nothing he can do about it, sunk in that dirt around third base with his head lowered to his chest, the crowd too stunned to react. It was one play, not the only play, but a symbolic play, symbolic of the feelings, the situation, everything.

If this were Hollywood, it would simply be part of a great script, the moment for a classic turnaround, a Rocky-like comeback, a fitting end for a season that has been like a mountain climb in your socks.

But this is not Hollywood. This is Detroit. Three games more, at best, and the Tigers must win them all. If that sounds almost impossible, it's because it is.

SAD FACES ARE SIGNATURE OF THE TIGERS' DEFEAT

October 13

One by one, they took their last at-bats of summer. Darrell Evans said goodby with a fly to right field, and Alan Trammell signed off with a hard line drive to shortstop. . . .

In a matter of moments, the Detroit baseball season would end the way it had begun six months earlier, on a cool Monday afternoon at Tiger Stadium. A loss then. A loss this day. But oh, what transpired in between! A magical regular season, full of twists and turns and rapid heartbeats; and a post-season that fell horribly flat, lost its sheen, and was finally packed away with a bouncer from rookie Matt Nokes to Minnesota pitcher Jeff Reardon, who threw to first for the out, the joyous leap, and the American League championship.

End of story. The Tigers went down badly in their final game, lost, 9-5, suffered the indignity of an explosive ninth inning by the Minnesota Twins, a team nobody expected, few respected . . . but now has won the AL pennant. "Nothing seemed to bother those guys," Sparky Anderson would say, shrugging. And he was right. Twins were everywhere, this day, this series, whacking hits, dashing around the bases, playing the infield like God's chessmen.

Did they make any wrong moves? Not that we remember. And when they jumped into that victory pile before a stunned Detroit crowd, no one could deny them their celebration. They had defeated, in four of five games, the team with the best record in baseball. "Outpitched us, outhit us, outfielded us and beat us," Jack Morris would say.

That about covers it.

End of story.

Here were some last glimpses of this remarkable Tigers team: Anderson, sitting in the dugout, expressionless, yet shaking inside, chewing sunflower seeds as his team was skinned to its last out; Darrell Evans, 40, the team leader, staring out to the field and beyond, perhaps wondering whether he'll ever see another of these championships; Kirk Gibson, whiskered, intense, desperate to make up for a lousy series, standing on first base, ready to run, ready to explode, but stuck there, stranded in the bottom of the ninth.

Sad faces. Disappointed faces. Yes. That is the signature of defeat. But when this was all over, when the Minnesota players were popping champagne and dumping Gatorade on themselves, the Tigers returned to their clubhouse, sighed, and thanked each other for a year that was too

275

good to be snubbed by any single series. Even a championship one.

Once upon a time, we had a hell of a baseball team. . . . That will be how these '87 Tigers are remembered long after the sting of Monday's defeat is forgotten. How far had they come? How unlikely a journey? Oh, my. Here was a group of third-place finishers in 1986, who had lost their catcher and leader, Lance Parrish, and done nothing to improve except age. Even the players didn't predict a high finish. They suffered a dismal April and May. Yet there began, what shall we call it? A small rumble? A turnaround. Minor at first, a few wins here and there.

Bill Madlock joined the team — cost the Tigers just $40,000 — and his bat went happy-go-lucky. Trammell clicked in his cleanup spot as no one had imagined. Chet Lemon, Larry Herndon, guys criticized for living on past laurels, began to create some new ones. Wins. More wins. Home runs. More home runs. And then Doyle Alexander, a quiet larceny, slipped on a Tigers uniform and won once, twice, three times, four times, and, look at this! First place was within reach. On Aug. 19 (against these same Twins in this same Tiger Stadium), the Tigers tasted that honey for the first time. From then on, it was a race for the hive.

And oh, how the lungs ached in this one! Remember? The Tigers won a game in Minnesota with a ninth-inning bases-loaded single by their rookie catcher, and another against Cleveland with just one hit. They lost a game to Milwaukee when Willie Hernandez walked in the winning run, and another to Toronto when Lou Whitaker threw wildly to home plate. And then, the finish. Humm-ba! The best final baseball chapter ever? Seven games against the Blue Jays? All one-run thrillers?

"It would have been a great story if we'd gone all the way, huh?" asked Trammell after Monday's defeat.

Hey. It's a great story anyhow.

And this is how it wound down Monday: A wild pitch by Eric King led to a Twins run. A throw to first baseman Evans grazed off his glove and rolled away, scoring another. Pat Sheridan, Evans, Trammell, all at the plate with men in scoring position; all walked back slowly to the dugout, snuffed out, dead.

"We just never played the way we could," said Lemon. "And they never let up. I think they won it by taking those first two games at the Metrodome. We had them down in that first game, 5-4, and we let them back. That was a big boost to them."

A boost? It was the story of this series. The Twins, picked by many to go down easily, were like one of those computer quizzes in an electronic arcade. An answer for everything. Clutch hit. Clutch pitch. Almost spookily successful. This is a young team? The worst record of any division winner?

Well. Yes. But if April through September is a safari, then October is a vine swing. Pick the right one and you get there first. The Twins got revved by their amazing crowd, and didn't stop until the champagne corks popped.

How different might this have been had the series begun in Detroit? How different if Trammell had swung like the MVP he is, or if Gibson had clicked, or if Morris and Walt Terrell had . . . ahh, why wonder? In the end, it was the Twins who won two on the road, a place where they'd won just nine games since the All-Star break.

End of story. During these final five games it was as if all the magic was gone, turned back to pumpkin. Alexander (who lost Games 1 and 5 of this series) was not the same Alexander as before. Madlock (only five at-bats all series) was gone, out of the lineup. Scott Lusader and Jim Walewander, the young spark plugs of that magical Tigers finish, were mere spectators. "We had the best record, but they won the series," said Gibson. "Does that make them the best? Does that make us horsebleep?"

Neither. What it makes things is over. The next Detroit baseball game is in Lakeland next spring. But no tears. Almost to a man, each Tiger had his moment in the sun, a big game, a big win.

And in a way, so did we all.

We grew older with these guys, lost hair worrying about their bullpen, lost voices screaming at Hernandez, lost composure with the giddiness of their title. We had our nerves rattled like jangled car keys with every late home run, every deadly double play, every weird error, ball through the legs, strikeout, leap for joy, high-five celebration. How good was this season? Think about how many games left you emotionally drained. Wasted. Exhausted. That's how good it was. We grew older and, in a funny way, we grew younger, too. That is what baseball will do for you.

One by one, when the sun was gone, the Tigers players filed out of the clubhouse in their street clothes, slapping backs, promising dinners, looking forward to spring, even as autumn hit full-stride. Behind them were the bats and helmets. And before them, waiting at the gates, were fans, shivering, holding autograph pads.

"You know," said Evans, who was greeted with a standing ovation in the first inning despite a terrible game Sunday night, "I woke up this morning, and someone had left a sign on my lawn. It said, 'Thanks for the thrills all year. Go get 'em.' No name. Nothing. Sometimes you forget that about these people, and then something like that. . . . "

For something like this. End of story. How, in days to come, will this crazy 1987 season be summed up? Who knows? Perhaps it will take a book, lots of chapters and pictures and quotes and stories. And perhaps it can be said this simply: Once upon a time, we had a hell of a baseball team. And once upon a baseball team, we had a hell of a time.

MINNESOTA'S HEROES EARN THEIR VICTORY LAP

October 26

MINNEAPOLIS — They were pouring champagne on each other's heads, screaming, laughing, celebrating in the usual way for world champions — when suddenly, amid this clubhouse euphoria, somebody screamed: "OUT TO THE FIELD!"

And out they charged, en masse, all these alcohol-soaked Minnesota Twins, the most unlikely World Series winners in some time, pushing through the tunnel and slapping hands and camera lights and finally, finally, emerging back to where it all happened, back to the Metrodome field where they had captured Game 7, a title, and the hearts of every Minnesotan and every closet underdog across the country.

Twins win. How about that? Beat the St. Louis Cardinals four times in seven tries. And here, on the turf, some in socks and undershirts, they leaped into each other's arms again — as they had on that final ground ball by Willie McGee that ended this 4-2 finale 30 minutes earlier. They leaped and yelped and grabbed a red-balled microphone to shout thanks to the thunderous fans, nearly all of whom were still here, they never stopped screaming, certain their heroes would return one more time.

"DID WE DO IT?" screamed Kent Hrbek, the homegrown first baseman, holding the microphone as a lounge singer would.

"YAAAAAAAH!" answered the crowd.

"WE'RE NUMBER ONE!" screamed center fielder Kirby Puckett, his body-builder frame popping out from his soaking T-shirt.

"YAAAAAAAH!" answered the crowd.

It was every party ever thrown rolled into the world's largest locker room. And well it should be. Why shower alone? The Twins owe much of this stunning World Series title to the undying crowd, which thumped and danced and roared and waved hankies until anything less than victory became totally impossible.

"That last inning was the weirdest feeling," third baseman Gary Gaetti would say. "It was so loud it didn't seem real. It seemed like I was out of my body, watching down, like some TV camera. It's like, 'I've seen this before on TV, teams win the World Series, but now, all of a sudden, I'm in it, man!' It's like. . . . I can't believe it!"

Believe it. Twins win the World Series. Cinderella found her slipper. Pinocchio is a real boy again. All things good come true for those who wait, and fans in this city have waited forever for this. They got it. The team that sported the worst record of all the division winners, the team that was mincemeat on the road, the team that carted around the nickname

"Twinkies" until a few weeks ago — and was 150-1 to win the World Series when this season began — is now champion of the baseball world.

How about that?

"We had a different guy contribute every night," said a beaming Greg Gagne, the shortstop, who drove in the winning run. "It's been that way the whole Series and playoffs. That's how we won."

Actually, how they won this final game of the year was less Minnesota style than St. Louis: a few runs, a hit here or there, a few walks, scrape and scratch and keep your pitching tight. No homers. No big innings. But, hey. It only figures. About the only thing the Twins hadn't done in this Series was beat the Cardinals at their own game.

"Bye Bye Birdies!" read a sign in the stands.

Crude, but true.

Back on the field, the players were joined by their families and friends. It was after 11 p.m. Tomorrow was a workday. Nobody cared. The crowd stayed.

"LET'S PARTY!" screamed right fielder Tom Brunansky.

And suddenly, spontaneously, the Twins took off for a victory lap, jogging together along the foul lines, laughing, carrying their children, holding their wives' hands, pointing and waving to the thunderous crowd. And in the middle was Frank Viola, the pitcher who had won Game 1, Game 7, and the World Series MVP.

"Amazing," mumbled a veteran reporter who has covered a dozen of these World Series, as he observed the scene.

Amazing. And typical. After all, these Twins have been called a "storybook" team; mostly by people who write stories for a living. And why not? Here is a classic cast of funny faces and funny bodies and foreign accents that wakes up this morning world champion of baseball.

Who knew of Gaetti, the tough-talking third baseman, before his excellent post-season? Who could identify the beefy face of Hrbek, or the fire-hydrant physique of Puckett, or the beard man, Bert Blyleven? Juan Berenguer put his sneering, mustachioed face on a most-wanted poster for next season, and Joe Niekro was caught smiling for the whole Niekro family (he is its first Series winner).

Don Baylor, the ageless veteran? Gagne, the reformed teenage drug-abuser? Tom Kelly, the youngest manager in the game? Face it. The Twins simply had an abundance of personality and, as any storyteller will attest, you need personality to make characters work.

They overcame plenty in this seventh game, as they have most of the post-season. The Cardinals scored two runs early, and when the Twins tried to retaliate in the second inning, they were robbed of a run by home plate umpire Dave Phillips, who called a sliding Baylor out at the plate when replays showed he was clearly safe. Puckett was thrown out trying for third base on a wild pitch in the fifth. Gaetti was nailed at home plate despite a crushing slam into Cardinals catcher Steve Lake.

Out. Out. For a while there, the Twins appeared to be seduced by the belief that they were beyond losing.

In the end, they were.

A moment here for the St. Louis Cardinals, who should also be painted in heroic colors, despite their loss. Here is the least-powerful team in the National League, missing half its power (injured Jack Clark and Terry Pendleton) and facing the home team in the year of the home team. The Cardinals' pitching was, by necessity, depleted down to its last throws, and Whitey Herzog did all he could just to stay afloat. It is true, the Cardinals have blown five straight chances to win a World Series (they led in '85 against Kansas City, 3-1, and this year, 3-2), but it is also true that they have made the sport's final dance three times in six years. No other team comes close.

"We got to the seventh game of the World Series," Herzog said. "If I could do that for the next 10 years I'd be happy." What more could he say? He was playing against power, pitching, karma, and 10 jet engines' worth of noise.

So here's where we leave the world champions, taking a victory lap as the music from "Star Wars" plays and the players turn into cheerleaders for the crowd. Heroes? You bet. Wherever they go for the rest of their Minnesota lives. Not for what they did, but how they did it: corralling destiny, tightening the rope, and saying: "You're coming with us." And dragging an entire state along as well.

So good for them. The fact is, it would have been a shame for the Twins to get this far and stumble. Nobody is calling them the best team in baseball. But they were the best in the post-season, and they wove a wonderful tapestry: a grand-slam opening, a quick 2-0 lead, then three losses in St. Louis, twice nickel-and-dimed to death, then a muscle-man display in Game 6, and finally this, Game 7, a dance with 55,000 partners.

And so ends a baseball season. It began with anger over free-agency collusion, and was marred by corked bats and scuffed balls, and yet still found time for hitting streaks, great pennant races, and the most exciting final two weeks in AL East history. It ends, as it should, in baseball — no talk of money, contracts or cheating — a euphoria brought on by a crazy, powerful, and finally teary-eyed bunch of victory-lappers, who prove that the game remains the thing. And they were one game better than everybody else.

How about that?

JAMIE MORRIS DESERVES A PERFECT ENDING

November 20

A NN ARBOR — We sat in a campus coffee shop, just a few days before the big game. Had this been a typical Wolverines season, Jamie Morris would have had little time for breathing, much less breakfast. Michigan-Ohio State? This Saturday? Wait. Shouldn't there be thunder when we say that?

"Last year," Morris admitted, taking a sip of juice, "no one spoke the entire week of practice before this game. The only word was when Bo called a play in the huddle. No smiles. Nothing. Just hitting. Huddle. More hitting. It was intense."

That game would become the biggest win of the season, the one that sent Michigan to the Rose Bowl as champion of the Big Ten. It would be glory and honor and tears and laughter. It would be singing "The Victors" in the locker room. It would be Michigan 26, Ohio State 24. It would be the highlight of Jamie Morris' college football career.

That was the upside.

The downside was he still had a year to go.

H ere is how it all began for Jamie Morris at Michigan. Spring practice. Freshman year. He ran a play the wrong way. Not once. Not twice. Four times. Guess who was watching?

"I must have been a FOOL!" screamed coach Bo Schembechler. "Will you SHOOT ME the next time I look at a 5-FOOT-7 TAILBACK?"

"Yessir," whispered Morris.

Perfect. Every football player at Michigan starts on Schembechler's dog list. The good ones work their way off. The very good ones win starting jobs. And the great ones? They try to reward the coach with a championship. Jim Harbaugh, the star quarterback who graduated last year, saw his fantasies realized with the trip to Pasadena.

And Morris, Harbaugh's backfield mate, the little tailback with the water bug moves, had the same dreams for this season: "I saw us winning the Big Ten, I saw us going to the Rose Bowl. I saw myself winning the Heisman Trophy."

The waitress came by with coffee. Morris crossed his arms and shrugged. He has put in his time, endured the bangs and bruises, and has pen-knifed out a mountain of yardage, more than any other rusher in Michigan history. He is 67 inches of speed, rock-solid, a toy soldier gone wild in the backfield. "A great player," admits Schembechler. And he's a senior. If life were fair, this would have been his year on the mountaintop.

It was not. The 1987 Wolverines were too inexperienced at some spots and too injured at others. The result is a 7-3 record going into the last regular-season game. Morris' Rose Bowl dream is gone; so is the Big Ten title, and any hope for the Heisman. Last year, with Harbaugh "guaranteeing" a victory, the Michigan-Ohio State game was larger than life. But that was last year.

"Sometimes I think I've failed," said Morris, ignoring his food, his boyish face turning suddenly serious. "I ask myself, 'What did Jimmy do differently? How come the team responded to him?' We made it to the Rose Bowl with him. That was a dream of mine as captain, to lead us back. . . .

"A lot of the guys on the team tease me. They say, 'You know, Jamie, if we had better leadership, we'd be in the Rose Bowl!' I know they're only joking, but I'm serious. And I guess . . . I have failed in that respect. . . ."

Nothing could be more untrue. Morris has been unselfish and hardworking. But you get four years in college, and you take what's given. If a professor goes on leave, you study under his replacement. And if your star quarterback — whose skill only makes you better — is due to graduate, well, he goes. And you stay. And make do with the new one.

In Morris' case, that was Demetrius Brown, a promising but inexperienced sophomore, who replaced Harbaugh (now with the Chicago Bears). Brown made his share of learning mistakes this season, including 15 interceptions. Some cost the Wolverines victories.

"Did that frustrate you?" I asked.

"In the beginning, a lot," Morris said. "Like the first game (a loss to Notre Dame) I was out there trying to win the game on every play. It was like: 'GET ME THE BALL. I can do it!' When Demetrius threw an interception, I would come to the sidelines saying, 'Why isn't he throwing it to me? There's nobody open downfield.' "

Morris sighed. "It's just that, Jimmy did so much for us last year. And it felt like everybody was turning to me for this year. . . . I finally had to accept that Jimmy played a different position from me. I can't control things like the quarterback. I don't determine who gets the ball."

It was an odd dynamic — Morris, an All-America, huddling up with Brown, a newcomer, a young kid looking for confidence. But Brown was quarterback. He had the reins. And while he was not the only reason for Michigan defeats this year, when he drove off the road, the other Wolverines had to go with him.

Seniors included.

You may remember some stories about Morris' childhood in Ayre, Mass. — how his military father would inspect the children's rooms, bounce quarters on the beds, wake up Jamie and his brother Joe (who now stars for the New York Giants) at 5 in the morning, just to tell them there was a spot on the floor they forgot to mop, and they'd better get down there and do it now. "He brought the Army home to us," Jamie said. "I wasn't crazy about it then. But I appreciate it now."

Sure. Compared to sweeping, painting, raking and mowing, scotch-taping your dreams back together is relatively easy. So it was that Morris and the other Michigan seniors, who obviously weren't going to win them all, decided to win all they could. "We had a meeting after the loss to Indiana (U-M's second Big Ten defeat)," Morris said. "We could have folded right then. But we dedicated ourselves to a strong finish."

Since then, the Wolverines have beaten Northwestern and Minnesota and Illinois. And Morris? Well. He may not control the scoreboard. But he has a way with numbers. He is averaging more than 130 yards a game, has 1,339 yards this season (the single-season team mark is within reach Saturday: 1,469, held by Rob Lytle, 1976). Two weeks ago, against Minnesota, he became Michigan's all-time leading rusher. In another time, another season, he might have been swamped with reporters. But most observers were following the progress of Michigan's arch-rival, Michigan State, which was cruising toward its first Big Ten title in more than two decades.

"It didn't bother me," said Morris, of the small group of reporters that stopped by his locker in Minnesota. "At the beginning of the year, when I dreamed about breaking the record, I thought there would be microphones everywhere. But then I started thinking: 'Why am I breaking this record?' I realized it's the blockers, the guys up front. I've been with some of these guys a long time. And when I broke the record, they recognized it, they congratulated me. That was enough."

He smiled, his fingers tapping against one another. "I don't know if I would have realized that had we been winning big and me getting all that attention."

A lot of fans fell in love with Morris during his time at Michigan. He was one of those "cute" rushers, too small to be doing what he was doing but — whoops! — there he goes, slamming into big bodies and bouncing off like a pinball. He was big in big games (witness last year's Ohio State showdown, and the 1986 Fiesta Bowl). And his attitude? Take Mr. Sunshine and Mr. Effort and let them marry Mr. Energy.

During that Minnesota game, there was a play where the Gophers came with a linebacker blitz. Morris picked it up, blocked the defender, and allowed Brown time to throw a touchdown pass. When Morris came off the field, Schembechler slapped his helmet, grabbed him and said: "That's why you're one of the best players in the nation!"

Morris beams at the memory. "At that moment," he said, "I could have ran through a wall."

So he has that in his memory box. And last year's championship, if not this year's. College, by nature, will always be tied to a calendar. You accomplish what you can in the time given.

And the time is about to end. Morris would like to play pro football. His brother has proved it can be done. Or else, maybe communications. Behind-the-scenes TV stuff. "Keith Jackson of ABC is my favorite college football announcer," he said. "He's doing the game Saturday."

"What would you like him to say about you?" I asked.

Morris seemed embarrassed. Then he flashed that laughing smile. "Well, like, if he said: 'That little scatback really hit that hole!' " He laughed at his imitation. "Oh man! I'd be going cra-zy!"

Time was late. Morris had a meeting. We grabbed our coats.

"What else?" I asked him finally. "If you could draw the perfect scene for Saturday, what would it be?"

He thought for a second. "First of all, we'd win. Second, I'd have a big game. I'm thinking 220 yards, maybe 29 carries. . . . I see the fans going crazy. I see us all singing 'The Victors' in the locker room afterwards, and Bo getting up on the chair and making one of his speeches like (he lowers his voice) 'What a wonderful game it was . . . ' and me just standing right beside him, kinda looking up, just soaking it all in. . . ."

"How about a final bow? Would you like to be taken out with a minute left, so you can be acknowledged with a big ovation?"

"No," he said. "I'd rather be on the field when the clock runs out."

"Why?"

"Because at Michigan, for four years they tell you it's the team and not the individual." He grinned. "I want to show them I've learned that."

We shook hands, he slipped on his coat and headed out the door. Jamie Morris, who finishes Saturday, may not have everything he wanted.

But he has everything he needs.

As Tigers' Mr. Nice Guy, Petry Was Always Angel

December 9

Baseball players can make you feel small. They see you walking around the clubhouse, asking questions, and they act like kings — they ignore you. Do not speak unless spoken to. "You know," some are fond of telling reporters, "I never even read the newspapers."

Dan Petry never said that. He always admitted he read the newspaper, this newspaper, every morning, and when an article caught his attention he would mention it. "That was pretty funny," he would comment. Or, "I didn't know that about. . . . " He never felt he was giving something up by doing that. People all around him were saying, "Nice effort," for his baseball. He just figured, why not say it back? That's the way he is.

Bye-bye, Mr. Nice Guy. A colleague of mine has this theory: "The good ones get traded." It's not always true. It's true about Petry. Detroit sent him to the California Angels Saturday for an outfielder named Gary Pettis. For the first time in his 12 professional years, Petry would be working for someone other than the Tigers.

He stayed up late that night, talking with his wife about where they would live and how it would affect their young son, Matthew.

"It's not so much the scenery in Michigan that we'll miss," Petry said a few days later, "but, well, I became an adult here, you know? Gosh, all our greatest memories of life are here. . . . "

By now most of us know Petry's story. Went from young pitcher to starting pitcher to great pitcher. Won 15, 19, 18 and 15 games in consecutive seasons. Helped the Tigers win a World Series. He even made it to an All-Star Game — he walked three batters. But that's OK. Petry was never good at glitz. He is more like the perfect next-door neighbor, seeking nothing more than a friendly hello, and the chance to lend you a rake.

Which is what made 1987 so hard. Petry slumped. Then he unraveled. Not pitching well and not knowing why led him to not pitching well and not knowing why. His record fell. He went into the bullpen. In a sport full of overstuffed egos, Dan Petry suffered an affliction more familiar to common folk: a lack of self-confidence.

"It got to the point when I felt like an outsider in the clubhouse. I even shied away when reporters would come in. I kind of felt everybody was talking about me, maybe in the press box, saying, 'Holy smokes, what's with this guy?' "

285

Nobody said that. Actually, what they said was: "Geez, I hope he does well tonight." That's about the highest compliment I can think of for Petry, because sports writers don't often root for guys they cover. Why are so many people in town going on about his departure? Why has every TV sportscaster used the word "class," every radio guy said, "Sad to see him go"? Dan Petry never bought us presents. He never drove us home.

He treated people with respect. Anyone. He would chat up the janitor, if that was who was around. Dan Petry looked like a golf pro, he dressed in greens and yellows and pinks, but he never — and I can attest to this — never behaved like a prima donna. I remember when he came back from elbow surgery, and he had in a small glass jar the little bone chips they had removed.

"What are you gonna do with those?" I asked.

"I dunno. Maybe put 'em on my fireplace."

He laughed. He was trying his best to get back to form. At one point, he had even told GM Bill Lajoie he would "do anything he needed" to try to make up for being injured.

"Like what?" I asked him Monday.

"Anything. Shuffle papers. Whatever."

There's a park near Petry's home in Grosse Pointe. Petry would take his son there on the off-days during the season. "It just hit me that I won't be going there anymore," Petry said, sadly.

Bye-bye, Mr. Nice Guy. Petry hails from Southern California, yet chose the snow of Michigan for his off-season home. He loved carpooling to games with fellow pitcher Walt Terrell. (I remember writing once how Terrell's favorite pose was with a beer can and a chicken wing. When I came in the clubhouse, Petry grabbed me and laughed like a kid. "You got him, all right! That's Walt!")

But there was a moment this year when the Tigers poured champagne, they had won the AL East, and I remember seeing Petry drenched, looking happy, but distant. He hadn't contributed much. You could tell that bothered him. Somehow, right then, I sensed he wouldn't be back.

And now he's gone. At age 29. Ready to begin a new phase. And this city, which has always loved the regular guy, says so long like a mom putting her kid on the camp bus. "I'm kind of embarrassed by all the attention. I mean, I'm not some Hall of Famer leaving town," he said.

Maybe not. But sometime this morning, Petry's wife, Chris, is due to give birth to their second child. And because this newspaper will be lying on the doorstep, I think the baby ought to know, right from the start, what kind of household it's getting into: The news, kid, is that Daddy is an Angel.

The truth is, a lot of us knew that already.

PERLES IN PARADISE: BEST WEEK, BEST YEAR, BEST JOB

December 30

NEWPORT BEACH, Calif. — The bus rolls off the avenue and into the crowded parking lot. The passengers peer out the window. Most of them are muscular young men wearing green satin football jackets. The coach, a round figure with silver hair, stands up in front.

"AWRIGHT, GUYS. YOU KNOW WHO YOU'RE GONNA SEE?"

Silence.

"YOU'RE GONNA SEE MICKEY MOUSE. MY MAN MICKEY."

Laughter.

"AND DONALD DUCK."

Laughter.

"AND ... AND. ..." He looks for help. "Who's that other guy?"

"Pluto?"

"YEAH ... PLUTO. YOU'RE GONNA SEE PLUTO. HELL OF A PULLING GUARD, THAT PLUTO."

The door opens.

George Perles is going to Disneyland.

Have you ever been at a point in life where every nerve in your body says this is it, where you belong, just get up, breathe, follow your heart and go live it?

Perles, the 53-year-old Michigan State coach, has found such a Shangri-la. This Rose Bowl journey is the best week of the best year of the best job he has ever had. The only job he ever really wanted.

Football coach. Michigan State.

He tried three times, and was turned down twice. He was criticized when he started and criticized as he went along. "Neanderthal," they called his offense. They moaned during the mediocre years. Some predicted he would lose the first five games this season. Critics called him slow, lacking charisma. They said his granite looks — somewhere between George Kennedy and Barney Rubble — were indicative of his imagination. And because he talked more about family and ethics than X's and O's, when he finally did win the Big Ten title and a trip to Pasadena — something MSU hadn't done in 22 seasons — they said big deal, the conference was mediocre.

To hell with them. He is here, in his fifth year on the job. Sunshine. Roses. The big rock-candy mountain. Shake hands with Mickey, coach.

WHO WE GOT HERE? . . . DONALD DUCK? . . . WELL, HELLO DONALD DUCK! . . ."

He is inside the front gates now, posing with real-life cartoon characters for hordes of photographers. Crowds stop and gawk. Which players are which? they ask. And who's the fat guy with the loud voice?

"HELLOOO, DONALD! . . . Heh-heh. . . . Oh, wait! What? You're not Donald. . . . You're . . . what's his name? Scrooge McDuck? . . . Sorry. . . . Scrooge, hey, WHERE'S MICKEY? . . . Oh, there's . . . MICKEY MOUSE, YEAH! . . . Hey, Mickey! Did you bring Pluto? No? He's not here? . . . FELLAS, GET IN HERE. Get the captains in here, make sure they get their pictures taken . . . HEY PLUTO, HOW YA DOIN'? . . ."

He pushes the players in front of the cameras. Soon he is behind them, out of the spotlight, his hands dug in his pockets, his ruddy face beaming. He is content here, in the shadow of the team he cherishes, the team he built, the team he left the pros to create.

"You know what it is," he says, watching the players mug for snapshots, "in high school, you coach 'em, then they go home to their folks. In the pros you coach 'em, they go home to their wives. But in college, you coach 'em, you eat with 'em, you watch them study. You're all they've got. You're their parent. . . .

"And I love playing parent."

The apartment was on Pitt Street near Vernor Highway in Detroit. A one-bedroom place. His folks got the bedroom. George, an only son, slept on a Murphy bed in the living room until he was 17 years old. His father, a Lithuanian immigrant, worked at the Ford plant, and under other circumstances, George would have wound up there, too.

College? To play football? Who went to college from the old neighborhood? The summer before, George had a job putting in fences that paid $3.67 an hour — more than his father was earning. So when college beckoned, his father hid the suitcase. Why leave for school, the senior Perles figured, when you're doing so well as a fence maker?

His mother sneaked the suitcase out when her husband went to work. And George went to MSU. Played football, got hurt his sophomore year, became a student coach, graduated, coached high school, then college, back to MSU as an assistant (under Duffy Daugherty), then to the Pittsburgh Steelers as defensive coordinator, 10 years — and now, finally, here, where he always wanted to be, his alma mater, head man, the Rose Bowl.

He remembers every step. Takes none of it for granted. Here is a guy who will never fire an assistant coach ("that's a disgusting thought"), who carries his own luggage, who has guests over so he can cook them

Lithuanian potato dishes. A few weeks ago he was invited to the governor's mansion and brought a half-dozen guys from the old neighborhood, three Ford workers, a fence man, a delivery truck driver, and they all ate and drank and sang songs till late into the night. When he walked on the field for his first Super Bowl he told a fellow coach, "Well, let's go fool 'em," and when he was about to be announced as head coach of the USFL's Philadelphia Stars, he whispered to the general manager, "Well, let's go fool 'em," and if you try to make football too complicated he gets red-faced angry. "It's a simple game for simple guys! Block and tackle! The only time you get into trouble as a coach is when you think you're some rocket scientist."

When he recruits he can be his own worst enemy, talking so much about academics and sacrifices that some players — such as quarterback Bobby McAllister — wondered "when's he gonna get to the good stuff?" But he doesn't have many problem kids, and you don't hear a lot of drug stories. All over the itinerary out here, people have been remarking how well-behaved this football team is compared to the others. And that's with Perles holding no reins. Heck. He's encouraging them to have fun. Live it up. The other night, upon returning from a huge prime rib dinner, he announced on the bus that "nobody will be allowed back in his room before midnight."

The players moaned. Finally he had to tell them OK, he was kidding.

HEY, WALT. WHERE WE GOIN'?"

He is talking now to the TV producer of the half-hour coach's show, a show Perles prizes, mostly because it helps him recruit. Today they get to film inside Disneyland. It's a coup.

"WALT? YOU KNOW WHERE WE'RE GOIN'?"

"Tomorrowland," says Walt, a heavy man with a cowboy hat.

"OH. OK."

And off they go. Past Main Street, a row of pseudo-New Orleans storefronts, past the monorail, past a pavilion marked "Star Tours." Perles has never been to Disneyland before. He can't believe the lines.

"Hey, coach!" yells a teenager in a gray MSU sweatshirt. "Beat USC!"

"OK. We'll try. Thank you."

"Sign my sweatshirt?"

He signs the sweatshirt.

Up a ramp, alongside the "America Sings" building, and here, overlooking everything, are the cameras and the lights, all set up. Perles is posed on a chair with the Matterhorn mountain over his shoulder, the little cable cars riding along. "THIS IS FUN, BOY. . . . THIS IS FUN."

Already he has filmed the "Today Show," been to the Tournament of Roses house in Pasadena, ridden a helicopter from there to practice. Heady stuff for a first-timer. But then, you have to remember whom you're dealing with. When he was working under Chuck Noll in Pittsburgh, Noll used to remark what a beautiful place Denver was, or San Francisco, or Miami. To which Perles would say: "Hey, Chuck, Pittsburgh is as far east as I go. Cincinnati is as far south. No more north than Minnesota, and no further west than Chicago. And if I have my way, I end up back in Michigan."

And his whole career, he stayed within those boundaries. The Good Witch of the North needn't tell Perles what to do with those ruby slippers.

When the filming is done, Perles is left alone for a moment, hands on the railing, looking down on the Disneyland masses. Hundreds of children with silver balloons, swarms of teenagers, old men, young women, mothers, grandmothers, the highest of high-tech rides all around, rockets, submarines, spinning tea cups, a Swiss mountain. This is a rare pose for a man. A chance to feel like king of the world he surveys.

"I tell ya," says Perles, "I could really use a hot dog."

And in a few minutes he is eating a hot dog and drinking a container of milk.

Let us clear something up right here. Perles never really predicted MSU would be in a Rose Bowl within five years of his taking over. What he said was, "Ask me in five years, I'll be better able to evaluate." But somehow the words got mixed up over the years, and all of a sudden, look, five years, a Rose Bowl. "It got so big I just ate it. But I never predicted this. Heck. I didn't know what was going to happen."

What he knew was, he was building with a core of "big-timers" — Lorenzo White, McAllister, Percy Snow — and a cast of also-rans. Many players on the MSU teams were recruits nobody else wanted. The kind Perles likes.

As he turns past the entrance to Adventureland, he bumps into five of his players. They all stop to say hello. Perles eats his popcorn as he listens.

"We went on Space Mountain."

"I'm nauseous."

"We're gonna eat pretty soon."

Perles asks them if they're having fun, asks as if he wants to make sure of it. Just before they leave, he reaches into his coat pocket and hands them his free meal ticket. "Go have an extra meal, split it up," he says.

The players leave. Perles walks on. "You know, my father always had a hard time saying I love you. I don't know if he said it twice that I can remember. His way was to cook for people. He'd give you his food, his drink. That was his way. I knew growing up, he'd make me a sandwich or something, I knew what he was trying to say.

"I'm no good at that stuff either, saying a lot. The words don't come out right. I guess that's why I cook, too."

He talks more about food. About Coney Island hot dogs. About Nemo's back in Detroit, and something called "Chili a la mode," which is chili with an ice cream-like scoop of onions on top. He laughs about how he and his friends eat that stuff up, night after night, the same guys he has known for years, what great guys, what a great school, what luck he has had.

"I love where I live," he says, shrugging. "You get to be an old guy, you gotta have a place to hang out."

Two hours after he arrived, Perles is ready to leave paradise. He has gone on no rides. Has walked through only a fraction of the Disneyland park. "It's beautiful," he says. "Super." But home beckons, and with five minutes to go before the first bus, he is inside the souvenir store closest to the gate, picking out stuffed versions of Mickey and Minnie for members of his family.

"HEY, WHICH ONE'S GOOFY? I GOTTA GET A GOOFY."

He turns to the people walking by, and just asks out loud.

"WHERE'S GOOFY?"

Nobody answers. Undaunted, he asks again.

"HEY, YOU KNOW WHERE GOOFY IS AT?"

Finally someone laughs and points to a shelf.

"THERE HE IS. GOOFY. MY MAN."

He takes one, and carries his little zoo over to the cash register. A woman cashier with frosted hair and thin glasses smiles at him.

"I'LL TAKE THESE GUYS HERE. TWO MICKEYS, TWO DONALDS. . . ."

He is not embarrassed, the everyday man on the everyday bonanza, a sweepstakes winner, and yet he knows how he got here and how long he'll stay and what life will be like when he returns home. George Perles, the guy who swears if they fire him from MSU, will come back the next year as a fan, every game, attend the tailgate parties and eat bratwurst and wear his green-and-white sweater. That's beyond loyalty. That's love. What a perfect movie it would make. This big, lumbering guy, laboring honestly in the shadow of more famous people, and some fairy godmother plucks him out and gives him a glorious moment in the sun.

Come to think of it, that's pretty much what happened.

"I bet you like your job here," Perles whispers to the woman behind the counter. "It's a happy place to work, right?"

"Yes," she says, nodding, "lots of little girls and little boys."

She hands him the bag with two Mickeys, two Donalds and a Goofy. He tucks it into his burly frame.

"Men ain't nothing but big boys," he says, and the woman smiles as he walks away.

THEY HAD THE BALL; THEY HAD IT ALL

January 2, 1988

PASADENA, Calif. — They had the ball! They had the ball! Todd Krumm was cradling it, dancing with it, raising it above his head and leaping into the arms of teammate Kurt Larson, and only gravity kept them from flying off into space. All the waiting, all the lean years, all the talk of Rose Bowl jinx — it was all crushed down and squeezed inside this little brown football, and now, Michigan State had it. God. At last.

"It was awesome! It was a relief!" Krumm would yell outside the locker room after Michigan State had stunned the disbelievers with a nail-biting 20-17 victory over USC in the Rose Bowl — the first time a Big Ten team has won it in seven years. Awesome? Relief? Tell us about it. Until that point — when Krumm recovered a Rodney Peete fumble with 1:37 left — destiny seemed sure to slip the Spartans a mickey.

Sure, they had played a powerful first half — an arresting display of rushing and defense — but like a tired runner, the Spartans' energy seemed to fade. A 14-3 halftime lead slipped to 20-17, and USC was a dragon down the stretch. Hot? Ho boy. Peete was directing the Trojans to a heroic finish, as surely as if a California screenwriter had called for it.

And then, the most miraculous thing. With USC on the MSU 30, Peete called for the snap — and never got it. The ball bounced, players fell on it, Larson kicked it, and on two bounces it landed in Krumm's waiting grasp, and damn if he was ever going to let it go.

"Kurt was hugging me, but I wanted to hug him," Krumm would say. And in the stands, MSU faithful were hugging one another. Was this incredible or what? They had the lead. They had one minute left. And they had the ball! They had the ball!

'm still nervous, can you believe that?" coach George Perles said after it was all over, after his Spartans had survived one final threat by USC, and had watched the clock turn to 0:00 and ring in the New Year better than it ever did in Times Square. "This feels great. For us, for the Big Ten, for everybody."

Raise your hand if you weren't at least a little moved by this fairy tale. That way we know who the dead people are. How long had all the parties waited for this? MSU hadn't been to Pasadena in 22 years. The conference hadn't won out here since 1981.

"What do you think about breaking the Big Ten jinx?" a reporter asked Perles.

"You've got to ask those other teams about the jinx," he answered. "I like the Rose Bowl."

I like the Rose Bowl? Too much. But then, this whole adventure was like that, this whole week of Spartans In Paradise. Here was the most unlikely of teams — nobody picked it to get this far — a group of nice, quiet, muscular guys coached by a ruddy-faced, basso-voiced man who said, "Hey, I don't care how Michigan and Ohio State did it. We're going to Disneyland and we're going to enjoy the hell out of it."

Yeah.

And the game? Oh, my. This was a lifetime in one afternoon. Sunlight to darkness, warmth to cold, a lead to a tie to a glorious victory that was not assured until the final snap. How much older was everyone when this thing ended? Ten years?

"It felt like the second half went on forever," admitted quarterback Bobby McAllister, who provided the most acrobatic play of the afternoon, scrambling to the sidelines, directing traffic, then leaping as he reached out of bounds and connecting on a 36-yard miracle to Andre Rison — a play that led to the winning field goal. He leaped? He threw it in midair?

"What do you call that?" he was asked.

"I call it. . . . "

He laughed.

"I call it, 'make something happen.' "

Perfect. Because that's what MSU needed. That pass — and another earlier bomb to Rison of 55 yards — kept the otherwise slow-grinding MSU offense from running out of steam. It was just one of countless memories for a Spartans scrapbook:

Here was a brilliant display of labor by Lorenzo White, who carried 24 times in the first half alone for 89 yards and two touchdowns. The quiet senior tailback, who had been denied the Heisman Trophy, played those first 30 minutes as if they might cast the award in his image next year. He finished with 113 yards, and more importantly, a victory in his last game. "We won, I'm done," he said. A pretty and effective final rhyme.

And from the rhyme to the reason: defense. Percy Snow. Sophomore linebacker. Seventeen tackles, 15 unassisted. If you're looking for a single reason for victory this day, you can start with his number. Despite its third-quarter drowsiness, the defense — the Spartans' forte all year — was a steel drum when it had to be. That's how you win big games.

What else? Lord. Who can remember it all? There were fake field goals — two by USC — and interceptions and a long punt return and a USC touchdown pass, Peete to Ken Henry, in which only a centimeter of shoe kissed the fair territory of the end zone. Thrills, chills, spills. A sellout crowd split down the middle, half green and white, half red and gold. So loyal that when one side began the wave, the other refused to carry it on. A Rose Bowl worthy of its tradition, for sure.

And finally, an MSU victory. This is one for the also-rans, the co-stars, the teams that live in the shadows of more famous programs. Listen up. Sometimes the underdog gets a shot. And sometimes the underdog wins. How fitting that the long, lamented Big Ten hex is broken here by Michigan State.

"I know we usually have the 24-hour rule," a happy Perles said after the game — reverting to the 24 hours of celebration or mourning he allows his team following games, "but I'm waiving that. They can celebrate from now until next spring for all I care."

Minutes after the game was over and the TV cameras had taken you to a commercial break, the MSU players began jogging off the field, then suddenly turned and headed back the other way, to the far corner, where sat thousands of Michigan State fans, who had waited, what, forever for this? And the marching band rose, and marched into the Michigan State fight song, and everybody, players, fans, joined in — "FIGHT! FIGHT! FIGHT!" — their voices crashing into the cool California darkness.

Beautiful. Here was the final scene of the dream: players and fans singing in unison, some of them crying, after a game that finally, finally, put an end to the old and a sparkle to the new. They had the ball. They had it all.